Achieving Civil Justice

Appropriate dispute resolution for the 1990s

edited by
Roger Smith

 Legal Action Group
1996

This edition published in Great Britain 1996
by LAG Education and Service Trust Limited
242 Pentonville Road, London N1 9UN

British Library Cataloguing in Publication Data
A CIP catalogue record for this book is available from the British Library

ISBN 0 905099 75 3

Typeset, from data supplied, by Datix International Limited, Bungay, Suffolk
Printed in Great Britain by Bell & Bain Ltd, Glasgow

Achieving Civil Justice

Appropriate dispute resolution for the 1990s

THE LEGAL ACTION GROUP (LAG) is a charity founded in 1971. Its purpose is to promote equal access to justice for all those members of society who are socially, economically or otherwise disadvantaged. To this end, it seeks to improve law and practice, the administration of justice and legal services by publishing a monthly journal, *Legal Action,* and a range of law books, providing professional development courses and promoting policy debate. Further information can be obtained by contacting the Legal Action Group, 242 Pentonville Road, London N1 9UN, UK, telephone (+44) 171 833 2931, fax (+44) 171 837 6094.

Contents

Acknowledgments

This book requires particular acknowledgment of the helpfulness of all the people mentioned in chapter 2 who gave generously of their time. Particular thanks are due to the following who gave hospitality and assistance beyond the call of any reasonable duty: David Baker in Toronto, Jayne Tyrrell in Boston, Gerry Singsen in both Boston and Washington, Forrest Mosten and Teresa Laird in Los Angeles, Rick Craig and Gordon Hardy in Vancouver, Jacques Fremont in Montreal.

RS

Introduction

This book is intended as a topical intervention into the debate on reform of our civil justice system. It has three linked themes: a response to the interim report of Lord Woolf published in July 1995;[1] an incorporation into domestic debate of North American experience; and, finally, the articulation of a programme of reform and study that is based on the needs of potential litigants, particularly those who are socially, economically or otherwise disadvantaged.

The organisation of the chapters may need explanation. The first sets out the context; the second recounts the findings of an empirical examination of innovations in North American courts; the third and fourth are examinations of the proposals in Lord Woolf's interim report by two eminent North American scholars who are, or have been, practitioners – Professor Carrie Menkel-Meadow of the University of California, Los Angeles, and Professor Garry Watson QC of Osgoode Hall Law School in Toronto, Canada; the fifth, sixth and seventh form a trilogy on the subject of alternative dispute resolution and are written in turn by Barbara Stedman, director of the multi-door programme at a court in Cambridge, Massachusetts; Karl Mackie, director of the Centre for Dispute Resolution (CEDR); and Marian Liebmann, former director and now projects adviser to Mediation UK, the umbrella group for community mediation; the eighth and ninth chapters are reflections on the previous content and argument. In these, LAG's director, Roger Smith, and its former policy officer, Anne Grosskurth, set out the group's observations on the way that policy should develop.

The book is being published at a particularly important time. Current debate on civil justice is dominated by Lord Woolf's interim report. By the end of July 1996, Lord Woolf should have published his final report. It might, therefore, be thought that debate on his earlier report will become rapidly outdated. In a sense, this will be right.

However, it is likely that, on many of the issues discussed in this book, Lord Woolf's final report will simply argue for implementation of approaches that he outlined in his interim version. It is unlikely, for instance, that he will recant from his fundamental argument that civil justice requires more judicial intervention or, in the words of Professor Menkel-Meadow, 'managed care'. Indeed, Lord Woolf may well move immediately to incorporating his ideas into rules. In that case, it remains crucial that debate continues. If Lord Woolf's recommendations are not correctly conceived and implemented, it is almost inevitable that yet another major investigation into the civil justice system will be established before we hit the millennium. As chapter 1 explains (p9), inadequate examination of underlying problems and the advocacy of ineffective solutions has dogged this area since the Judicature Act of 1873 gave us something not that different from our current court structure.

This book follows previous publications in which LAG has already developed some of these themes. For instance, the importance of education in the workings of the law and courts was argued as a general proposition in *A Strategy for Justice*.[2] It was discussed more specifically in *Shaping the Future: new directions in legal services*,[3] which contained a report on the pioneering work of the People's Law School in Vancouver. Both ADR and class actions, two concerns of this report, were also the subject of contributions in *Shaping the Future*.

Some comment on chapter 2 is required. This is a report more in the genre of journalism than academic treatise of a month's fact-finding visit to the United States and Canada in the summer of 1995. Full, some might say adequate, treatment of its themes would require considerably more time, research and reading than such a short trip could provide. The limited amount of background work is a danger that the reader should always bear in mind. Any comparative study of the operation of the law faces major danger of oversimplified understanding of other jurisdictions. The unavoidable superficiality of this one makes it likely that this report is more prone to such deficiencies than most. However, it is hoped that two factors will combine to outweigh these problems. First, the fundamental focus of this study is unashamedly domestic, the search for innovation of relevance to England and Wales. Second, it is important that there should be rapid transmission of information about new developments in other countries.

Some further limitation of the content of this book as a whole needs to be made specific, particularly for readers familiar with the

Legal Action Group and its concerns. The contributions to this book do not, in the main, consider publicly funded legal services, although the first chapter indicates the importance of such provision in any meaningful attempt to increase access to justice. Furthermore, the book concentrates on developments within, or close to, the courts. Although the first chapter also argues the importance of non-court adjudication by institutions such as tribunals, such narrowness of focus is deliberate. The purpose of this book is to concentrate on courts. LAG has set out in various other places its policies more generally.[4] It hopes soon to return to other issues relating to civil justice.

The idea both of looking abroad for inspiration and the particular choice of North America may also require explanation. In its two previous major projects that gave rise to the books referred to earlier, LAG has found that it can be enormously stimulating to bring experience from other jurisdictions into discussion of domestic policy. Countries with similar political, economic and social backgrounds face similar problems. Lessons must be learnable and transferable from differing responses to the same issues. Yet the opportunities are often ignored.

The choice of North America over, say, Australia is more arbitrary and, in truth, largely dominated by the relative cost of travel. North America has, however, significant attraction as a source of comparison with the UK. Canadian and US courts, in some ways, face more extreme versions of British domestic problems. Legal aid is generally less available for most civil litigation. Even so, the situation seems to be deteriorating fast. In the course of June 1995, British Columbia's New Democratic Party (roughly equivalent to Britain's Labour Party) was pushing through a legal aid cut of over 5 per cent; the Progressive Conservative Party took power in Ontario with a pledge to make cuts of around a third in the legal aid budget to provide money for tax cuts; Quebec's lawyers were working to rule against proposals of cuts to a similar magnitude; and, in Washington, the Legal Services Corporation was preparing for massive cuts in its funding, possibly amounting to its abolition, by the Republican majority in the Senate and House of Representatives.

In such circumstances, it is not surprising that individuals interested in experimenting with new ways of providing legal services have found occasional haven in the courts. The language, for instance, of Noreen Sharp, working on innovative ways of providing legal information to Arizona's litigants in person, mirrors some of that heard in the early days of law centres: 'We are working to put ourselves out of business' (see p39).

In this country, eligibility for legal aid is falling fast. A benefit which was available in 1979 on income grounds, albeit on payment of a contribution, to almost four-fifths of the population is now available, even on government figures, to well under half.[5] It is no longer credible to see legal aid as the only means required to create a level playing field in the civil courts between those with and without financial resources. More fundamental attention to the consequences of the imbalances of power is required. It is precisely because North American courts operate in the absence of adequate legal aid that there may be lessons to be learnt from their experience.

Furthermore, North American experience, particularly that of the United States, has a powerful influence on developments in Great Britain. The law is no exception, for all the traditional British superiority over what is traditionally portrayed as the excesses of US litigation. Lord Alexander made a specific reference to the desirability of US 'multi-door courthouses' in a 1995 Child and Co lecture.[6] Lord Woolf was clearly much influenced by US experience, particularly of case management, in producing his report. He specifically recommended that: 'Developments abroad, particularly those in the United States, Australia and Canada, in relation to ADR should be monitored . . .'[7] He was also evidently impressed by the electronic kiosk pioneered in the USA (see p41).[8]

It is important to note that politics in North America are moving fast. Assaults on legal aid could be followed by attacks on other aspects of civil justice. In the USA, there is already an avowed campaign by forces associated with the Republican Party to produce what the legal director of the American Civil Liberties Union has called 'a legal counter-revolution'.[9] On this agenda are various deterrents to restrict access to justice. There are proposals to prevent litigation by individuals against corporations; to appoint more conservative Federal judges and to cut back on the power of the courts. Many of these found expression in the Common Sense Legal Reforms Act proposed by the Republican House of Representatives in 1994 and 1995, and described by the *New York Times*[10] as 'a grab bag of measures intended to strengthen defenses against torts, lawsuits seeking damages – what Corporate America sees as an unprincipled attack on property and enterprise and what many consumer groups see as their leverage against corporate power'.

This publication provides the culmination of a year-long project which has been generously funded by the Nuffield Foundation. Its grant paid for Roger Smith's visit to North America, a conference and two seminars held in London in November 1995 at which the three North American contributors spoke on their r pers. Our profound thanks are due to the Foundation for its support.

References

1 Lord Woolf, *Access to Justice: Interim report to the Lord Chancellor on the Civil Justice System in England and Wales* (Woolf Inquiry Team, 1995).
2 LAG, 1992.
3 LAG, 1995.
4 eg, *A Strategy for Justice.*
5 R Smith (ed), *Shaping the Future: new directions in legal services* (LAG, 1995), p20.
6 See 'Who dares to resolve, wins' Lord Alexander of Weedon QC, *The Times*, 14 March 1995.
7 Woolf (above), recommendation 62, p227.
8 See Woolf (above) p87.
9 Steven R Shapiro, quoted in R Perez Pena, 'A rights movement that emerges from the right', *New York Times*, 30 December 1994.
10 27 January 1995.

CHAPTER 1

The context

ROGER SMITH

The economic, social and political problems of the late 20th century have impacted on the justice system in England and Wales, just as on most other facets of modern society. Uncertainty now reigns where once doubt was unknown. As a consequence, the voice of Lord Hailsham, Mrs Thatcher's first Lord Chancellor, as expressed in his 1983 Hamlyn Lectures, now comes across as a plaintive cry for a bygone age: '. . . to exist at all, law must have at least a certain durability. Authority and tradition demand more than a casual respect. A state which hopes to survive cannot be in a state of constant turmoil. Its institutions, its customs and traditions, its national personality must be seen to endure and maintain their identity in the midst of change.'[1]

The symptoms of a deep, underlying unease are many. We are in the midst of a major battle between the judiciary and politicians on the respective roles and powers of each, so constitutionally deep that it transcends party political lines (see below). What is more, a respectable and growing body of opinion even seeks to challenge the fundamental assumption that the civil, publicly-provided courts are the best place to adjudicate civil disputes. In some US courts, the pursuit of alternative dispute resolution out of the courts is mandatory before cases are allowed before a judge. In this country, report after report extols the virtue of avoiding formal court adjudication if this is possible. Dissatisfaction with court proceedings is so great that the government has launched a second 'fundamental' review of civil justice within a decade. In the same time-span, legal aid, as important in enabling litigation for the poor as any court procedure, has been subject to two green papers proposing major reform and faces the prospect of an imminent second white paper and, consequently, a second major Act of Parliament.

The underlying cause of concern is financial. The cost of litigation has always prevented access to justice for the poor unless they could 7 get access to subsidy or assistance. Costs have now risen to such levels that even multi-national corporations balk at litigation if it can possibly be avoided. Above all, the cost of courts, judges and lawyers has become an increasingly important issue for government. The control of cost has dictated a raft of government policies on the law, encouraging in its wake a greater managerialism and control over the provision of the publicly funded services provided by both courts and lawyers. Lord Mackay's proposal to introduce contracts for legal aid providers and Lord Woolf's assertion of a need for greater judicial control over litigation represent similar reactions to similarly perceived problems.

The crisis of the courts, both in terms of proposals for government-imposed reform and the self-doubt of existing participants, should, therefore, be linked more widely to the identity and funding crisis of much of the current welfare state. Providers of state-funded services – whether legal aid practitioners, judges, social workers, teachers, professors or doctors – face common and combined externally created crises over funding which are reflected in an internal loss of faith over their identity and role. We are in an age when the resources needed to fulfil Lord Hailsham's plea for traditional conservatism are simply politically unavailable. Widespread turmoil is not only shared by different professional groups remunerated by public funds within this country. It is equally apparent in other developed countries of the world whose economies and attendant politics are changing as rapidly.

In many ways, the age is one of pessimism for those committed to the extension of rights and services to all those in society. The optimistic assertions of equality of access that were so motivating an element in demands made in the 1960s and 1970s are fading away in the face of more deeply divided societies. Change is, however, by no means all bad. It gives the opportunity for innovation and experiment that has not previously been possible. There has, after all, never been a golden age in the past when all members of society have had equal access to justice. From this comes the value of studying the response in other countries to their manifestations of what are essentially the same consequences of economic change. In a pattern of experience which is generally depressing, there are glimmers of light in the darkness as some people, in some institutions, in some countries seize the opportunity to advance the democratic engagement in providing greater access.

This chapter seeks to set out an analysis of the current state of the civil justice system in this country and its problems. This requires description of such structures as the High Court and the county courts. It also involves some coverage of relevant contemporary debates and political initiatives. No claim of comprehensiveness is made. Some important questions, such as the debate over the appointment of the judiciary and its composition in terms of sex, class and race, have largely been ignored, despite detailed proposals for change made by the Labour Party. Some, such as the future of administrative law and multi-party actions, have been raised only briefly, although they are both under active review. The central concern is with those who are excluded from equal access to justice by reason of social or economic disadvantage and the reforms which are necessary to provide more appropriate means of dispute resolution for these groups than those which exist at present.

The structure of civil justice

It is, of course, a mistake to see civil justice solely in terms of the courts. Adjudication of civil disputes in England and Wales is provided by the state through a bewildering array of at least 25 interlocking institutions. The vast majority are tribunals but there are no less than three virtually separate courts: the judicial committee of the House of Lords, the Supreme Court (consisting in civil of the High Court and the Court of Appeal) and the county courts. Such organisation is explicable only in terms of history. The Supreme Court is, for instance, not supreme at all: appeals from its appeal court are heard by the House of Lords. It inherits its name because those framing the Judicature Act 1873 intended it to be supreme but were beaten by a reactionary backlash following the defeat of Gladstone's Liberal government at the 1874 election.

As a general rule, the prestige of courts is in inverse proportions to their workload. In 1994, a little over 150,000 writs were issued in the Queen's Bench Division and 570 cases determined after trial. By contrast, 2.7 million cases were begun in the county courts and over 110,000 cases disposed of by trial or arbitration. Bottom of the heap are the myriad of tribunals. In 1993, the General Commissioners of Income Tax disposed of 322,279 cases, social security and disability appeals and medical appeals tribunals 109,708 and industrial tribunals 21,440. The prestige of the adjudicator follows a similar pattern. At the top are the ten Lords of Appeal in Ordinary plus the Lord Chancellor, then the 32 Lord Justices of Appeal, 95 High Court judges, 520 circuit judges and 1,014 district judges. Again at the bottom are the tribunals and the 255 chairmen of industrial tribunals, and the 142 chairs and 830 members of the Independent Tribunal Service.[2]

These statistics are quoted to a purpose. Prestige bequeaths power and influence. It is the powerful who tend to define the problems and, hence, dominate discussion of the solutions. To its credit, the government has recognised the importance of representation in tribunal proceedings in its recent legal aid green paper, as did the Labour Party in its 1992 election manifesto. Nevertheless, the two most recent reports on aspects of the civil courts have come from eminent judges: Lord Woolf, who is a Lord of Appeal in Ordinary, and Sir Philip Otton, who is a Lord Justice of Appeal.[3] Both have focused on the Supreme Court. Neither deals in any depth with the state of affairs in the county court. This can lead to misleading responses, whether deliberate or unintended. For instance, the Otton report argues that there is a particular problem with litigants in person in the Court of Appeal. Bowing to the recommendation of the report, Lord Mackay, the Lord Chancellor, agreed a welcome major grant to the advice bureau in the Royal Courts of Justice. Nothing was, however, done about the plight of litigants in person in the county courts, where much larger numbers of people encounter problems and where, as described below, an outstanding recommendation of the Civil Justice Review still awaits implementation.

The county courts

Official disdain of the county courts is regrettable because they are the workhorse of the court system. Overall, their major function is the collection of debt. In 1994, just under half of all summons were issued by the Summons Production Centre, which processes the debt-collection work of 125 banks, finance houses and other large commercial lenders. 92 per cent of all cases issued were default summons, ie, debt cases to which no defence was expected. 171,000 actions related to the repossession of land. About half of these were mortgage possession cases.

The trend of work is changing. Five years ago, the 1989 *Judicial Statistics* reported that 'in the last fifty years there has been a steady increase in the work of the county courts, and a more rapid rise in the last decade'.[4] Thereafter, the workload rose sharply as reforms introduced by legislation in 1990 transferred large amounts of business, particularly personal injury cases, from the High Court. 1991 represented the peak, with over 3.5 million cases begun. Levels have now fallen back virtually to what they were in 1989, though with more debt and fewer housing cases. The precise causes are unclear, though they undoubtedly include continuing economic recession, the decrease in the public rented sector and restrictions on the rights of tenants.

In the last few years, the largest internal change to county courts has been the increase in small claims arbitrations conducted by the lowest level of the judiciary, district judges, formerly known as registrars. The number of full trials has stayed relatively constant. In 1989, 22,267 cases were disposed of by trial and 49,829 by arbitration. In 1994, the comparable figures were 24,219 and 87,885. This reflects the doubling of the small claims limit, under which cases are automatically sent to arbitration, from £500 to £1,000, following publication of the Civil Justice Review in 1989 (see p15). In January 1996, the limit was tripled to £3,000, indicating that the number of arbitrations is likely to rise still further, if the district judges can cope with increased numbers of hearings. In 1994, over three-quarters of arbitrations related to debt; 3,783 concerned personal injury; 7,435 other negligence and 1,250 non-possession housing disputes. A large part of the county courts' work is enforcement. Just under 1 million warrants of execution against goods were issued.

In the early 1990s, many county courts were overwhelmed by the enormous increase in work arising from a general rise in litigation and the particular consequences of cases being shifted down the court structure. To some extent, the downturn in litigation, probably caused by the depth of the economic recession, has saved them, but the statistics suggest that all might not yet be well. Over five years, from 1990 to 1994, the time that it has taken from issue of a summons to start of trial has dropped by a fortnight, from 81 to 79 weeks, around 18 months. However, the small decrease in time appears largely due to the parties and their lawyers. They have reduced the time from issue to setting the case down for trial by five weeks. By contrast, courts have extended the period of waiting from that point to when the case actually starts by four weeks, from 17 to 21 weeks.

Reports from practitioners suggest that the statistics reveal a genuine problem. The courts are struggling to cope with too limited resources. In particular, their complaints include the following:

– difficulties of access for poor litigants because of the closure of local county courts and the regionalisation of provision (ten have been closed in five years);

- the quality and training of staff;
- inconsistent practice between courts and the consequent inappropriate importance of the quality of the chief clerk;
- too many judges without specialist knowledge of distinct jurisdictions, reflecting a reluctance to allow judges to specialise either in civil cases as a category or within civil cases on, eg, housing;
- lack of assistance for litigants in person;
- inadequate implementation of new technology, giving rise to the continuing phenomenon of the lost file and the judge without access to computer assistance;
- the need, in some areas, for more active court users' groups and in others, of more notice being paid to their recommendations;
- continuing unacceptable trial delays;
- overloaded listing of cases, particularly on housing possession days in inner city courts, when 40–50 cases may still be allocated for hearing within an hour; and
- lack of management of judicial time so that judges come to court hearings without having read the documents.

The High Court

The High Court is divided into three divisions: Chancery, Queen's Bench and Family. Only the first two are considered here. The first-instance work of the Queen's Bench Division has been dramatically affected by transfer of work to the county courts. The issue of cases peaked in 1990 at around 370,000. This number had more than halved in 1994.[5] Again, most of the cases related to debt collection, with 77 per cent in the combined category of debt and return of goods. Other categories included breach of contract (6 per cent of the cases begun in London); personal injuries (4 per cent); recovery of land (4 per cent); and other negligence (which accounted for only 299 of the 37,450 cases begun in London); and defamation (418 cases).[6] The Queen's Bench Division also hears judicial review cases. In 1994, there were 3,208 applications for judicial review. Just over a third of applications were allowed. Most were then settled. Judicial review was granted in 441 cases after trial.

The 63 High Court judges (plus the Lord Chief Justice) determined 570 cases after trial (330 related to personal injuries) and, alone or in a divisional court, decided 747 judicial reviews. Reflecting the continuing, though diminishing, dominance of personal injury cases, High Court litigation typically pits an individual (3,520 out of the

4,420 plaintiffs whose cases were disposed of after being set down for trial) against a corporate defendant (2,550 out of 4,420 defendants). Contrary to the position in the county court, delays in cases coming to trial in the High Court arise more in the period from issue of proceedings to setting down than subsequently. Over five years, the average of the first rose from 105 weeks in 1990 to 137 in 1994: the wait for a trial stayed constant at 40 weeks. Overall, the time between issue and trial rose, therefore, from 145 weeks to 177, taking it from under three years to well over.

The Chancery Division has a smaller, more specialist jurisdiction. The total number of cases begun in 1994 was only 38,867. This is down from a 1992 peak of about 48,000 but, in contrast to the Queen's Bench Division and county courts, well above the level of activity during the 1980s when, for most of the decade, well under 30,000 cases were begun each year. Around 30 per cent of all actions related to bankruptcy; 27 per cent were heard in the semi-autonomous Commercial Court and the major categories of the rest were land, business and industry, intellectual property, professional negligence and trusts, wills and probate. The division's 17 judges (plus the Vice-Chancellor) saw 974 cases disposed of after trial or at hearings outside the specialist areas of commercial cases, bankruptcy and patents.

The administrative jurisdiction

The major way in which the High Court impacts on poor people is, now that personal injury cases have largely been removed and discounting its not inconsiderable role in debt collection, through the administrative law jurisdiction of the Queen's Bench Division. Challenges to immigration decisions account for well over a quarter of all applications for judicial review.[7] Just over an eighth relate to homelessness.[8]

In direct consequence of its importance, this role of the court as champion of the individual against the executive is under challenge from politicians of both the left and the right. Conservative Central Office became so keen on the attack that it beguiled the *Times* and the *Daily Telegraph* into reporting a speech never given by Lord Mackay, in which he was variously alleged to have told the judges to 'toe the line', according to the former, and 'to keep in line' in the apparently independent words of the latter.[9] The resulting ridicule dented the credibility of all those involved.

A more considered, and thereby more worrying, attack on the

judiciary had been made a few weeks earlier by a Labour politician, the Lord Chancellor in waiting, Lord Irvine. In the course of a scholarly analysis of judicial review made to the Administrative Law Bar Association, he argued for a fundamental rolling back of assertions of judicial power. He even went so far as to question the role of the courts in supervising the tribunals, so important in the determination of the rights of the poor: 'An interventionist approach to judicial review for error of law may, in part, undermine the raison d'être of the system of specialist administrative tribunals, which are intended by parliament in most cases to replace, and not merely supplement, the decision-making powers of the court.'[10]

The reactionary implications of this line of argument can be indicated by comparing it with the decision of Lord Denning in one of the early test cases undertaken with the support of the Child Poverty Action Group (CPAG) and designed precisely to encourage the judiciary to raise standards in tribunals. He said: 'If [the point in issue] were to be regarded as a strict point of law, there is much to be said ... for judicial intervention ... but ... This seems to me a good instance where the High Court should not interfere with the Tribunal's decision, even though it may be erroneous in law.'[11] Considerable work was undertaken by CPAG and others before Lord Denning's successor as Master of the Rolls, Sir John Donaldson (as then he was), was to accept seven years later, in another case in which CPAG was instructed and the relevant government department sought a restrictive ruling of judicial non-intervention in line with the earlier case, that: 'It is inappropriate in my judgment that the Court should seek to define the limits of the review jurisdiction of the Divisional Court.'[12] By then, successful judicial reviews had forced much higher standards of first-level adjudication and the introduction of a right of appeal where none had previously existed.

Legal aid

The overall role and importance of legal aid in funding civil non-matrimonial litigation in the courts is hard to judge. Legal aid is important in the Queen's Bench Division. 1,140 plaintiffs (about a third of all individuals) received legal aid. In 80 cases both sides were legally aided and the defendant alone in 60 cases.[13] In 1994–95, a total of 193,747 legal aid certificates were issued in non-matrimonial civil proceedings. 31 per cent of these related to personal injury and a further 7 per cent to medical negligence.

The number of legally aided litigants is increasing. Between 1984–85 and 1990–91, the number of legal aid certificates in civil non-matrimonial cases doubled. Since then, the rate of increase has slowed but 21 per cent more certificates were issued in 1994–95 than five years previously.[14] Legal aid is, however, increasingly available in civil cases only to the poorest. The percentage of certificates which are free and thus given to those with incomes at or around the levels entitling them to means-tested benefits has risen from 80 to 85 per cent in the last decade.[15] As stated on p4, less than half the population is currently eligible, even with payment of a contribution, compared with around three-quarters in 1979.[16]

More significant perhaps than the availability of legal aid within the courts is its non-availability outside them. Legal aid is not available for arbitrations in the small claims court, hence the attraction for government in raising its jurisdictional limits. The only recommendation of Lord Woolf's interim report which the government announced it would immediately implement was a tripling of the small claims limit from £1,000 to £3,000. The consequences of the absence of representation in tribunals was definitively examined by Professor Hazel Genn in 1989. For instance, she found overwhelming statistical evidence that lack of representation in industrial tribunals brought lack of justice: 'where the applicant has no representation and the respondent is legally represented, the applicant's probability of success is reduced by 10 per cent'.[17]

The Civil Justice Review

Projects for reform of courts and civil procedure since the major Judicature Acts of the 1870s have a long and inglorious history. Well over fifty reports have called for varying degrees of change. The potential effects of many have proved to have been over-estimated by their progenitors. The most recent major report was that of the Civil Justice Review, established by Lord Hailsham when Lord Chancellor in 1985, which reported in 1988.[18]

Lord Woolf quotes the *Supreme Court Practice 1993* in its enthusiasm for this report: '. . . a great leap forward . . . a landmark in the ongoing history of English civil procedure . . . it may be claimed that a change is effected by these provisions . . . more profound and extensive since the Judicature Acts of 1873 and 1875.'[19] This is only marginally less positive than press coverage at the time of its publication with headlines such as 'REVOLUTION IN THE COURTS' and copy like: 'The cost of going to court is to be cut in a free-market revolution for the legal profession unveiled by the Government this afternoon'.[20]

A review as fundamental as it was claimed to be should not have needed reworking well within a decade of publication. Its main recommendations are summarised below; it argued for the transfer of cases down the system: personal injury cases were to be largely removed from the High Court, the small claims limit was to be increased and the status of the lowest level of the judiciary, the registrars, raised to deal with a greater workload. To some extent, the review's final report was a disappointment. In the face of opposition from the Bar and the judiciary, it resiled from the one major reform suggested in the course of its extensive consultation exercise, the unification of High Court and the county courts. Furthermore, it proposed no continuing procedure or institution for maintaining the pressure for change. The ten-strong review team was disbanded on publication. History may yet agree with the reaction of *Legal Action*, at the time of the review's publication, which said that its 'major value may not be its actual content but its raising of public expectations'.[20A] Within five years of its publication, the Bar and the Law Society had published a report arguing for further reform.[21]

Lord Woolf's current inquiry into civil justice has its origins directly in the Civil Justice Review. He was originally asked to implement one of its still outstanding recommendations, integration of the rules for county court procedure with those of the Supreme Court. With typical gusto, he widened his terms of reference into a broader investigation; set up a rolling programme through 1994 and early 1995 of seminars around the country; acquired a Lord Chancellor's Department secretariat; and published the interim report referred to above (p1); and is due to produce his draft rules and final report in the summer of 1996.

Reform: the 'bureaucratisation' of justice

A consistent trend in recent programmes of reform for civil justice has been the hope of a solution to the problems of delay and cost by what Carrie Menkel-Meadow terms the 'bureaucratisation' of justice (see p93). Reliance is placed on a combination of stricter procedural rules requiring greater disclosure and more judicial intervention to enforce them. This was reflected in the approach of the Civil Justice Review, which argued for greater court management of litigation and for such procedural changes as the exchange of witness statements. In doing so, it was echoing well-established earlier arguments for reform, eg, in Justice's 1974 proposals for the incorporation of affidavits of evidence with pleadings.[22]

Currently, Lord Woolf's interim recommendations provide the focus for any contemporary discussion of civil justice. These will soon be overtaken by those in his final report, but they are unlikely to change other than in their detail, if at all. They are summarised below because they provide a precise set of proposals on which to focus discussion of the kind set out by the two North American commentaries in chapters 3 and 4. Lord Woolf's are not the only proposals that are relevant at present. They are thus summarised in conjunction with relevant proposals from a recent report of a committee of the Judges' Council which considered the position of litigants in person and was chaired by Sir Philip Otton ('Otton' below), the government's green paper on legal aid published in the spring of 1995 ('green paper') and its white paper on divorce ('white paper'), released almost simultaneously with Lord Woolf's interim report.[23]

Summary of Lord Woolf's proposals

Procedure

– 'There should be a fundamental transfer in the responsibility for management of civil litigation from litigants and their legal advisers to the courts.' (Recommendation 1, p223)
– There should be three tiers of cases: those in an enlarged small claims jurisdiction; a fast track; and a multi-track.
– The small claims arbitration limit should initially be raised from £1,000 to £3,000 and subsequently to £5,000 if procedures prove effective.
– The fast track will primarily apply to cases with a value of less than £10,000 and will provide for determination within 20–30 weeks from issue of proceedings. Discovery will be limited; trials will last no more than three hours; there will be no oral expert evidence; costs will be fixed.
– Multi-track management will be conducted by teams of judges managed by a master or district judge and based around two hearings: one immediately after receipt of the defence and the other immediately pre-trial, to be conducted normally by the trial judge.

- There should be heavy investment in information technology to assist with case management.
- There should be more specific pleadings; more limited discovery; replacement of witness statements by summaries; more control of expert evidence by the court.

Litigants in person

- 'The provision of assistance to litigants should be an invariable obligation of the courts.' (Recommendation 47, p266)
- Help should be provided through a court-based duty advice scheme funded by the Legal Aid Board at 'each of the courts identified as handling housing and debt work'; general advice should be available from advice agencies in those courts where there is a need and, at least as an experiment, by the introduction of information technology kiosks.
- The citizens advice bureau in the Royal Courts of Justice should receive greater funding. (Otton)
- The Bar and Law Society should organise a *pro bono* assistance scheme in the Royal Courts of Justice. (Otton)

Legal aid

- Legal aid costs should be capped, allocated to regions and divided between providers who compete for bulk contracts. (green paper)
- By implication, legal aid should be retained for personal injury cases above £1,000, with cases up to £10,000 being dealt with under the fast-track procedure.
- Advice provision of the kind described above should be funded through legal aid.
- There should be a debate on whether successful unassisted parties might be able to obtain costs against legally aided opponents.
- Voluntary organisations providing alternative dispute resolution services, such as Mediation UK, should receive more funding.
- Consideration should be given to use of ADR being covered by a legal aid certificate and whether the existence of ADR as an alternative way of resolving disputes should be taken into account in the decision to grant a legal aid certificate.
- Legal aid funds currently being paid to lawyers in divorce cases should be diverted to mediators. (white paper)

Mediation and alternative dispute resolution (ADR)

– Courts should encourage litigants to use private ADR and un-
  reasonable refusal to do so may be a factor in the award of costs.
– There should be experiment with the use of 'judicial mini-trials' of
  key elements of some complex cases.
– The Lord Chancellor and the Court Service should be under a duty
  to keep the public aware of the possibilities of ADR.
– Mediation should be introduced into divorce procedures. (white
  paper)
– 'Civil magistrates' might be appointed to provide, among other
  services, 'alternative means of resolving disputes within the courts
  by conducting arbitrations, inquiries, mediation or conciliation'.[24]
– There should be better funding for community mediation schemes.

Structure

– There should be a new Head of Civil Justice with a presiding role
  somewhat like the President of the Family Division.
– Each circuit should have a presiding judge with responsibility for
  civil work.
– There should be no change to the High Court/county court
  division nor amalgamation of the Chancery and Queen's Bench
  Divisions of the High Court.
– There should be a Civil Justice Council to oversee the implementation of Lord Woolf's reforms.

Access to justice

A number of threads bind the four reports cited above together. One
is the theme of 'access to justice'. This is the title chosen by Lord
Woolf for his report. It has also served in recent months both as the
title of the Labour Party's document on its civil justice policy[25] and, in
terms of increasing it, as the Conservative government's aim as stated
in the very first paragraph of its green paper on legal aid.[26] This states
explicitly enough, 'the aim of the government is to improve access to
justice'. For good measure, *Access to Justice* was also the title of a
document produced by the Liberal Democrat Lawyers Association in
October 1995.[27] Politicians of all parties thus find themselves in
agreement that greater 'access to justice' is desirable, yet the
phrase requires some discussion.

Such apparent universal political agreement should alert us to a problem about precision of meaning. Can all these players of the political scene believe in and be describing the same thing? LAG has previously discussed some of the problems with the phrase.[28] For LAG, commitment to access to justice implies acceptance of two objectives:

a) a procedural fairness in the determination of rights and the enforcement of duties so that, in the words of the oath taken by US federal judges, we 'do equal right to the poor and the rich'. The respective wealth, power, culture, resources or class of two parties to a dispute should make no difference to the result of its determination; and

b) an inherent and substantive fairness in the nature of rights and duties.[29]

Lord Woolf, commendably, appears to share such a formulation. He accepts that the civil justice system should be 'just in the results it delivers', implying a concern with substantive social justice, and 'fair, proportionate, speedy, understandable, responsive, certain and effective', concepts that relate to procedural justice and the creation of 'level playing fields'.[30]

Access to justice as a concept was publicised, if not devised, by Professors Cappelletti and Garth as the unifying concept behind an ambitious global review conducted in the late 1970s. They asserted that it designated a 'worldwide movement to make rights effective'.[31] They saw it as subsuming earlier phases at solving the problem of unequal access to justice through, first, the provision of legal representation and, then, various mechanisms for representing what they called 'diffuse interests' in society: 'the emerging "access to justice approach" to legal reform . . . includes, but goes beyond, advocacy, whether inside or outside of the courts, and whether through governmental or private advocates. Its focus is on the full panoply of institutions and devices, personnel and procedures, used to process, and even prevent, disputes in modern societies.'[32]

The professors identified three particular barriers to justice. They were not cost, complexity and delay. They were cost (including delay); deficiencies in the capacity of some prospective parties (including lack of financial resources, knowledge and relative experience – identified as the imbalance between 'one-shot' litigants and 'repeat players'); and the particular problems of 'diffuse interests', 'collective or fragmented interests, such as those in clean air or consumer protection'.[33] Professors Cappelletti and Garth made two further relevant points. First, there is a pattern behind many of the barriers to justice: they 'are most pronounced for small claims and for isolated individuals, particularly the poor'. Difficulties were often most extreme in relation to the 'new substantive rights which are characteristic of the modern welfare state [which] . . . involve efforts to bolster the power of citizens against governments, consumers against merchants, people against polluters, tenants against landlords, and employees against employers (and unions) [where] the money interest of any one individual – as plaintiff or defendant – is likely to be small.'[34] Second, solutions need to integrate different approaches: 'many access problems are related, and changes aimed at improving access in one way can exacerbate barriers in another'.[35]

Exclusion and excess

The argument about the meaning of 'access to justice' is immediately relevant to the terms of reference of Lord Woolf's inquiry. Its aims are stated to be: 'to improve access to justice and reduce the costs of litigation; to reduce the complexity of the rules and modernise terminology; to remove unnecessary distinctions of practice and procedure'.[36] In furtherance of these, Lord Woolf is clear about the 'key problems facing civil justice'. They are 'cost, delay and complexity'[37] thus providing a further link with the Civil Justice Review by echoing its terms of reference. These were: 'To improve the machinery of civil justice in England and Wales by means of reforms in jurisdiction, procedure and court administration and in particular to reduce delay, cost and complexity'.[38] Though it included a chapter on 'access to justice' in its final report, the review's final report necessarily concentrated on the three elements highlighted in its terms of reference.

There are grave dangers in too facile an assumption of the problems of civil justice that will inevitably lead to inadequate solutions. The key issues are not cost, complexity and delay: they are better characterised as exclusion coupled with excessive cost, complexity and delay.

Exclusion

The bias of Lord Woolf's report, like the Civil Justice Review before it, is its concern with the fate of existing litigants. Yet, those who receive least justice in society are those who have had no access to the remedy available to meet the wrong that they face. *A Strategy for Justice*[39] discussed the extent of failures to take up certain avenues for the enforcement of rights, arguing, for example, that 'it is still the case that only a small majority – probably no more than 10 per cent –

of those injured other than on the roads or at work make a claim'.[40] A consultation paper for the Civil Justice Review compared the known state of repair of tenanted houses and the number of actions, then 1,500 a year, taken for disrepair by tenants. It accepted a major lack of take-up and explicitly worked on 'the assumption' that 'many more . . . might seek a remedy through the courts'.[41]

Exclusion from justice can arise from a number of causes. These include economic barriers, as for example in relation to those now ineligible for legal aid due to the sharp decline in eligibility.[42] It may arise from cultural and social barriers felt by those so unfamiliar with court procedures and bureaucratic expectations that they do not feel able to take small claims actions even using the existing available assistance. The Otton Report quotes Professor Hazel Genn at length on the potentially devastating effects arising from exclusion from representation and assistance that may afflict litigants in person:

> Parties who appear in courts and tribunals without the benefit of representation may be seriously disadvantaged within the justice system. This disadvantage derives from the fact that unrepresented parties, in common with most citizens, are unlikely to have experience of court proceedings or to have general knowledge of the area of law with which their case is concerned. Unrepresented parties may therefore lack the following: comprehension of court procedures; familiarity with the language and specialist vocabulary of legal proceedings; objectivity and emotional distance from their case; skill in advocacy; ability to undertake cross-examination and test the evidence of an opponent; understanding of the complexities of common law and regulations.[43]

Exclusion may occur from simple lack of education and information. This is why the example of some North American courts, such as Arizona, is so stimulating (see pp38–42). Alternatively, exclusion may arise from the failure of the civil justice system to provide an adequate remedy, eg, for classes of people to take actions in relation to a defective drug, again an area where North American experience has much to offer.

Excessive cost, complexity and delay

It is a simple, but important, point that problems arise only over *excessive* cost, complexity and delay. For instance, complex procedures and complex law may be required to cover complex situations, eg, the regulation of alleged patent infringement. Similarly, a degree of delay may be beneficial in some sorts of litigation. For example, the government proposes to retain a period of delay in the obtaining of a divorce. The white paper on its proposals extolled various reasons in favour of such a delay, including time for emotional processing and reconsideration: 'The period will allow the parties time to consider marriage guidance . . . This will mean that those who initiate the divorce process as a "cry for help" will be more likely than in the present system to receive the help they need. The period will provide many opportunities to withdraw from the process . . .'[44]

Manifest difficulties arise from dealing at too general a level with the problems of the civil justice system, a tendency encouraged by too easy an acceptance of the 'cost, complexity and delay' litany. Lord Woolf himself describes in detail the fiasco that has arisen over the attempt to save costs by changing procedure so that written witness statements replaced the giving of oral evidence-in-chief. Indeed, the Commercial Court Users' Committee reported that 'it was having a devastating effect on costs . . . because statements were being treated by the parties as documents which had to be as precise as pleadings'.[45]

Government policy and court fees

Government policy is not always internally consistent. Lord Woolf clearly took a deliberate and political decision to play down the consequences of the government's recent decision to raise court fees so that they meet not only the administrative costs of the civil courts, as has always been the expectation, but also the cost of judicial salaries. This is a controversial approach which has been rejected, for instance, in the United States (see p36) and Australia, where a government-appointed committee recommended:

> that fees should neither encourage nor be perceived as encouraging decisions by court administrators designed to maximise revenue. Accordingly, we are firmly of the view that there should be no budgetary link between revenue raised by the collection of fees . . . and the appropriate use of monies.[46]

For 1995–96, as a first step, the Court Service has been instructed to raise 75 per cent of such full costs from litigants. The equivalent was 60 per cent in 1994–95. In consequence, court fees are set to rise significantly. Increases to the existing fee structure were announced late in 1995. A consultation document on the possibility of introducing daily fees for court hearings is expected to be issued early in 1996. Increasing court costs in this way is likely to provide an additional barrier to justice for poor people. This is the basis of opposition to the policy of raising fees to this extent both in North America and Australia. Currently, fees are remitted automatically for litigants on income support. Fees may also be waived where they would cause undue hardship for a litigant. This waiver appears to be relatively little used, at least in the High Court. The Otton Report found that in a three-month period from mid-November 1994 to mid-February 1995, only 28 fees were remitted to litigants in person on the issue of 8,500 writs. For a comparable period in 1991, only one fee was remitted.

The government's policy is objectionable not only in pragmatic terms because it erects new barriers to justice for the poor, but also in terms of constitutional logic. Civil litigation, particularly in a common law jurisdiction, takes place not only for the benefit of the particular litigants concerned but also to set precedents by which unknown numbers of non-litigants then regulate their affairs. Furthermore, some litigation takes place directly to enforce a public interest and a public right, eg, judicial review challenges to government decisions. Requiring litigants in such cases to pay the full cost of hearing such cases is, implicitly, to re-categorise them as private cases of interest only to the parties concerned.

The problem of resources

Lord Woolf's approach to reform is variously described by two of the North American contributors to this volume as a move to 'managed care' (Professor Menkel-Meadow) or to 'a cost and control model' (Professor Watson). It might be characterised as a move from 'due process' to 'due progress'. The courts will be much more involved in the administration and management of cases. This raises a key issue over resources, to which Lord Woolf is alive. He told the Law Society annual conference in October 1995 of his response:

> It is said that the proposals will be defeated by lack of resources. I, of course, would prefer to see the government providing a substantial injection of resources but I have known throughout that there is no prospect of this. Both main political parties [have] made their attitude clear. . . . But this does not mean the proposals are doomed. They can be achieved by the redeployment of the existing resources and pump-priming.

And yet, resources remain a problem. It should be noted that Lord Woolf is deliberately blunting the impact of his point: pump-priming still requires extra resources, albeit limited to a start-up period. Greater case management and increased judicial control of litigation are bound to mean additional costs for the courts. The whole strategy is, essentially, to shift costs from the parties, who bear them disproportionately in an adversarial system, to the court, which bears them disproportionately in an inquisitorial and court-controlled system. The effect of this can be seen in Annex V to Lord Woolf's report. This lists court and lawyer fees in Germany. The lawyers' fees are significantly lower than in England and Wales, which is the reason for the use of the figures, but the court costs are astronomically higher. For instance, a claim for up to the equivalent of about £5,000 incurs court costs of £318 and lawyers' fees of £806. A claim for just under £1 million incurs court costs of about £12,000 and lawyers' fees of about the same amount.

Throughout his report, Lord Woolf notes that, although many of the recommendations of the Civil Justice Review have been implemented, 'the system of court control of case progress . . . has not'.[47] The reason for this is precisely that the resources have not been made available. In practical terms, therefore, Lord Woolf's proposals have to be considered on the basis that the government will continue to make no additional resources available. We have to consider the extent to which that will impair their effectiveness.

Research

Projects for reform of the civil justice system are bedeviled by inadequate research. Lord Woolf has evidently done what he could with a limited budget. He has organised assessors and academics to assist him. Nevertheless, the absence of a capacity for detailed research inevitably colours his approach. It has, no doubt, biased him towards the broad-brush approach of his different tracks of litigation. One issue that is, in consequence, rather swept aside is the fact that the level of litigation's complexity is not necessarily commensurate with the level of damages at stake. Oddly for an administrative lawyer of his eminence, Lord Woolf does not indicate how a judicial review of national importance but without any financial claim for damages would be allocated to an appropriate track. The content of such a case could vary between a simple point of legal construction and a highly complex argument involving totally new jurisprudence.

Lord Woolf's approach, no doubt dictated by lack of resources, notably differs from that of the Civil Justice Review. The latter was criticised for over-dependence on management consultants with insufficient knowledge rather than more thorough academic study but, in comparison with Lord Woolf, its commitment to empirical analysis is striking. Factual studies were commissioned in the areas of personal injuries, small claims, debt enforcement, the Commercial Court and housing cases. The results played a part in the determining the review's final recommendations. As Lord Woolf approaches the second part of his report so the difficulties over lack of research capacity may tell even more. One of the subjects of his concern, for instance, is to be multi-party actions. These raise very difficult questions linking together issues about procedure, funding and substantive law. Many jurisdictions have considered the issues in some detail as part of the process of making a decision. The Scottish Law Commission has, for instance, published a report by a working party and a discussion paper on the subject.[48] Ontario's Law Reform Commission produced a similar report, followed by another report from a government-established committee, before implementing its recent class action legislation.

Lord Woolf faces the very real danger of proposing over-simplified solutions developed in the absence of adequate background research. This was a problem widely foreseen by a number of commentators from the outset, once the form of the inquiry became clear.[49] This book is, in part, a contribution to domestic debate by providing a way of feeding a broader range of research and experience, including in particular that of North America, into domestic discussion. With contributions from eminent practitioners and academics, it is also a plea for more consideration and research before inadequately analysed reforms are implemented.

Mediation and ADR

A key issue facing civil justice is the relationship of traditional litigation in the courts and forms of alternative, or appropriate, dispute resolution. This is particularly apparent to anyone familiar with the United States, where ADR has been one of the major developments of recent years. A number of problems, however, beset the possible integration of mediation and ADR into court processes. These arise largely from the inherent contradiction between the two different reasons why ADR might prove attractive.

For some litigants with some problems, ADR may represent a better, non-confrontational way of resolving their problems. Indeed, there is some evidence that some litigants are seeking redress that the legal system may be completely ill-fitted to provide. The National Consumer Council found in a survey conducted jointly with the BBC Radio 4's programme *Law in Action* that 'out of every 100 people involved in a civil dispute, only 32 are primarily seeking financial compensation. Another 25 are mainly trying to prevent the same thing happening again. Yet our civil justice system is largely geared to providing – at great expense – financial compensation'.[50]

ADR's attraction for government, however, is that it appears that it might be cheaper than court proceedings. It is, for instance, the likely intention of the Lord Chancellor's Department that legally aided mediators in divorce cases will be paid less than the lawyers currently instructed. The danger of suggesting any experiment with court-annexed ADR is shown by Lord Woolf's indication of what is likely to be the government's reaction: a possibility that 'the use of an appropriate scheme of ADR, where there is one, should be taken into account when the grant of legal aid for court proceedings is under consideration'.[51] The implication of this is that poor litigants might effectively be forced into ADR by a requirement of their legal aid certificate, leaving the courts only to the rich who have the resources to choose.

In these circumstances, a way forward is difficult. A number of chapters deal with this topic. Carrie Menkel-Meadow discusses the effect of integration or non-integration into the court structure (pp98–108). Professor Karl Mackie outlines the history of commercial mediation in the UK (chapter 6) and Marian Liebmann that of community mediation (chapter 7). In chapter 5, Barbara Stedman provides a description of a sophisticated ADR programme in a court adjacent to Harvard University, home of one of the academics who were early proponents of a changed approach. Finally, chapter 8 includes an assessment by Anne Grosskurth of what, in all the circumstances, seems a reasonable way forward in this country.

Advice, assistance and representation

No discussion of civil justice is complete without consideration of how ordinary people of low or modest means, or others facing other barriers to justice, can get access to the resolution of their disputes. Both Lord Woolf and Lord Justice Otton indicate the problem of litigants in person who are in need of advice. The latter is particularly concerned with the appeal courts. The Civil Justice Review considered that advice provision was required in the county courts. Lord Woolf records the fate of its recommendation and that of the detailed work on the proposal undertaken for the Legal Aid Board. The cost, which might have been £1.7 million at its highest at 1991 prices, was the reason for its veto by the Lord Chancellor. The cost would, presumably, now be around £2 million at the maximum level. This could and should be met by the Legal Aid Board.

As legal aid eligibility has plummeted, so the need for litigants in person to receive some form of advice and assistance has increased. Such a cut in provision cannot be made with impunity and some form of compensating advice provision is required. Lord Justice Otton's specific recommendation was that the citizens advice bureau in the Royal Courts of Justice should receive sufficient funding to extend its opening hours from the current four mornings to five full days a week.[52] This required better accommodation, assistance with equipment and some help with additional salary costs. The Lord Chancellor has now given additional funding for this. LAG, of course, deplores the cuts to legal aid eligibility and recognises that these have now bitten to such an extent that many are deprived of access to the courts. The minimum action needed is that advice provision must be extended to the county courts.

Class and multi-party actions

It is currently unfashionable to talk of 'unmet need for legal services'. Though deployed freely in the 1970s, the underlying implications of the phrase have been consistently attacked as problematic since the need for legal services tends to be defined by providers rather than recipients.[53] However, bearing in mind such reservations, one current area of unmet need, or at least procedural and financial deficiency, can be identified in the handling of cases of the kind that arise in relation to defective products or accident disasters with multiple litigants.

The need for reform of multi-party or class actions has been apparent in the United Kingdom since the problems encountered by the Thalidomide cases of the 1970s and pressing since the Opren cases in the mid 1980s. Lord Woolf will consider this issue in his final report.

Unfortunately, recent domestic history indicates some reluctance to grapple with the admittedly difficult issues involved. The Civil Justice Review ducked the issue in 1988 by calling for more investigation:

> The Lord Chancellor is invited to institute a separate study by one of the law reform agencies of the case for extending the availability of representative or class actions, or establishing other procedures, to be available in cases where there are large numbers of litigants whose claims or defences

have a common basis. The study should extend to the funding of such cases.[54]

Lord Mackay responded to continuing pressure by requiring the Legal Aid Board to examine the issue. The board produced a report in 1991. The board, still at the time a very young institution, took a narrow view of its remit. It devoted only three paragraphs of its report to the interrelationship of court procedures and funding, arguing in the same terms as the review team three years earlier: 'It is desirable that a review of how multi-party action cases are handled in the High Court should take place.'[55]

LAG has consistently argued, in the words of its submission to the board in 1989, that the issues of procedure and funding were 'so closely interlinked they cannot and ought not to be separated'.[56] The subsequent experience of the Legal Aid Board suggests that this is correct. The board incurred costs of between £30 and £35 million before deciding that legal aid should be withdrawn in abortive litigation regarding the effects of the tranquiliser Benzodiazepene. This spurred it to renewed consideration of the issues. Recognising that adequate reform required changes to procedure as well as legal aid, it suggested that 'the Lord Chancellor's Department should address the procedures for handling these actions in the courts'.[57]

The board's concern at the inadequacies of current procedures appears to have been shared by the judiciary. The Supreme Court Procedure Committee, responding to the very practical problems of taking multi-party actions produced in 1991 a guide to procedure, noting, however, that 'the existing law is in some respects uncertain' and reform overdue.[58] Chapter 2 reports on developments in such litigation in Canada where similar rules about cost indemnity mean that experience is likely to be more relevant in the United States where, generally, litigants are liable only to pay their own costs and not those of their opponents, even if they lose.

Comparison

This survey of contemporary domestic issues provides the basis for the proposals for reform advanced in the final chapter. It also gives some background for comparison with the review of innovation in the United States and Canada set out in the next chapter. This deals with developments in many of the same themes discussed above, with one notable exception. The key issue of the lessons from Canada and the United States in the deployment of various forms of bureaucratised justice is left to Carrie Menkel-Meadow and Garry Watson, acknowledged experts in their own jurisdictions.

References

1 Lord Hailsham, *Hamlyn Revisited: the British legal system today* (Stevens, 1983) p85.

2 The court statistics are taken from Lord Chancellor's Department, *Judicial Statistics Annual Report 1994* (HMSO, Cm 2891, 1995), as are all 1994 court figures unless otherwise stated. The tribunal figures are taken from Council on Tribunal's *Annual Report 1993/94* (HMSO, 22, 1994). The number of Law Lords in taken from *Whitaker's Almanac 1995* (Whitaker, 1994) and those for the other judiciary from Lord Chancellor's Department, Court Service *Annual Report 1994–95* (HMSO, 579, 1995). The figures are as at 1 April 1995.

3 Lord Woolf, *Access to Justice: Interim report to the Lord Chancellor on the civil justice system in England and Wales* (Woolf Inquiry Team, 1995) hereafter referred to as 'Lord Woolf's report') and *Litigants in Person in the Royal Courts of Justice, London: an interim report of the Working Party established by the Judges Council under the Rt Hon Lord Justice Otton* ('the Otton report') (Judges Council, 1995).

4 Lord Chancellor's Department, *Judicial Statistics 1989* (HMSO Cm 1154, 1990).

5 To 157,453.

6 Statistics of type of case are only published in relation to the 20 per cent or so of cases begun in London.

7 935 out 3,208 in 1994.

8 447 out of the 3,208.

9 Reported on 8 December 1995.

10 'Judges and decision-makers: the theory and practice of *Wednesbury* review', unpublished.

11 *R v Preston Supplementary Benefit Appeal Tribunal ex p Moore and Shine* [1975] 1 WLR 624, CA.

12 *Howell v Chief Supplementary Benefit Officer* (1982) unreported.

13 *Judicial Statistics 1994.*

14 Legal Aid Board *Annual Report 1994–95* (HMSO, 536, 1995).

15 Ibid, table Civil 9, p62.

16 See *Shaping the Future*, chapter 3, and *A Strategy for Justice*, chapter 2.

17 H Genn and Y Genn, *The Effectiveness of Representation at Tribunals* (Lord Chancellor's Department, 1989) p99, and see *A Strategy for Justice*, chapter 6.

18 Civil Justice Review, *Report of the Review Body on Civil Justice* (HMSO, Cm 394, 1988).

19 *Supreme Court Practice 1993* vol 1 pvii.

20 *Evening Standard*, 7 June 1995. See also C Glasser, 'Civil Justice – a time for change' in *Shaping the Future* (above) chapter 15.

20A July 1988 p3.

21 *Civil Justice on Trial – the case for change* (Law Society/General Council of the Bar, 1993) usually known by the name of its co-chairs as the Heilbron/Hodge report.

22 Justice, *Going to Law: a critique of English civil procedure*, 1974.

23 Lord Chancellor's Department, *Legal Aid – Targeting Need* (HMSO, Cm 2854, 1995) and Lord Chancellor's Department, *Looking to the Future: mediation and the grounds for divorce* (HMSO, 1995).

24 Woolf Report para 18.27.

25 Labour Party, *Access to Justice: Labour's proposals for reforming the civil justice system*, 1995.

26 *Legal Aid – Targeting Need* (HMSO, Cm 2854, 1995) para 1.1.

27 *Access to Justice: a comment and some proposals* (Liberal Democrat Lawyers Association, 1995).

28 eg, in R Smith (ed), *Shaping the Future: new directions in legal services* (LAG, 1995) at pp11–14.

29 Legal Action Group, *Access to Justice: an initial response to Labour's proposals for reforming the civil justice system*, 1995, para 3.

30 Woolf Report, para 3.

31 See M Cappelletti and B Garth, *Access to Justice, Volume 1: a world survey*, (Sijthoff & Noordhoff, 1978) chapter 1.

32 Ibid, p49.

33 Ibid, p18.

34 Ibid, p20.

35 Ibid, p21.

36 Woolf Report, Introduction.

37 Ibid, para 3.1.

38 Civil Justice Review (above), para 1.1.

39 LAG, 1992.

40 Ibid, p44.

41 Civil Justice Review, *Housing Cases* (Lord Chancellor's Department, 1988) p23.

42 See, eg, *Shaping the Future* (above) p20.

43 Quoted in Otton Report, para 1.1.2.

44 *Looking to the Future: mediation and the ground for divorce* (HMSO, Cm 2799, 1995) para 4.35.

45 Otton Report (above) para 22.6.

46 Access to Justice Advisory Committee, *Access to Justice: an action plan*, 1995, p387.

47　Woolf Report, para 5.12.

48　Scottish Law Commission, *Multi-Party Actions: report by working party set up by Scottish Law Commission* (1993) and *Multi-Party Actions: court proceedings and funding* (1994).

49　See, for example, Professor Michael Zander's contribution to Lord Woolf's access to justice seminar on 27 January 1995; C Glasser, 'Civil Procedure: time for a change' in *Shaping the Future:* (above).

50　National Consumer Council, *Civil Justice and Legal Aid,* 1995, p13.

51　Woolf Report para 18.35.

52　Otton Report para 4.7.

53　See, eg, P Morris, R White, P Lewis, *Social Needs and Legal Action* (Martin Robertson, 1973).

54　Recommendation 27, Civil Justice Review, *Report of the Review Body on Civil Justice* (HMSO, Cm 394, 1988) p156.

55　Legal Aid Board, *Report on Proposals to the Lord Chancellor relating to the Legal Aid Aspects of Multi-Party Actions* September 1991, page unnumbered.

56　Legal Action Group, *Response to the Legal Aid Board's Consultation Paper on Multi-Party Actions,* 1989, p1.

57　Legal Aid Board, *Issues arising for the Legal Aid Board and the Lord Chancellor's Department from Multi-Party Actions,* May 1994, p1. See also Civil Litigation Committee, *Group Actions made Easier* (Law Society, 1995).

58　Supreme Court Procedure Committee, *Guide for Use in Group Actions,* May 1991, p4.

CHAPTER 2

Access to justice: innovation in North America

ROGER SMITH

> The Judicial Conference should undertake to examine *de novo* the role and mission of the federal courts as well as the goals that will carry them into the future. Such a 'fresh start' renewal ensures that the federal courts are neither trapped by the choices of earlier planners nor oblivious to the new forces – and new voices – within and outside the judicial branch that shape their role in government and society.[1]

So ends a 'long-range' planning document of the Federal Judicial Center of the United States published in March 1995.

The US judges are not frightened to reveal their highly political agenda or reveal a certain delight in constructing the consequences of its rejection:

> It is 2020 . . . Austerity is a way of life . . . The queue for civil cases lengthens to the point where federal judges rarely conduct civil trials. User fees proliferate and would be judged onerous by 20th century standards. As a consequence many litigants seek justice from private providers. Overworked and underpaid administrators defer maintenance on court-houses and no longer update library collections. Most vacancies on the federal bench go unfilled for long periods of time because capable lawyers, once attracted to a judicial career, are no longer willing to serve . . .[2]

The US judges raise this nightmare vision only, of course, to provide a more optimistic future, based both on more adequate financial resources and on the development of existing innovative practices, such as alternative dispute resolution. Many of these are discussed in more detail later in this chapter and in chapter 4. However, the very existence of such a report provides an interesting contrast with domestic experience. Here, the task of examining the courts' future was given to one judge alone, Lord Woolf.[3]

Policy and objectives

Comparative consideration of judicial engagement in policy immediately raises constitutional differences between the United Kingdom and the United States. The constitutions of Canada and Great Britain have greater similarities. The US constitutional doctrine of the separation of powers enunciated in a written constitution, ultimate construction of which is given to a Supreme Court, gives the judiciary a greater autonomy, if short of complete independence, from the executive and the legislature. A British judge operates within the confines of a constitutional theory fundamentally unchanged since Francis Bacon prescribed the judiciary's position as 'lions beneath the throne', albeit that sovereign monarch has become sovereign parliament.

In consequence, those who are, or aspire to be, government ministers are usually keen to emphasise the constitutionally limited nature of the independence of the British judiciary. As a recent innovation, the judges formed a vehicle, the Judges' Council, to let off steam at Lord Mackay's assault on the privileges of the Bar. Senior judges like the Master of the Rolls and the Lord Chief Justice make occasional forays into political debate. But, there remains no organisational voice that represents the judiciary as a whole. The executive is not particularly concerned that there should be one. It was notable, for instance, that in establishing the Court Service as an administrative agency in April 1995 neither government ministers nor service officials paid much attention to the views of the judiciary on the service established to administer the courts in which they work. The judges are not mentioned in the service's *Framework Document* in the list of those relevant to the notion of 'accountability'.[4] They are not even accorded the shadowy status of 'stakeholders' in its operation.

By contrast, the different position of the US judiciary encourages the sort of wide-ranging political intervention represented by the document quoted in the opening section. The judiciary has fought to maximise its influence through, for instance, the successful establishment in 1967 of a Federal Judicial Center with a continuing brief to provide education and training, research and publications and material in other media.[5]

The Center has grown into a large, well-established and well-resourced operation. It occupies a prestige building in Washington; has an overall brief 'to further the development and adoption of improved judicial administration'; advertises a catalogue of 157 currently available publications; reported that in 1994 it had 'completed

33 research or planning projects and continued work on 84 others'; had a turnover of around $18 million and around 150 employees, some 30 or so of whom work in its research department.[6] The Center has been mandated by the US Congress to monitor the effects of its Civil Justice Reform Act 1990 in requiring federal courts to introduce 'expense and delay reduction plans'. It has, accordingly, produced a large 400-page tome reporting on progress.[7] It has undertaken and published a large amount of research on ADR, to which reference is made below.[8]

The Center thus plays a powerful role in supporting the Judicial Conference of the United States, the formal body representing the federal judiciary. Deployment of its resources and personnel has enabled the Conference not only to foster judicial research and education but also to develop its own long-term planning in a way which would be unthinkable in a British context. A conference committee on the subject is, accordingly, in the process of consulting on such a plan and has produced a 175-page set of proposals.[9]

Such long-term views of judicial developments have become somewhat fashionable in recent years. State-based commissions in both California and Massachusetts (see also p121) have recently attempted similar exercises. The latter, for example, provides an enthusiastic view of a revived justice system 'that creates and reflects the values of a just society . . . equality, the inherent dignity of every human being, mutual respect for difference, fairness, full participation in political and social life, and an ethic of shared responsibility for one another.'[10]

Canada has indulged less in such flights of imagination, yet provides an interesting contrast with Lord Woolf's inquiry into civil justice. An equivalent civil justice review has been undertaken in Ontario. It has been conducted by way of two tracks of work. One has led to a report recommending immediate reforms: the other to the publication of a study paper raising more long-term issues for the civil justice system.[11] Such an approach is not without problems or, indeed, critics. It is difficult to produce long-term analysis which is sufficiently detailed and specific in its discussion to maintain a relevance to the concerns of policy-makers and practitioners orientated to the problems of today. Nevertheless, the widespread consideration of future policy contrasts strongly with the situation in the UK.

North American jurisdictions, both in Canada and the United States, appear more willing to accept a wider role for courts than the simple processing of cases submitted to them. Courts and the judiciary are more accepted as having a symbolic importance in relation to the justice system as a whole. British Columbia's commitment to educational work is discussed in some detail below. The Massachussetts commission on the future of the courts emphasised the same point: 'Education is the means to independent thinking, to self-respect, to connection to society, to participation in community life. We recommend programs to link schools with courts, to enable judges and other court personnel to visit schools, and to encourage students to visit and work within the courts.'[12]

Greater autonomy perhaps encourages the judiciary to take a broader responsibility for access. The rise in court fees to full 'user pays' is regarded in Great Britain as a wholly domestic matter for the Lord Chancellor. By contrast, the Judicial Conference of the United States discussed whether court costs should be raised to meet running costs a couple of years ago and rejected the idea.[13] The idea, also rejected by an Australian commission on justice,[14] was anathema also to a senior administrator in Massachussets who considered that charging full-cost fees would breach constitutional rights contained in the provision that: 'Every subject of the commonwealth ought to obtain right and justice freely, and without being able to purchase it; completely, and without denial; promptly, and without delay, conformably to the laws.'

Courts and education

British Columbia

British Columbia's commitment to a broad view of the role of courts is striking. Across the street from the People's Law School, described by its director in *Shaping the Future*,[15] is another major provider of law-related education, the Law Courts Education Society. Its offices are integrated inside Vancouver's superb central court building, conceived overall as a public space with a startlingly beautiful atrium, roof gardens and a water-covered glass roof over the small claims waiting area. In harmony with the building, the creation of the Society was an expression of a desire, in the words of its director Rick Craig, 'to create a partnership between the judges and the Attorney-General's Department within an agenda of changing the culture in the courts. We are not preaching the system. We are trying to open it up to response.'[16]

The society, established in 1989, has the formal purpose of maintaining:

a bridge between British Columbians and the court system in order to broaden public understanding of the court system and how it works.

Its objectives are to:

(a) provide the public, both within the education system and otherwise, with greater understanding of the legal principles and processes in action through the court system;

(b) assist court personnel in understanding the legal education and information needs of different communities of British Columbians and involve court personnel in the delivery of legal education programs to meet these needs;

(c) identify areas in which better knowledge and understanding of the court system is required.[17]

The Society is well resourced (current annual funding is just short of 1 million Canadian dollars or around £500,000) and well supported by the judiciary. Many give up part of their lunch hours from time to time to talk to the school parties brought in to watch the courts at work. British Columbia, unlike England and Wales, has sought to incorporate law within its national curriculum. It figures as a compulsory component within the social studies curriculum taken in one secondary school year and as an optional course available in another. Law is taught more generally in earlier years. Rick Craig explains: 'Our ideal is to bring a school child into contact with a court at least twice before he or she leaves school.' Such has been the backing for the society that the Vancouver court was built with three seminar rooms available for use as mock courts: it is government policy for all new courts to have similar accommodation. In 1994–95, the society organised 413 mock trials, for which it has a number of standard programmes, and 1,189 courtwatching sessions.

A distinctive emphasis is given to the Society's work by the particular circumstances of British Columbia. The Society has put considerable resources into the preparation of material for native communities and also for new immigrants to the province. However, it handles the interaction between courts and the public in a way that provides a generally applicable example. It is responsible for much of the training given to court staff and the judiciary, eg, on multiculturalism. Rick Craig reports: 'We are doing a lot of cultural awareness work with staff. It tends at the moment to be a bit ad hoc but we are trying to develop a model for it. We are working towards a five-year plan and taking the province city by city so that we can orientate our provision to local need. We are working on a pilot of the theme of "developing awareness into action". The training day ends with the drafting of an action plan. We hope to persuade the court to roll up these into its annual report.'

Ontario

A commitment to legal education and information is also manifest elsewhere in Canada. Ontario's Civil Justice Review reported in March 1995, conducted jointly by the Ontario Court of Justice and the Ministry of the Attorney-General. It made a number of recommendations on education, arguing that 'the Ministry of Education, elementary and secondary schools, universities and community colleges play a greater role in the education of the public with respect to the purpose, values and processes of the civil justice system'. It also advocated the development of videos on family law and procedure 'that could be purchased by lawyers and community resources. Viewing of this video would become a mandatory pre-condition for entering the Family Law court process, with exceptions for emergency applications.'[18]

Courts, litigants and new technology

Canada may provide the best example of a link between conventional education and the courts. Unsurprisingly, it is the United States that makes the best use of new technology. The most interesting provision is made in Arizona, set in the USA's sunbelt and one of its fastest-growing areas. Despite the rapid influx of newcomers, the state remains small in absolute numbers, with a population of just under 4 million. It has, however, a staggeringly high divorce rate – around 30,000 per year, a rate of one divorce per 133 inhabitants. (The comparable rate for England and Wales is around one for every 333.) Noreen Sharp of the Superior Court of Arizona in Maricopa County (based in downtown Phoenix) explains some of the consequences which have encouraged innovative provision of assistance to litigants:

> Only 8 per cent of divorce cases now have lawyers on both sides. We have judges that do not see a lawyer for six weeks. 80 per cent of cases go by default and 80 per cent of those come back within a year.[19]

What is particularly interesting about Arizona is that two courts have responded to the same problem in different ways. The court in Maricopa County, the area that contains Phoenix, has employed Noreen Sharp to establish a 'self-service' provision, including a 12,000 square foot centre on the fourth floor of its court building. Meanwhile, the Arizona Supreme Court, with headquarters a little further down the street, has begun an experiment with electronic self-service kiosks, discussed below.

Ms Sharp has a bold strategy and a $1 million budget. She wishes to dispense three types of services: information on such matters as court locations and hours, and tips on self-representation and court procedures; court forms and instructions; and information on lawyers, ADR providers and duty advisers. These services are currently available in four forms. Details have been printed which can be obtained from the court. They have also been recorded on around six hours of tapes through which callers can move by way of an automated telephone system and hopefully find the information that they need. All services are currently available through an electronic bulletin board accessible through E-mail. Newly operational is an internet version with hypertext cross-referencing.

The intention is to develop the court premises, in Ms Sharp's words, as a 'mother site' which then feeds 'secondary' sources of information based in places such as community colleges, local libraries and lower level courts. Access is also available at the 'primary' level of individual homes and offices through the internet, computer bulletin board and the automated telephone system. She is proposing a high-tech, low-staff operation with ambitious targets: 'I see this as a three-year project. We are spending the first developing our information, court forms and instructions in hard copy at the mother site as well as on the bulletin board and the internet. In the second, we will develop the secondary sites and increase public awareness of access through homes and offices. After that, we hope to have increasing use of primary and secondary sites and less use of the court site.' Obsolescence is already built in. Ms Sharp sees the bulletin board, for instance, as only a temporary solution to the communication problem: 'I don't expect it to last more than a couple of years.'

Ms Sharp's long-term hope is the potential of the internet to deliver to widely available sources. She is undeterred by those who say that many people will not feel competent to access its treasures: 'You can bring in a mentor to help you if you cannot use it yourself.' She anticipates that video will soon be easy to add to internet information and sees no problem in adding such things as touch-screens to help accessibility.

Linked to the courts' approach to litigants in person is the profession's response to the same phenomenon. In 1994, the State Bar of California produced *The Pro-Per Counselling Handbook* to encourage attorneys to assist litigants in person, at a profit. It explains: 'how you – a California lawyer – can expand your practice by providing a valuable service to the many consumers who . . . lack affordable access to our civil justice system.'[20] This approach is very much that of the 'unbundled' services advocated in Forrest Mosten's contribution to *Shaping the Future*.[21] The State Bar of Arizona has become sufficiently aware of the issues relating to unbundled legal services that it has issued guidance on the ethical considerations of acting for 'pro per' litigants, reminding its members of such issues as client confidentiality and lawyers' inability to get clients to agree in advance to waive their liability for negligent advice.[22] It has, however, been broadly supportive and attorneys are on the courts' referral lists.

Proponents see the provision of unbundled services combined with court assistance as a way of lawyers clawing back a market currently threatened by paralegals. One attorney was quoted as saying that they were 'finding a way to bring . . . consumers and lawyers back together again'.[23] Maricopa's chief court administrator even sees unbundling as a desirable backwards move: 'To a certain extent it is getting back to the way lawyering was practised many years ago in small communities where someone needing legal advice could seek out a lawyer who was simultaneously a friend or acquaintance, ask for advice in a particular subject or issue, and get billed only for that particular interchange.'[24]

Meanwhile, the Arizona Supreme Court favours its electronic kiosks. These were described in one of the contributions to *Shaping the Future: new directions in legal services*.[25] The idea of the kiosk has been enthusiastically received. Lord Woolf recommended that 'information technology kiosks should be introduced on a trial basis in selected courts'.[26] The recent green paper on legal aid speculates that under its proposals: 'it would be feasible to deliver legal services in ways which are either rare or not possible under the current scheme. For example, use could be made of telephone advice lines or electronic information kiosks.'[27]

A number of experiments were made with this technology before Arizona began its co-operation with North Communications Inc of Los Angeles that led to the current generation of kiosks. An early variant is used in Vancouver's provincial court to help litigants through small claims procedures. It displays options on a touchscreen which allow users to follow their way through the procedure. It does not, however, use visual or video material. There were signs, apparent on visiting it, that this kiosk was not well used: the touchscreen did not function in one area; the racks for small claims literature that surround the machine were empty, particularly noticeable because the

Vancouver courts generally employ a computerised tracking system for display literature and elsewhere had leaflets well available.

The North Communications kiosk is considerably more sophisticated. In the summer of 1995, three *QuickCourt* kiosks were operational, all in courts in Arizona – Tucson, Mesa and Scottsdale. North Communications was on the point of selling more to Arizona and a large order to the state of Utah. More orders were in the pipeline. A number of other orders were being negotiated. The company produces a range of other products using the same technology, including *AutoClerk* dealing with traffic cases. It also has a range of kiosks dispensing government and tourist services. For instance, a North Communications kiosk stands in Santa Monica's main street for the guidance of tourists.

The exact current use made of *QuickCourt* is hard to determine. Statistics for the three Arizona kiosks are available for 1993, during which 1,751 people accessed its information on court overview, 6,112 on small claims and 3,098 used it to complete and print divorce forms. The court has been sufficiently impressed to decide that it should order another 135. These will, however, be different. Utilising the kiosk technology to process credit and debit cards, these will charge an estimated $30 (about £20) for the process of producing divorce forms. The court appears to have reached this figure by halving the usual $60 fee which it estimates is the market level for paralegal 'docu-prep' services. Certain improvements may be made in the kiosks. For instance, it is hoped that the kiosks will be incorporated in desks which allow the user to be seated during the average 20–30 minutes or longer that it takes to go through the whole process of completing and printing a divorce form.

The three kiosks have not been equally successful. I watched the one in Scottsdale for around an hour. Two people used it and it did not have the information that either of them sought. Location seems, however, to be important. The Scottsdale court does not, in fact, have a divorce jurisdiction so it is perhaps unsurprising that there were few people wanting to use its assistance on this topic. Jeanie Lynch, the manager of the contract for the courts, says: 'Success with the kiosks depends very much on the audience. For Tucson, the technology is too sophisticated. In Mesa, it seems about right.'[28] Furthermore, other matters are relevant, says Ms Lynch: 'My concern is that the court must have a "buy in" to it. The kiosk that works best is in Mesa, where it is set up in a law library and supervised by its staff. They keep a list of problems and make appointments for people to use it.'

It seems, therefore, as if the kiosk should be seen as complementary to other advice provision rather than as an alternative. Ms Lynch reports other issues that have arisen. These include the owner-ship of the intellectual property in the finished script as between the court where it originated and the publisher/manufacturer. There are conflicts of interest over payment, advertising and sponsorship. There are differences over emphasis. Ms Lynch says: 'The volume of need is in landlord and tenant cases and small claims, not just divorce which is the area that has been seized upon.' Nevertheless, the court is enthusiastic over the development. Contrary to some press reports, it has not gone sufficiently gung-ho to wish to place the kiosks in shop-ping malls: these are not thought appropriate. Indeed, the demands from the Mesa court have been for more privacy for users.

It has been argued that the kiosks, which have until now used laser disks, represent rapidly outdated technology. North Communications is now moving to digital reproduction of its information and, beyond that, is preparing for services which can be provided on-line.

Court-annexed alternative dispute resolution

One of the distinctive developments in US courts over the last 20 years has been, as Carrie Menkel-Meadow pointed out in her contribution to *Shaping the Future*,[29] the increasing use of a range of alternative methods of dispute resolution. The cause of alternative dispute resolution (ADR) has been advanced by a number of factors. Its emergence can be dated to the intellectually appealing nature of the 'multi-door courthouse' advanced by Professor Frank Sander in the late 1970s. He projected the vision that, by the year 2000, a court-house be:

> not simply a courthouse but a Dispute Resolution Center, where the grievant would first be channelled through a screening clerk who would then direct him/her to the process (or sequence of processes) most appropriate to his/her type of case. The room directory of such a center might read as follows: screening clerk – room 1; mediation – room 2; arbitration – room 3; fact-finding – room 4; malpractice screening panel – room 5; superior court – room 6; and ombudsman – room 7.[30]

Professor Sander's idea was matched on the ground by a range of community-based mediation programmes and neighbourhood justice centres which saw themselves as outside the court process and deliberately deployed lay mediators.

As the 1980s progressed, the US judiciary and legislature became increasingly interested in the potential of ADR within programmes to reduce delay and increase the level of court management over cases. In 1983, the federal judicial rules were amended to provide for the use of 'extrajudicial procedures to resolve the dispute'.[31] In 1988, Congress authorised 20 federal courts to offer ADR, half on an 'opting in' basis and half through semi-mandatory 'opting out' schemes. In 1990, the Civil Justice Reform Act (CJRA) listed ADR as one of six desirable principles of case management. By the end of 1994, 'at least two-thirds of the [94] courts now authorize one or more forms of ADR'.[32] Congress also required the Federal Judicial Center and an independent research operation, the RAND Corporation, to study ADR.

ADR attracts scepticism as well as true believers. Opposition is rampant among legal classicists like Professor Owen Fiss who objects to the substitution of judgment by settlement that results from 'trivializing the remedial dimensions of a lawsuit, and also by reducing the social function of a lawsuit to one of resolving private disputes'.[33] Professor Abel represented another strand of objection in his book *Informal Justice* and other writings in the early and mid 1980s: 'Until [the] millennium comes, formality is the best, often the only, defense against power.'[34] He confirmed during an interview that his view has not really changed: 'ADR is only desirable in very precise and limited circumstances.'[35]

Within a domestic UK context, LAG has been historically committed to the rights-based approach exemplified by Professor Abel. Outside matrimonial cases, it has given little consideration to the potential of ADR. There are signs in the US of a greater acceptance of ADR techniques among those who might in the past have been more hostile. The *Clearinghouse Review*, from which Professor Abel's quote comes, has more recently published more welcoming assessments of ADR and advocated a pragmatic approach: 'Picking and choosing among programs, and deciding which clients and problems can benefit from them, requires both knowledge and sensitivity on the part of legal services advocates.'[36] The support of Alan Houseman, director of the influential Center for Law and Social Policy and a guru of the legal services movement, for this argument is particularly significant.

Pragmatism was also in evidence in discussion with Bill McNeill of the Employment Law Center, funded by legal services, in San Francisco:

> Clients often don't understand about litigation. They often think that filing the law suit is the end not the beginning. We tend to use early neutral evaluation and mediation. Two cases in particular have been very successful for us. ADR procedures are more client-orientated and friendly.

Neutral evaluation can also help to move clients to be more reasonable. If ADR works well, it can save the parties cost; save the courts some expenditure; help to clarify issues and help settlement. Our experience of arbitration is not so good. Former judges appointed as arbitrators tend to think that they are still judges. I don't think that they are adequately trained or orientated.'[37]

The appropriateness of a pragmatic approach was confirmed by two observed court-annexed ADR sessions. One was a mediation; the other a court-ordered neutral evaluation. The mediation did appear to add to the quality of the process: each of the three sides in the disputes got a chance to express their version of events in a considerably less formal way than they would have in court. As a result, it seemed to me that they were participating in the debate much more than they would in a court. The evaluation seemed, in contrast, to be pointless. The case involved liability for a complicated road accident. Both parties were clearly uninterested in compromise and were ready for court. They seemed to be going through motions because they had been ordered to do so. A major difference between the two was the role of the lawyers and the neutral. The evaluation was dominated by the lawyers and was managed very like an informal court hearing. The mediation was much more in the hands of the parties.

During the trip, it was possible to visit four ADR schemes, all different but all highly respected. They had the following characteristics.

The Middlesex Multi-Door Courthouse in Cambridge, Mass

This is the subject of Barbara Stedman's chapter 5. She gives definitions to various forms of ADR, such as mediation (p127), case or early neutral evaluation (ENE) (p128), complex case management (p128), arbitration (p128) and summary jury trial (p129).

The District Court for the District of Columbia

This court ADR programme began in 1989. It offers mediation and early neutral evaluation. These are governed by the following principles:

* The parties enter ADR by consent;
* any judge on the Court may participate in the program; the individual judges select the cases and recommend them for either ENE [early neutral evaluation] or mediation;
* the mediators and evaluators are highly-qualified attorneys who serve the Court without compensation;

* all mediators and evaluators are carefully trained before they begin to handle cases, and they attend periodic in-service training sessions;
* all mediation and ENE proceedings are confidential.[38]

The ADR process appears to have handled around 800 cases between 1989 and 1992. The programme has flourished with the support of the DC Bar, which provides funding for training and has developed standards. An experimental third programme was developed in 1992 and 1993 which included the mandatory referral of motor vehicle personal injury cases to a mixture of ENE and mediation.

A distinctive feature of the programme is the *pro bono* involvement of the mediators and neutrals: 'Litigants often react very favorably when they realize – sometimes midway through a mediation or evaluation – that the neutral is working on a *pro bono* basis. The realization that the volunteer believes in the process and is spending considerable personal time on the problem breaks through the cynicism with which some people approach ADR and often infuses new energy into the discussions,' reports the programme's administrator.[39]

The programme has achieved some spectacular successes. The largest mediated settlement resulted in the payment of $38 million (about £25 million) for alleged discrimination in the employment practices of the Potomac Electric Power Company:

> Participants on both sides of the case hailed the settlement as a strong vindication of the use of mediation in large, complex employment disputes. One lawyer praised the 'extremely skilled' mediator assigned to the case, who 'kept us talking when we were still having problems and led us to find a way to resolve some very difficult issues.'[40]

The appellate mediation program for the United States Court of Appeals for the District of Columbia

This is a part of a larger programme in the DC courts. It handles less than 100 cases a year yet claims 'a significant impact on the court's caseload'.[41] The parties can request mediation and are screened about six weeks after filing. Again mediators are volunteers. Mediation is confidential. 'The primary role of program mediators is to make every effort to help parties resolve some issues in the case. If settlement is not possible, the mediators will help parties clarify or eliminate issues to expedite the litigation process.'[41A]

The ADR programme of the Northern District of California

This contains elements of a mandatory programme of court-annexed ADR in an ADR Multi-Option Pilot. The court-annexed arbitration programme was first established in 1978. It was designated under the CJRA 1990 as one of five 'demonstration districts' for review of ADR between 1991 and 1994. In 1989, it prepared a booklet on ADR procedures. It also has a list of private ADR providers. The booklet is given to all plaintiffs at the time of issue of their summons. Court orders require service of the booklet on defendants.

The court sponsors seven and recognises eight ADR procedures, all of which are confidential and non-binding:

1) *Early neutral evaluation*   50 per cent of all cases in the following categories are automatically assigned to ENE:

> contract (including business contracts, insurance coverage, Miller Act, negotiable instrument, stockholders suits and contract product liability); torts (including motor vehicle, motor vehicle product liability, personal injury, personal injury – product liability, and fraud); civil rights (employment); intellectual property; antitrust; racketeer influenced and corrupt organizations; and securities/commodities exchange.[42]

Exceptions proposed in draft court rules would exempt some categories that would otherwise be included: 'Class actions, cases in which the principal relief sought is injunctive, or in which one or more of the parties is proceeding in pro per'.[43]

Others can opt for ENE. Evaluators provide the first four hours free, as volunteers, thereafter the cost is $150 (about £100) an hour. Mandatory ENE has been imposed for the last two years.

2) *Mediation*   This is confidential, non-binding and may be mandatory. Costs are as for ENE.

3) *Arbitration*   This is mandatory 'for contract or tort cases involving not less than $150,000 (exclusive of punitive or exemplary damage, interest and costs)'.[44] It can also be used voluntarily. Costs are as for ENE.

4) *Trial by a magistrate*   A party may consent to trial by a magistrate rather than a judge.

5) *Settlement conferences conducted by a judge or magistrate*

6) *Non-binding summary jury or bench trial*

7) *Appointment of a special master to perform a specified task*

8) *Private dispute resolution*

A court booklet explains: 'There are numerous dispute resolution providers in the private sector offering a variety of services, including arbitration, fact-finding, conciliation, mediation, negotiation, and private trials. The role of the "neutral" can be played by retired judges, law professors, former government officials and experienced attorneys . . .'[45] This procedure has become widely, and somewhat disrespectfully, known as 'rent-a-judge'. This programme is included in an evaluation of 10 similar schemes researched by the Federal Judicial Center.[46]

ADR: a preliminary assessment

The Federal Judicial Center suggested the following as 'points of agreement' in a recent pamphlet on ADR:

* Although there is considerable evidence about user perceptions of ADR, research findings are currently insufficient on the cost and time consequences of ADR and cannot fully inform that part of the debate that revolves around cost and time. Research should not in any case displace other sources of guidance . . .
* ADR provides substantial benefits to litigants by satisfying their need to tell their story to a neutral. Courts should be responsive to the importance litigants place on a meaningful and fair forum . . .
* Efficiency should not be the overriding principle . . .
* Fair procedures and case outcomes as well as litigant and public satisfaction with the courts require that any court-based ADR programs provide high quality service . . .
* There appears to be a value in an early screening process to determine case needs and party preferences and to educate attorneys and litigants about their case-processing and dispute-resolution options.
* The outcomes of court-based ADR procedures, particularly mandatory procedures, must be nonbinding and must preserve access to trial without penalty, unless the parties voluntarily agree to a binding outcome.[47]

A number of themes emerged from interviews with those concerned in these schemes. These are discussed below. An assessment of the relevance of ADR in the context of UK domestic courts is set out in chapter 8.

The importance of mediation

Professor Sander called mediation 'the sleeping giant of the civil justice system' in a reference to its enormous potential. The Federal Judicial Center's Donna Stienstra confirmed: 'The numbers do suggest that mediation is the most popular form of ADR.' Judge Peter Agnes of Middlesex County, a committed ADR supporter, wished to be more discriminating: 'Mediation works best when the aim is to maintain a relationship, particularly in relation to children. It is also better than adjudication when the issue is how much someone should pay rather than whether they should pay anything.'

North California's Stephanie Smith gave two reasons for this: 'First, mediation is facilitative, intra-space and non-evaluative. Second, people define it so broadly that everything is included.' Her last point has some validity, particularly as there seemed widespread agreement that mediation was generally developing towards a more evaluative rather than facilitative form. This is no doubt helped by the growing domination in court-annexed ADR of lawyers as neutrals. This, in its turn, raised for Judge Agnes an important policy issue to be decided: 'whether the decision is entirely up to the parties. Are they free to agree whatever they want? The purists would say, "Yes". The other view is that the courts have a fundamental responsibility to be fair and to stay within the solutions permitted by the law.' Not surprisingly, courts seem to be coming to agreement on the latter position.

An interesting effect of the popularity of mediation is a consequent change in lawyers' practices. Forrest Mosten, a contributor to *Shaping the Future: new directions in legal services*, now proclaims his Los Angeles specialist matrimonial firm as 'attorneys and mediators'. Two lawyers in Boston said that mediation was now a substantial part of their practice. Both enjoyed it. One particularly liked the comradeship involved in being a member of a small group of mediators that met for 'brown bag lunches' and co-operated in their work rather than taking the adversarial position adopted by lawyers. He also admitted that the $150 an hour (about £100) that he could earn as a mediator was not that far below the $175 an hour (about £115) he charged when not operating on a contingency fee.

ADR has considerable support within a broad band of the US legal profession, as illustrated by consistent support for it by the American Bar Associations and local groups like the Beverly Hills Bar. This has a committee on ADR attended by general practitioners and a number of specialists in fields as diverse as patent and family law. There is some concern, however, at its effect. Judge Agnes reports some opposition from 'lawyers who fear that ADR involvement early in a case will lessen the costs that can be obtained from clients. They are concerned about what will happen to the practice of law.'

A number of people talked of early neutral evaluation and other arbitration-orientated techniques in terms of their being a 'reality check' for litigants on the strength of their case. The value of this in a British context, where legal aid and the indemnity cost rule provide such a check, might be significantly less.

A settlement climate

There is little evidence that incorporation of ADR saves money for courts, particularly those which have hired senior lawyers to run their ADR schemes. Donna Stienstra says, however, that 'judges report fewer motions', implying less procedural wrangling. Judge Agnes admitted that 'the impact on the number of trials is little if any'. He argued, in accordance with much other data, that 'there certainly is evidence of the effect of ADR in getting cases to settle earlier' though he added that 'early court intervention is what counts. I could not say that it is just ADR.' San Francisco employment lawyer Bill McNeill developed the same point in a slightly different way: 'It is true that cases settle when lawyers look at the file. Early ADR certainly makes you do that. It starts you off with the principle that settlement is not a problem.'

As a result, it would seem that any cost-benefit analysis of the potential effect of the introduction of ADR domestically should concentrate on savings in fees to clients and to legal aid rather than to the courts.

The importance of individuals

It was my clear, though unprovable, observation that the success of ADR schemes depended both on the skills and personality of their directors and of the individual mediators. ADR seemed to be very much in a pre-institutional, charismatic phase in which the personality and qualities of the particular individuals played an important part in the quality of provision.

The three permanently appointed directors of the programmes visited were all powerfully in command of their jobs and commanded considerable respect. Nancy Stanley in Washington DC's federal court in particular needed this, as a part of her work involved intervening in cases that had already been decided and were now under appeal. She selected likely candidates for settlement on the basis of whether there might 'be an underlying problem or a commercial interest' in coming to an agreement, a role that took considerable personal judgment. Practitioner McNeill paid tribute to Stephanie Smith's team: 'They are forceful. They ring you up. They keep the pressure on.'

My observation of the two neutrals at work in the ADR sessions that I saw convinced me that there was considerable variation and individuality in approach and effectiveness. Interestingly, both used exactly the same words in a bid to establish .credibility: 'I've been round the block a few times and . . .' The success of ADR seemed to me likely to be as dependent on the personal qualities of the neutral as any other factor.

ADR can be abused but the problem is not significant

A number of practitioners differed from Professor Sander's assertion to me that few lawyers tried to use ADR sessions to further their client's case by finding out the opposition's case while not disclosing their own. However, a Boston mediator and lawyer, Jeffrey Petrocelly, commented: 'One side can come to learn the other side's case. I would say that it might happen 10 per cent of the time. It just makes me feel disappointed. I have never been a lawyer who holds cards close to his chest so it does not really prejudice me. It just makes it a waste of time.'

Representation complements ADR

There was considerable agreement that court-annexed ADR was not an excuse for doing away with legal representation. Nancy Stanley reported that she 'discourages mediation for those without representation. We have been criticised for that but it puts the mediator in a difficult position. Each side needs its own representative. In addition, a very high percentage of *pro se* [unrepresented] litigants are emotionally very difficult. Sometimes a judge will require a *pro bono* advocate for someone who really needs it.' Bill McNeill confirmed that in his experience 'ADR does not work well with litigants in person'.

Some cases are unsuitable for ADR

Most ADR administrators were content for ADR to be mandatory in the sense that litigants had to opt out of participation, but all schemes also had cases for which they recognised that ADR was unsuitable. Most matrimonial schemes, for instance, excluded cases where there were allegations of domestic violence or the parties were manifestly unequal.

Payment

The observed ADR schemes had different policies in relation to the payment of mediators and neutrals. The Washington federal court scheme had no problem in obtaining *pro bono* volunteers from among the area's plethora of lawyers. The others paid varying amounts. Professor Sander raised questions about the profit required by the private providers. He feared that a prime motivation would become the desire of the owners to build up a large business so that they could, at the appropriate moment, sell it off for capital gain. He thought that raised issues on quality levels.

There were also different policies on whether litigants should pay. Terry Jones, acting head of the Washington Superior Court scheme, thought that 'it would be better to charge. We have well-off people who are not paying. Those sessions take the longest because they have the most to argue about. They come because we are good and have a good reputation. I would like to have a sliding fee, though it would be an administrative nightmare to take fees.' Judge Agnes argues that 'everyone should have access to ADR. We argue that the state constitution requires that we enter cases into the whole spectrum of settlement. Everyone should have the choice as to what is more appropriate. We recognise that acceptance of this might take time and, in the short run, we are prepared to expand our current system where people who can pay cross-subsidise others.'

Other issues

ADR faces a range of other current issues, such as qualification, training, referral methodology, the degree of acceptable compulsion, confidentiality and ethics. These are not, however, pursued here.

Class actions: mass markets and collective obligations

As discussed in the previous chapter, the English legal system is manifestly not finding it easy to adapt to one of the characteristics of modern society: the development of mass markets and collective obligations. Such actions involving a collective element can cover a wide spectrum of subjects. The Supreme Court Procedure Committee listed eight different examples of situations in which 'class actions' might arise.[48] The range of potential cases is not limited to private law. In 1993 the Law Commission raised the related issue of the role of group and public interests in the context of legal standing to take actions for judicial review.[49]

A study by the Ontario Law Reform Commission set out its understanding of why multi-party or class actions should have become a contemporary problem:

> It is the development of a highly complex, interdependent society that has impeded the capacity of each person to vindicate his legal rights. No longer are we faced with only a single individual or small business against whom we have some grievance . . . we live in a corporate society,

characterized by mass manufacturing, mass promotion and mass consumption. The production and dissemination of goods and services is now largely the concern of major corporations, international conglomerates, and big government . . . Inevitably, dramatic changes in production, promotion and consumption have give rise to what may be called 'mass wrongs' – that is, injury or damage to many persons caused by the same or very similar set of circumstances.[50]

From this position, an advisory committee deduced the need for a class action 'in which many similarly injured persons join together [and which, therefore,] can provide an effective and efficient means of litigating such mass claims . . . the presence of effective remedies must contribute to a sharper sense of obligation to the public by those whose actions affect large numbers of people. This is the case whether the obligation is owed by an aircraft manufacturer, a pharmaceutical company, a financial institution or even a government.'[50A]

The committee supplemented such utilitarian reasoning with a more political justification, that we:

live in a society that strives to maximize access to justice for its citizens. Sophisticated and highly evolved rights and obligations are of little value if they cannot be asserted and enforced effectively and economically. Of what value is a right or obligation, or the judicial system itself, if the users be told that the right is 'too small' or 'too complex' or 'too risky' to justify its enforcement?[51]

Class action procedures are, thus, designed to increase 'access to justice' by providing a practical procedure for cases which otherwise prove extremely difficult to be handled by the courts. For the prospective plaintiff in a mass product liability or disaster case, they have disadvantages that must be recognised. First, they can operate to provide a cap on the liability of, for instance, the manufacturer of a defective product. If a global award of damages is made, then the manufacturer at least knows the outer limits of the cost: it will be the amount of the collective award plus costs plus any payments to plaintiffs who opted out of the class action.

The desirability of such an effect has been seen as an advantage even by such a proponent of class actions as Judge Jack Weinstein, who saw through settlement of the Agent Orange litigation in the US. He accepts that at least 'particularly large disasters probably require a cap on the total cost to defendants . . .'[52] Such a position represents, however, the triumph of pragmatic over theoretical justice.

A class action is intended to bring together a large number of otherwise individual cases. This has its dangers for members of the group concerned: the fate of a large number of litigants rests on the one key case chosen as representing their class. For this reason, a plaintiff lawyer like Mike Eizenga, based in London, Ontario and taking a number of class actions under Ontario's new legislation cautions: 'Class actions are not the be all and end all. It is sometimes better to proceed against a defendant on a case-by-case basis.'[53]

Furthermore, class actions unavoidably subordinate the individual to the group. Decision-making, even at the nominal level, is taken from individual litigants and given to the professionals – the lawyers and judges concerned. The disempowering consequences of this move were demonstrated very clearly in the Agent Orange litigation, when various of the campaigning veterans groups were highly dissatisfied with the settlement worked out by the lawyers and the judge over the weekend before the trial was due to begin. One of the key plaintiffs expressed his dissatisfaction thus: 'A reporter calls me at 7 am Monday morning and tells me the case has been settled. We had no say in the settlement. Is it a lawyers' case or the clients' case? . . . The veterans got nothing.'[54]

As a result of this sort of experience, class actions are anathema to common law classicists. Professor Patrick Glenn of McGill University in Montreal criticised the Quebec scheme on its establishment, questioning why class actions should be 'allowed to distort the traditional adjudication process . . . when concepts of legal aid, small claims courts, administrative tribunals, arbitration and conciliation have left it intact, and have still greatly widened the dispute resolution process'.[55]

Professor Glenn remains convinced that class actions cannot give the 'exquisite care' possible, at least in theory, in cases with individual and identified litigants. He has 'a theoretical objection because courts are unable to deal with the circumstances of the individual'. He also raises a very practical problem: 'There is no research. No one knows what really happens in class actions. There are problems in relation to the ethics and conflicts of interest of the lawyers involved. There are also problems if we accept the notion that courts dispense "rough justice" in cases.'[56]

Class actions tend to reverse the usual lawyer-client relationship. As a result, the lawyers dominate the litigation. This is clear from Peter Shuck's brilliant account of the Agent Orange litigation.[57] This becomes particularly so when the lawyers are being paid by contingency fees. In Agent Orange, this led to lawyers dividing into two groups, with strikingly different interests when it came to settlement and the determination of costs, those who operated simply as bankers and put up money to keep the litigation going as against those who actually undertook some of the work.

Class actions raise, therefore, complex issues. For the purpose of this report, there are three questions to be addressed, at a very basic level:

a) What is the current (1995) state of class actions in the three provinces of Canada visited, British Columbia, Ontario and Quebec?

b) What is the experience of those involved in their operation, particularly in Quebec where there has been the longest period of operation?

c) What has Canadian experience to tell us in relation to ways of funding class actions?

Procedure

Canadian class action legislation is perhaps best approached through that of the United States which provided the original model. Rule 23 of the US Federal Rules of Civil Procedure has provided the basis for all Canadian legislation. It reads:

> One or more members of a class may sue or be sued as representative parties on behalf of all only if . . . the class is so numerous that joinder of all members is impracticable . . . there are questions of law or fact common to the class . . . the claims or defenses of the class, and . . . the representative parties will fairly and adequately protect the interest of the class.
>
> An action may be maintained if . . . in addition:
>
> (1) the prosecution of separate actions by or against individual members of the class would create a risk of . . . inconsistent or varying adjudications . . .
>
> (2) adjudications with respect to individual members of the class which would as a practical matter be dispositive of the interest of other members. . . .
>
> (3) the court finds that the questions of law or fact common to the members of the class predominate over any questions affecting only individual members, and that a class action is superior to other available methods for the fair and efficient adjudication of the controversy . . .

The US rule was introduced in 1966. It inspired legislation on class actions (*recours collectifs*) in Quebec in 1978 which added a funding mechanism through a class action fund (*Fonds d'aide aux recours collectifs*). Ontario followed in 1992 with a less generous funding mechanism. Most recently, British Columbia enacted legislation in 1995 with a variant of Ontario's legislation on class proceedings but without any funding mechanism other than contingency fees. Undoubtedly, momentum for change has been given by the pressing need to bring Canadian litigants into the US settlements of class action litigation in such cases as those relating to the Dalkon Shield and breast implants.

A major difference between litigation in the USA and Canada is the existence in the latter of a British-derived indemnity cost rule under which the loser of a civil action is generally liable for the costs of the victor. This adds another dimension to the considerations relating to litigation. It is the reason why this chapter examines only Canadian, and not US, class actions in any detail.

The three Canadian provisions are generally similar. A number of the differences that exist are not material to general consideration of their appropriateness as a model for domestic British implementation. However, some differences are noteworthy. The Quebec and British Columbia legislation applies only to plaintiffs: that of Ontario to both plaintiffs and defendants.

The British Columbian legislation is the most recent. Its drafters sought to take into account the problems seen to have arisen in Ontario and Quebec. It requires a court to certify a class action if:

(a) the pleadings disclose a cause of action;

(b) there is an identifiable class of two or more persons;

(c) the claims of the class raise common issues, whether or not those common issues predominate over issues affecting only individual members;

(d) a class proceeding would be the preferable procedure for the fair and efficient resolution of the common issues; and

(e) there is a representative plaintiff who

    (i) would fairly and adequately represent the interests of the class,

    (ii) has produced a plan for the proceeding that sets out a workable method of advancing the proceeding on behalf of the class and of notifying class members of the proceeding, and

    (iii) does not have, on the common issues, an interest that is in conflict with the interest of other class members.[57A]

The three provinces allow potential class members to opt out of the class to preserve their individual rights. The legislation also seeks to maintain a wide ambit for class litigation. For instance, the Ontario statute specifies that the following do not provide, by themselves, any justification for refusing certification:

1. The relief claimed includes a claim for damages that would require individual assessment after determination of the common issues.

2. The relief claimed relates to separate contracts involving different class members.
3. Different remedies are sought for different class members.
4. The number of class members or the identity of each class member is not known.
5. The class includes a subclass whose members have claims or defences that raise common issues not shared by all class members.[58]

The legislation allows a number of orders to be made by the court relating to the proceedings, in relation to notice provisions. The Ontario statute specifically allows statistical information as evidence even though this would not otherwise be admissible. The Quebec code allows collective and/or individual recovery. Two Quebec lawyers explain the difference: 'Collective recovery means that a defendant will be condemned to pay a single amount for the benefit of all the group's members, no matter how individual members will later be paid. A judgment for individual claims, on the other hand, implies no immediate conclusion either as to the total liability of the defendant or as to the amount to each member. In such a case each member must present a claim following the judgment and the defendant's final bill is known only when the last of these has been dealt with.'[59] As an alternative or supplement to damages, the court may order some other form of reparation.

Initial judicial reaction to class proceedings was very hostile and suspicious in both Quebec and Ontario. Early judgments in Ontario have indicated a somewhat inconsistent judicial approach. Quebec went through a similar period of judicial suspicion but now, according to former *Fonds* administrator Yves Lauzon, now private practitioner advocate, this has been overcome:

> The legislation is now working well but this has not been the result solely of its wording. For the first five years we had basically the same words but very conservative judges. In the period between 1979 and 1985, a large percentage of applications for certification as a class proceeding were denied and many defendants successfully appealed many of those [applications] granted. Then we had a landmark judgment in the court of appeal in the Dalkon Shield case. That changed everything. If we were doing it again, I would ensure that the judges were given more information about what was intended.[60]

Funding

The three Canadian jurisdictions have different provisions in relation to funding. British Columbia has followed the US model and intends that litigation using its newly created class action procedure will be funded by contingency fees. An official commented:

> We have had contingency fees in British Columbia for quite a while. We have found that they are a good way to provide access to the legal system. We went for a 'no way' costs rule [ie, generally no order for costs in any event]. There was a committee amendment for a 'one way' cost rule where only the plaintiff could be indemnified for costs but that was rejected as unfair. Academic literature recognised that a 'two way' costs rule [as applies in the UK] was a deterrent in class actions. We have a lot of common law which deters 'frivolous and vexatious' litigation.[61]

At the other extreme is the situation in Quebec. Its *Fonds d'aide aux recours collectifs* (*Fonds*) has operated since 1979. The *Fonds* is a small organisation, legally required to be administered by three people including a president and with a full-time administrator. Application can be made to the *Fonds* for funding either before or after the court has certified a class action. The *Fonds* can meet all or part of the costs, including all the applicant's legal costs. It operates a flexible means test without formal rules. The relevant provision states that:

> The Fonds shall study the applicant's application and it may, for that purpose, hear the applicant or his attorney.
>
> In order to determine whether to grant assistance, the Fonds shall assess whether the class action may be brought or continued without such assistance; in addition, if the status of representative has not yet been ascribed to the applicant, the Fonds shall consider the probable existence of the right he intends to assert and the probability that the class action will be brought.[62]

Administrator Louise Ducharme explains: 'The applicants have to produce information on their means and that of any other members of the class who are known. It is a very flexible test, much more flexible than legal aid.'[63]

The *Fonds*, if it accepts the case, agrees a budget to cover judicial fees, disbursements, notice costs and lawyers' costs up to $100 an hour (roughly £50). In return, the *Fonds* is subrogated to the lawyers' right to costs in the event of success. It is also liable for costs in the event of failure but the level of these is set at the lowest possible tariff (the one applicable for cases with a value of $1–3,000). Lawyers can agree an uplift on their normal costs with their clients but court approval is required.

The effect is to set up a double check on a class action. The lawyer involved requires the consent both of the court and of the *Fonds* to take a case. Consent is also now required to settle a case. Louise Ducharme explains: 'There was a settlement problem of lawyers settling in their own interest and not of the *Fonds*. In an attempt to counter this, they now require the consent of the *Fonds* and the court. The proposed settlement is the subject of a hearing by the *Fonds*.' For Ms Ducharme the role of the *Fonds* provides an important check on abuse by lawyers of the class action procedure:

> Public funding makes class actions less of a gamble and speculation. In the United States it has become a business. Here in Quebec, a mix of lawyers are taking class actions. Pensions lawyers are beginning to get involved. Class actions are regarded seriously. People do not think of them in an extreme way. We don't think of a class action as way of blackmailing even though it is a very powerful tool. Courts don't panic any more.

The *Fonds* operates on a small budget with what appears to be a creditable success rate. Its budget in 1993 was only a little over $750,000 (£375,000): its total cost over 15 years has only been around $14 million. As the largest cases begin to settle or are decided, so the percentage of recovered costs rises: it is currently around 12 per cent. Between 1979 and 1994, it assisted in 313 cases, the numbers rising as the procedure has become established and overcome judicial conservatism. 163 cases have come to a conclusion: 67 of these were successful.[64] They covered an impressively wide range of different matters including 'manufacturers' misrepresentations, non-delivery of goods, interruption of cable service, illegal strikes in public transportation, and damages caused by pollution . . . (t)ravellers frustrated by delays or false advertising, patients struggling to get the care and services to which they have a right, and workers seeking to recover unpaid wages from directors of a bankrupt company'.[65]

Ontario was sufficiently inspired by the Quebec model to seek to follow it. Its recent legislation established a Class Proceedings Fund. However, this fund is limited in its role to the payment of disbursements, though it does provide a costs indemnity for the litigant. The fund has been relatively little used, a fact explained by litigator Mike Eizenga:

> The problem is essentially that the financial deal is not good enough. There is only $500,000 [about £250,000] in the whole fund for disbursements. In return the fund gets the right to reimburse itself with 10 per cent of an award of settlement. It is too much of a take. This will be reconsidered in January 1996. A lot of people are waiting to see what will happen then. A fairer percentage would be two to three per cent. There also needs to be more for disbursements.

The Ontario fund is intended to work in conjunction with contingency fees, which would provide the lawyers' income above cover for disbursements. Another source of uncertainty for lawyers like Mike Eizenga is the percentage that courts will allow them to take. This is currently uncertain because of the lack of experience of the courts in dealing with these new procedures. There is some scepticism in Ontario as to how successful the new legislation will be in encouraging class actions.[66]

Which way forward?

It is not the purpose of this report to provide a comprehensive treatment of all the complicated issues relating to class actions that have arisen in the three pioneering Canadian jurisdictions examined. However, two conclusions can be advanced, even from such a rapid and superficial study. First, British courts could beneficially add to their armoury of procedures the possibility of class litigation. The experience of Quebec suggests that this does allow a modest extension of the wrongs that can more easily be righted through litigation. Second, the experience of Quebec suggests also that there is considerable value in state funding of such actions. Not only does this assist poor litigants; it also adds considerably to what the Quebec *Fonds* administrator called the 'seriousness' of the procedure, helping to avoid the excesses of contingency fee funding.

Management

The next two chapters respond to Lord Woolf's proposals for reform of domestic procedure in the light of experience in Canada and the United States of various innovations in handling otherwise unmanageable caseloads.

References

1 Committee on Long Range Planning, Judicial Conference of the United States, *Proposed Long Range Plan for the Federal Courts*, 1995, p136.
2 Ibid, p19.
3 Woolf Inquiry Team, 1995.
4 Court Service, *Framework Document*, 1995, pp5–7.
5 See R Wheeler, 'Empirical research and the politics of judicial administra-

tion: creating the Federal Judicial Center', *Law and Contemporary Problems*, Summer 1988 pp31–54.

6 Federal Judicial Center, *1994 Annual Report*, and interview, D. Stienstra, 9 June 1995.

7 Federal Judicial Center, *Civil Justice Reform Act Report, Appendix II*, 1995.

8 Eg, D Stienstra and T Willging, *Alternatives to Litigation: Do they have a place in the Federal Courts?* (1995), D Rauma and C Krafka, *Voluntary Arbitration in Eight Federal District Courts: an evaluation,* and B Meierhoefer, *Court-Annexed Arbitration in Ten District Courts* (1990).

9 Note 1 above.

10 *Report of the Chief Justice's Commission on the Future of the Courts* (Supreme Judicial Court, Commonwealth of Massachussetts, 1992), p64.

11 *Civil Justice Review: first report* (Ontario Court of Justice and Ministry of the Attorney General, 1995) and *Study Paper on Prospects for Civil Justice,* (Ontario Law Reform Commission, 1995).

12 Op cit, note 10 p71.

13 Interview with D Stienstra.

14 Access to Justice Advisory Committee, *Access to Justice: an action plan,* (1995).

15 LAG 1995, chapter 6.

16 Interview, 22 June 1995.

17 Law Courts Education Society of BC, document undated.

18 Ontario Court of Justice and Ministry of the Attorney General, *Civil Justice Review: first report* (Ontario Civil Justice Review, 1995) p385 and p276.

19 Interview, 12 June 1995.

20 p1.

21 Chapter 4.

22 State Bar of Arizona, *Assisting Pro Per Litigants: ethical considerations,* undated.

23 Quoted in M Budinger, 'Court Self-Service Center: a paradigm shift', *Maricopa Lawyer*, January 1995.

24 As in note 19 above.

25 p82.

26 *Access to Justice: interim report* (Woolf Inquiry Team 1995) recommendation 49.

27 *Legal Aid – Targeting Need* (HMSO, Cm 2854, 1995) para 6.21.

28 Interview, 12 June 1995.

29 Chapter 16 pp221–228.

30 Quoted in D McGillis, *Major issues involved in the development and operation of multi-door courthouse centers* (unpublished).

31 Through amendments to Federal Rule of Civil Procedure 16.

32 D Stienstra, 'ADR in the Federal Trial Courts', *FJC Directions*, December 1994, p5.

33 O Fiss, 'Against Settlement', *Yale LJ 1085*, quoted in S Goldberg, F Sander and N Rogers, *Dispute Resolution: negotiation, mediation and other processes* (Little, Brown and Co, 1992) p144.

34 R Abel, 'Informalism: a tactical equivalent to law' 19 *Clearinghouse Review* 383, quoted in Goldberg et al (above).

35 Interview, 19 June 1995.

36 L Singer, M Lewis, A Houseman and E Singer, 'Alternative Dispute Resolution and the Poor' *Clearinghouse Review*, May/June 1992, p153.

37 Interview, 15 June 1995.

38 United States District Court for the District of Columbia, *Dispute Resolution Programs*, undated.

39 L Finkelstein and N Stanley, 'A US District Court ADR Program: a success story', *World Arbitration and Mediation Report 1993*, p72.

40 *1993 Highlights: ADR Programs in the US District Court for the District of Columbia.*

41 US Court of Appeals for the District of Columbia Circuit, *Appellate Mediation Program* (1992), p1.

41A US Court of Appeal for District of Columbia Circuit, *Appellate Mediation Program* (1992) p3.

42 *Dispute Resolution Procedures in the Northern District of California*, undated, p4.

43 *Proposed Revised Local Rules of the United States District Court for the Northern District of California*, 20 January 1995, rule 5–2.

44 *Dispute Resolution Procedures in the Northern District of California*, p6.

45 Ibid, p16.

46 B S Meierhoefer, *Court-Annexed Arbitration in Ten District Courts* (Federal Judicial Center, 1990) and D Rauma and C Krafta, *Voluntary Arbitration in Eight Federal District Courts: an evaluation* (Federal Judicial Center, 1994).

47 *Alternatives to Litigation: Do they have a place in the Federal Courts?* Federal Judicial Center, Long-range planning series No 4, 1995, pp10–11.

48 Supreme Court Procedure Committee, *Guide for Use in Group Actions*, May 1991, pp5–6.

49 Law Commission, *Administrative Law: judicial review and statutory appeals* (HMSO, 1993) section 9.

50 Ontario Law Reform Commission, *Report on Class Actions* (Ministry of the Attorney-General, 1982) volume 1, p3.

50A Attorney-General's Advisory Committee on Class Action Reform, *Report* (Ministry of the Attorney-General, 1990) pp16–17.

51 Ibid.

52 J Weinstein, *Individual Justice in Mass Tort Litigation: the effect of class actions, consolidations and other multiparty devices* (Northwestern University Press, 1995) p22.

53 Interview, 29 May 1995.

54 Quoted in P Schuck, *Agent Orange on Trial* (Harvard University Press, 1987) p169.

55 P Glenn, 'Class Actions in Ontario and Quebec' 62 *Can. Bar Rev.* 1984.

56 Interview, 27 June 1995.

57 Note 54 above.

57A Class Proceedings Act 1995 (BC) s4.

58 Class Proceedings Act 1992 s6.

59 S Potter and J-C René, 'Class Actions in Canada – Quebec's Experience and Ontario's Proposal' *Class Action Reports* Jan–Feb 1991, p9.

60 Interview, 26 June 1995.

61 Phone conversation, 23 June 1995.

62 Loi sur le recours collectif (LRQ c. R–2.1) art 23, as quoted in L Ducharme and Y Lauzon, *Le Recours Collectif Québecois* (Yvon Blais, 1988).

63 Interview, 26 June 1995.

64 Draft *Annual Report 1993–94*.

65 S Potter and J-C René, op cit note 59 above, p12.

66 See, eg, Garry Watson, 'Class Proceedings' in Watson and McGowan, *Ontario Civil Practice* (Carswell, 1995).

CHAPTER 3

From an adversarial to a managed system of litigation: A comparative critique of Lord Woolf's interim report

GARRY D WATSON, QC

Garry Watson is Professor of Law at Osgoode Hall Law School, an expert on civil procedure and Director of Professional Development at Blake, Cassels and Graydon, Toronto.

FOR JACK JACOB

> There once was a man, a Lord no less, who believed that a nation's litigation culture could be changed by edict and judicial education, and that the citizenry would be better served by a regime based on judicial discretion rather than the Rule of Law. To paraphrase an old song, 'maybe he's right and maybe he's wrong'.

Lord Woolf has proposed fundamental and radical changes to the way litigation should be conducted. His diagnosis is that civil justice is in crisis because (among other things) it takes too long, costs too much money and, even when people win, they are unhappy with the process. Although this analysis is far from new,[1] I agree with it. I also agree with Lord Woolf that radical change[2] is needed, not cosmetic surgery. However, reforming the civil justice system for the better 'ain't easy'.[3] This is why, despite some sixty reports in England on aspects of civil procedure since 1851,[4] there has been no lasting solution to the twin problems of cost and delay. The same is true of North America. Our predecessors were neither foolish dullards nor acting in bad faith; reform is simply very difficult. The challenge is not simply to propose change: it is to propose reforms which significantly improve the current position.

Civil procedural reforms that will reduce cost and delay certainly 'ain't easy' if we wish to adhere to certain basic principles such as the maximisation of due process, regulation by rules rather than discretion and the right of parties to choose how much procedure they want. This is the context of the legal culture in which the reform of 63 civil procedure has been approached to date. It follows a 'due process' model currently exemplified by the procedural rules in all common law jurisdictions, for example the Rules of the Supreme Court, the United States Federal Rules of Civil Procedure and the rules of the various provinces in Canada. This is ultimately based on the value and primacy of process values. It is important that, win or lose, the parties feel content with the process and, in consequence, believe that they got 'a fair shake'. Hence, the due process model, though designed by (and possibly for) lawyers, invokes client satisfaction as its rationale and objective.

But what do you do if most parties are in fact unhappy with procedures that purport to maximise their due process? The answer, Lord Woolf in effect concludes, is to break the mould and to opt instead for a 'cost and delay control' model. He believes that this is much more likely to maximise client satisfaction. Such a change of direction involves a shift in values similar, though strangely opposite, to that in contemporary western politics. Generally, there is a move away from the welfare state and its social safety net to debt reduction and an emphasis on individual entrepreneurship. By contrast, Lord Woolf proposes a shift from lawyer-driven adversarial combat (representative of entrepreneurship) to judicial case management (surely, a form of socialised law). In both cases there are, or will be, casualties.

I feel somewhat uncomfortable in the role of the conservative (or perhaps liberal) critic, questioning radical reform proposals. I am used to proposing reforms or criticising judges for being too timid. Be that as it may, I offer a critical assessment of Lord Woolf's proposals and others can judge its worth. I concede the possibility that, overall, Lord Woolf's bold new regime might work and even be an improvement over the present state of affairs. However, such an achievement will require adequate resources and careful effort in the drafting of appropriate rules. As a proceduralist who both has no responsibility for the English litigation system and believes in empirical experimentation, I would be selfishly delighted to see Woolf's proposals implemented. North Americans would be provided with a cost-free social experiment that might help us understand where to go and where not to go.[5]

This chapter begins with an overview of Woolf's proposals, then takes a closer look at specific procedural reforms, followed by some general comments and critique. In closing, I offer some suggestions as to where the reform process should go from here. My central theme is that, while one of Lord Woolf's major goals is to reduce cost and delay, the reforms he is proposing are unlikely to do that.

An overview of Lord Woolf's report

Lord Woolf's recommendations fall into several broad groups: a wholesale movement to case management, a range of procedural reforms (dealing with pleadings, discovery, exchange of witness statements, experts, offers to settle and costs), some structural changes and, most importantly, a change of culture.

Case management

Lord Woolf sees this as his central and most important proposal. From a North American perspective, the introduction of case management is hardly novel, let alone radical. Some form of case management has been an established practice for some time throughout Canada and the United States. But Lord Woolf's concept of case management is possibly broader, and potentially more intrusive, than its North American counterpart.

Across the Atlantic, case management takes many different forms. However, it typically focuses on ensuring that a set timetable for events is followed and that settlement is fully explored. Nevertheless, it takes place within the context of an adversarial system in which the parties retain primary responsibility for conducting the litigation. At the centre of Lord Woolf's report appears to be the profound wish to see the adversarial system give way to one in which judges will become central and 'run the show'.

Lord Woolf wastes no time considering the possible problems associated with such a wide-ranging programme of case management. In the United States, though not as yet in Canada, serious questions have been raised as to the methods and objectives of case management. Most of these have come from academics rather than judges or practitioners.[6] For example, in reviewing case management in the United States, Professor Elliott concluded[7] that the essence of managerial judging is *ad hoc* action by judges to impose costs on lawyers. He saw it is as a response to a fundamental design flaw in United States procedure, namely the lack of incentives for litigants to narrow issues for trial. He further argued that, recently, managerial judging has rapidly evolved from a set of techniques for narrowing issues to a set of techniques for coercing settlement. Case management as practised in the United States may well be a special case, responding to particular problems. In Canada, where case management is much younger, similar excesses have not appeared, at least as yet. Relevant to the central role that Lord Woolf proposes for case management is

Professor Elliott's further observation: 'What makes the managerial judging movement coherent is not so much the existence of specific techniques on which all management judges agree. Rather, managerial judges are distinguished by common themes in their rhetoric. Managerial judges believe that the system does not work; that *something* must be done to make it work; and that the only plausible solution to the problem is *ad hoc* procedural activism by *judges*.'[8]

Structural changes

Lord Woolf rejects outright the merger of the county courts and High Court (on elitist grounds) but the different rules for the two courts are to be unified. A new, more fluid approach to questions of jurisdiction and the 'allocation' of procedure emerges. In place of the traditional approach – a hierarchy of courts, each with their own jurisdiction and procedure, and party autonomy to decide where the case fits in – a rather different regime is proposed. While there remain two levels of courts, a case can be started in either court. The so-called uniform set of rules really encompasses three levels of procedure (small claims, fast-track and multi-track; see p17).[9] Then comes a major conceptual change. While there are jurisdictional and procedural guidelines, ultimately it will not be for the parties to choose which court will process the case or which procedure (or how much) they will get. Instead, this will be decided by the court.[10] Even when these basic decisions have been taken, judicial discretion, as opposed to legal rules, will reign. Judges will decide whether the pleadings are adequate; to how much discovery the parties are entitled; and even whether witnesses are to be called and whether or not they may be cross-examined. Lord Woolf discusses alternative dispute resolution (ADR) at some length and makes various suggestions as to how it might be used; but stops short of mandating it as part of a multi-door courthouse. He does recommend that such developments in other common law countries should be monitored.

Cultural change

A need for cultural change is to be coupled with all of this reform. Lord Woolf concluded that 'the unrestrained adversarial culture of the present system is to a large extent responsible' for the present state of affairs.[11] Attitudes and culture must change. Combat must give way to co-operation. There must be a fundamental shift in the responsibility for the management of civil litigation from litigants and their legal advisers to the courts. Consequently, this transformation will involve not only a different progress for cases within the system but also 'a radical change of culture for all concerned'.[12] Great responsibility is to be placed on judges for the way in which a case proceeds through the system to a final hearing, including even the form of the final hearing itself. In short, the adversarial system is largely to give way to a managed system.[13] For judges, Lord Woolf recommends training. On what is to be the mechanism for changing lawyers' culture, he is quite unclear.[14]

As already noted, though less explicitly discussed by Lord Woolf, many matters are to be regulated by judicial discretion, rather than by hard and fast, or sometimes apparently any, rules.

Delay

Delay in litigation is of two quite different kinds. *Lawyer/litigant delay*, the time it takes the parties to ready the case for the ultimate trial, is attributable to the conduct of the parties. *Court-based delay* is the time that parties who are ready for trial must wait until the court has a judge and courtroom ready to try the case. Lord Woolf is very concerned, in the English context, with lawyer/litigant delay[15] but largely unconcerned with court-based delay.

From a North American perspective, the most startling aspect of the report is the minuscule space devoted to problems of court-based delay and the inability of the court to offer a timely trial date for cases which are ready for such disposal. Lord Woolf dispenses with this matter in a few paragraphs, concluding that this is not a problem since the High Court can, on average, offer parties a date within 40 weeks of the case being set down for trial.[16] In many Canadian jurisdictions, such a short waiting time is unheard of. Delay is more likely to be in the order of two or three years. Hence, court-based delay is often a serious and pervasive problem. North American reports similar to Lord Woolf's will generally devote considerable space to attempting to work out solutions to the problems of court-based backlog and delay. An example is the recent Ontario Civil Justice Review.[17]

Where the courts repeatedly and systemically fail to provide cases with a timely hearing, the task of a civil justice review is more complex and frustrating than that faced by Lord Woolf's inquiry. The extent and nature of the problems are much greater. Court-based delay raises a whole range of complicating factors: questions of court and judicial efficiency; the adequacy of existing levels of government financing and court resources or the more difficult issue of the ability of courts and judges to do better with existing 'inadequate' resources; attempting to fathom how court 'queues' behave and why and how that behaviour can be changed or modified without further threatening access to justice. This has led North American courts to focus heavily on techniques to increase the disposition of cases without a trial: aggressively to pursue settlement; to compel parties to resort to ADR and so on.

Freed from the problem of combating court-based delay, Lord Woolf had the luxury of looking at civil justice reform in a different light. Unfortunately (for North Americans), because he does not perceive court-based delay as a problem, he does not analyse the subject in any depth. We do not learn directly from his report how court-based delay has been combated and solved. At least part of the answer would seem to be found in the use of deputy judges. In 1994–95, approximately 35 per cent of all sitting days in the Queen's Bench Division and 18 per cent in the Chancery Division were by deputy judges. In Canada, the use of deputies is not possible on constitutional grounds. Our constitution requires that judges have tenure 'during good behaviour' to age 75. If the use of deputy judges, increasing judicial manpower, has been the key to England's solution to the problem, this should be of major interest across the Atlantic. One of the current North American dogmas is that problems of court-based delay cannot be solved by increasing manpower. The emphasis has been on such solutions as improving court administration.

Procedural changes

Lord Woolf devotes eight chapters to a range of procedural reforms discussed below. However, in addition, he has in effect provided a generic 'simplified' procedure for what will be a large percentage of cases. This arises from the special procedure for fast track cases. This provides for limited discovery, determination within 20–30 weeks, trials restricted to no more than three hours, exclusion of oral testimony and fixed costs.[18]

Pleadings

Lord Woolf states that pleadings fail to fulfil their basic function, which is succinctly to state the facts relied upon. He proposes that the primacy of this requirement be re-established. This is to be achieved through a handful of reforms.[19] In an attempt to bring increased veracity to pleadings, they are to conclude with 'a declaration . . . of belief in the accuracy and truth of the matters put forward'. The pleading rules relating to the defence should require defendants to set forth their own version of the facts so far as they differ from those stated in the claim: bare denials would no longer be acceptable. The most dramatic recommendation is that, in effect, pleadings are to be 'settled' by the court, another managerial solution. In all cases, after a defence is filed, the pleadings are to be considered by the procedural judge, who will give directions on points to be clarified. If they are so unclear that the matters in dispute cannot be properly identified, the judge will hold a case-management conference with the aim of producing an agreed statement of the issues in dispute. The rationale is that 'experience shows, mere exhortation and amendments to the rules of pleading, unaccompanied by real judicial scrutiny, will achieve no improvement' because 'the defects in pleading do not arise from the defects in the rules of court, but from the repeated failure of parties and lawyers to observe the rules and of the court to police them'.[20] To aid in the process of change (cultural change again), pleadings are no longer to be referred to as such. Instead, they are to be called 'statements of case'.

The difficulty with these proposals is cost. How many defences are filed each year in England and how much time will each procedural judge spend reviewing pleadings and extracting agreed statements of fact? How much lawyer time, and hence private costs, will be incurred in preparing and participating in the conferences and in complying with directions on pleading? Will the benefits achieved outweigh those obtained under the present regime (where pleadings are challenged, and scrutinised by the court, only when one of the parties is dissatisfied with them) and if so, at what cost?

Discovery of documents

Lord Woolf makes perhaps his most interesting proposal in the field of discovery. He found a general consensus that in more complex litigation, documentary discovery is a real problem because of the sheer volume of documents, with resulting high costs. Across the Atlantic the issues are much the same. Again Lord Woolf finds his answer in judicial management and discretion:

> As part of the case management process, the judiciary will have both the means and the responsibility to ensure that discovery is limited to what is really necessary.[21]

The court is to retain jurisdiction to order full discovery of the kind now presently available, but it is anticipated that this will be rare. Discovery will generally be more limited. Woolf's proposals depend upon distinctions he would draw among what are today considered relevant and hence producible documents. These would fall into four categories:

1) the documents which a party will rely on to support its case;
2) documents which to a material extent adversely affect a party's case or support the other party's case;
3) documents which are relevant to the issues in the proceeding but do not fall into the preceding categories; and
4) those documents which are not in and of themselves relevant but could possibly begin a 'train of inquiry' leading to relevant documents.

Documents in the first two categories (directly supporting or adversely affecting a party's case) are to be available as 'standard discovery', while the documents in the second two categories (relevant or possibly relevant) are only available as 'extra discovery'. In fast-track cases, the parties will normally only be required to give 'standard discovery'. In multi-track cases, discovery is to be tailored to the circumstances of the particular case and it will be for the procedural judge to decide if and when 'extra discovery' will be available. Lord Woolf realises that this highly innovative approach carries with it some difficulties:

> The core of the problem is that conscientious lawyers and their clients might feel obliged to trawl through all category (3) documents in order to eliminate the possibility of overlooking category (2) documents. To do so would be to defeat the aims of controlled discovery.[22]

He resolves this matter by stating that 'initial disclosure should apply to documents of which a party is aware at the time when the obligation to disclose arises'.[23] The court and the parties, he says, will have to work out in practice the appropriate balance between what should properly be disclosed under that test and what can legitimately be left for the opponent to canvas on an application. The need for reform in this area is great, if only because of cost considerations. At first blush, it is a little worrying to hear Lord Woolf saying that a party is *not* required to 'trawl through' all the documents in its possession to find out if adverse documents exist, since this may open the door to the non-production of damaging documents. However, trading off this risk against reduced discovery costs may be a reasonable one. Again we are told that discovery 'is an area where the culture has to change' but again Lord Woolf is silent on what the mechanism will be which will cause this to happen.

Witness statements

Lord Woolf traces the relatively recent history of the development of the English practice of the exchange of witness statements, and their use at trial as the evidence-in-chief of the witness rather than oral testimony.[24] He notes that this development has caused problems and has been the subject of much criticism. Because lawyers spend an enormous amount of time ironing and massaging witness statements, their preparation has had a devastating effect on costs. The exchange of these statements, he also observes, allows lawyers to spend hours preparing cross-examination and can lead to prolix examinations.

Notwithstanding the criticisms, Lord Woolf strongly endorses the continued use of the practice as providing early mutual disclosure leading to more just outcomes, earlier settlements and permitting judges (now charged with case management) to be familiar with the case from the start (thus empowering judges).[25] Lord Woolf sees as the major cause of problems surrounding this practice the failure, until recently, to permit sufficient scope for supplementing these statements. If this is permitted and 'a more relaxed attitude is adopted by the court to the statements', the new industry devoted to the creation of witness statements will, in his view, more likely wither.

This conclusion is questionable. The root of the problem lies in moving beyond the use of witness statements as merely a vehicle of mutual disclosure to using them as the evidence at trial in lieu of oral testimony. While doing this may at first seem cost-efficient (since trial time is not consumed having the witnesses examined-in-chief), it may result in great inefficiency. The reason why lawyers spend so much time polishing witness statements is because they realise that under such a regime the statements become *their whole case*. Given this, Lord Woolf's statement that 'they are not intended to be drawn with the precision of affidavits' is bizarre. Typically, the statements will end up being the evidence upon which the very outcome of the case (not some mere interlocutory application) will be decided.[26]

A further problem, to which Lord Woolf does not allude, is the enormous front-end loading of costs that results from requiring the early preparation and exchange of witness statements. Lord Woolf recommends that witness summaries should be exchanged in fast-track cases within 28 days of the delivery of the defence. As in North America, the vast majority of these cases will settle long before the trial date. Requiring such early exchange of witness statements builds up the costs in cases which, if left alone, would settle without this considerable expense.[27]

In the chapter on exchange of witness statements, Lord Woolf declares that it will be the judge who 'will decide which witnesses he wishes to be called' and that 'cross-examination on the contents of witness statements should only be allowed with leave of the judge'. We may need to move away from some elements of the adversarial system in the direction of a managed system, but these recommendations go too far. Some rudiments of due process must be retained. Clients will not be satisfied by a process where they are denied the opportunity to 'tell their story' or to question the witnesses against them. The right of confrontation must surely count for something. To propose such sweeping powers for judges assumes an omniscience on their part which should not be conceded. Lawyers who have lived for months or years with a case are likely to be better placed to make these kinds of judgments than a judge who is just becoming familiar with it. There is a real risk that judges exercising this power will too often just 'get it wrong'. Lon Fuller's observation remains apposite:[28] 'an adversary presentation seems the only effective means for combating [the] natural human tendency to judge too swiftly in terms of the familiar that which is not yet fully known.'

Expert witnesses

Unhappy with the role currently being played by expert witnesses, Lord Woolf proposes a range of reforms. The calling of expert witnesses is to be subject to the complete control of the court ('all power to the judiciary' again). The court is to have discretion, with or without the agreement of the parties, to appoint an expert to report or give evidence (discretion again) as well as a wide power to appoint assessors.

Lord Woolf's central complaint at this point is a current lack of independence and an increased partisanship on the part of experts:

> Expert witnesses used to be genuinely independent experts. Men of outstanding eminence in their field. Today they are in practice hired guns: there is a new breed of litigation hangers on, whose main expertise is to craft reports which will conceal anything that might be to the disadvantage of their clients.[29]

Lord Woolf's lament is right about those experts, such as forensic accountants and some engineers, who have gone 'into the business' of being court experts. It tends not to apply to most doctors, who have wider professional roles. While Lord Woolf makes interesting proposals to curb the partisanship of experts who testify, including removal of privilege from the instructions received from lawyers, we may need to go even further and remove the privilege surrounding those experts who have been consulted but abandoned. Experts who are in the 'witnessing business' have become so pliable and partisan that they are well aware that they will be dismissed if their opinion does not strongly favour the party consulting them and they know that the fact they were even consulted will never have to be disclosed to the opposing party or the court. Moreover, non-compliant professional witnesses soon see their business dry up. Entrepreneurship in witnessing ill fits a system that hopes to find the truth.

Whether Lord Woolf's proposals will solve what is a genuine problem is doubtful. Sweeping aside the objections made to him on the use of court-appointed experts, he optimistically and unabashedly states that the 'court is perfectly capable of deciding which cases would be appropriate for a court expert and then of appointing an expert with the necessary qualifications and ensuring that he is used effectively'.[30] One of the concerns he noted, but swept aside, is the 'inability of a court expert to deal with the situation where more than one acceptable view can be held on a particular issue'.[31] Anyone who has been through the process of retaining experts realises that this occurs not infrequently, and is hardly the exception, even among experts who are not in the 'witnessing business'. Steps to make the whole expert witness process more transparent are more likely to be acceptable to the profession and its clients, and more likely to aid accurate fact-finding, than resort to the use of court-appointed experts.

Offers to settle

The one-sided payment-into-court device is to be replaced with a regime of offers to settle. Under this regime, instead of the defendant alone being able to make an offer of settlement resulting in costs consequences if refused and the refusing party does no better at trial, both parties may do so. Either party can simply deliver a written offer to settle and it is no longer necessary for the defendant to pay money into court. As Lord Woolf notes, this device is now well established and working well in Canada.[32] Indeed, reported Canadian cases suggest that now in virtually all cases going to trial the parties will have each delivered serious offers to settle. As in any common law jurisdiction, the vast majority of cases settle without a trial and these settlements now typically arise from the delivery of written offers to settle.

(While similar rules exist in the United States, they play no real role in litigation because the courts lack a general power to award an indemnity, or cost-shifting, for lawyers' fees.)

A caveat that must be made is that the device carries with it the same aspect of potential unfairness as does payment into court. To have the intended effect of 'forcing' parties to settle, courts must apply the prescribed cost sanctions virtually automatically if a party does less well at trial than the offer. Arguments that the ultimate recovery was close to the offer or reasonably refused must generally be unavailing.[33]

Costs

Lord Woolf's general proposals in the area of costs seem sensible. He recommends the retention of the general rule of cost-shifting (loser pays). He also wants greater transparency in information on lawyers' fees so that clients will be better informed and there will be scope for more competition. Lawyers should be under a professional obligation to explain to prospective clients how their charges for litigation will be calculated; to estimate what the overall cost might be; and to give reasonable notice if that estimate is to be exceeded. Legal professional bodies should encourage their members to undertake litigation on the basis of fixed fees, either for the proceedings as a whole or for stages in the proceedings.

For cases under the fast-track procedure there is a more radical cost proposal.[34] The provision of such a straightforward and limited procedure is designed to make it possible to introduce standard fixed costs representing the extent of a party's liability to the opponent. Moreover, the same amount would generally constitute an appropriate amount of solicitor-and-own-client costs payable to a party's own legal adviser, except in cases where there has been an explicit agreement to pay more which has been fully explained to the litigant. Lord Woolf states: 'The results should be that not only would a party know what his maximum liability in relation to costs could be to the other side, he should be able to obtain legal representation for no greater sum than he would be liable to pay to the other side. I envisage that the costs would normally represent a percentage of the claim and that there would be a basic fixed minimum of costs.'[35] Lord Woolf indicates that this recommendation is inspired by a similar regime that exists in Germany – an approach, he indicates, which does not appear to have had a deleterious effect on the income of German lawyers.

The proposal certainly will have the effect of forcing lawyers to be economical in terms of the time spent on cases. Discussion with

German lawyers suggests that their system is somewhat different from that portrayed by Lord Woolf and has certain characteristics which make it more amenable to a fixed-cost regime. The cost system is more complex and costs are higher than suggested. In addition, smaller cases are almost exclusively handled by young lawyers and procedure is quite different from common law systems. Lawyers are called on to do much less: for example, they do not usually interview witnesses, have to give documentary discovery or secure the attendance of witnesses (a task undertaken by the court).

Some general reflections

Overall, the Woolf report recommends stern medicine for what is seen to be an extremely severe illness. The report raises two general issues: are such draconian remedies necessary or desirable and will they achieve their stated objective of reducing cost and delay?

Desirability

There is bound to be disagreement as to the desirability of Lord Woolf's proposals. Yet, we have to come to grips with the fact that reforms introduced to date have done little, if anything, to alleviate the problems of cost and delay. Surely it is time to try something 'completely different'. Case management, at least directed towards enforcing timetables and moving the case along, seems desirable while hardly amounting to radical reform. To the extent that Lord Woolf's proposals reduce the autonomy of lawyers and increase the power of the court, at this stage of the legal system's development (or dilemma) they seem a path worth trying.

Efficacy

The likely efficacy of Lord Woolf's proposals is more problematic. Reforms do not always lead to a change for the better.[36] The greatest concerns are threefold: the very real possibility that Woolf has seriously underestimated the need to increase resources in order to give effect to his new regime; the movement from rules to discretion; and just whether and how the reforms will reduce cost and delay.

Resources

Though Lord Woolf devotes a short chapter to the question of resources,[37] his conclusions may be over optimistic. His recommendations call for a dramatic increase in judicial activity at a time when, so it would appear, judicial resources are already in short supply (witness the extensive use of deputy judges). While recognising that case management is not just to be 'fitted in', he calls for what seem to be far too modest increases in judicial manpower: no new High Court judges and 'some new appointments' of district judges. His analysis on this point appears to be driven by élitism (fear of diluting the quality of the High Court bench) and over-optimistic expectations of the efficiencies that will result from case management, such as increased settlements, reduced interlocutory activity and shorter trials.

Discretion

Concern about replacing rules with discretion is based less on philosophy than efficacy and efficiency. Lord Woolf spends little time discussing directly the proposed shift from rules to discretion, but even within his report, there is evidence to suggest that this might be problematic. He refers to research by Professor Baldwin identifying four different approaches by district judges to the conduct of hearings in small claims:[38]

a) 'going for the jugular' (identifying the central issues at an early stage and sticking to them);
b) 'hearing the parties' (allowing the parties greater latitude to develop their arguments in their own way);
c) 'passive' (talking to each of the parties like a solicitor interviewing clients); and
d) 'mediatory' (encouraging the parties to agree their own solution).

Lord Woolf treats this as a particular problem, peculiar to small claims, which can be solved by training. He does not seem to appreciate that this same phenomenon is just as likely, perhaps bound, to occur under highly discretionary case management.[39] Later,[40] he also notes an observation from the Heilbron/Hodge Report (see p16) on the serious lack of uniformity that existed amongst judges on the issue of whether exchanged witness statements should stand as the evidence-in-chief of the maker when judges were given a general, undirected discretion in this matter. Notwithstanding this, Lord Woolf then goes on to propose giving judges the breathtakingly broad discretion to determine which witnesses will be called at trial and who will be subject to cross-examination.[41]

Unbridled and undirected discretion, tantamount to leaving matters to the length of the Chancellor's foot, can result in confusion, inefficiency and an increase in costs. Lord Woolf will need to pay particular attention to the issue of discretion when he comes to drafting rules. Rules that give judges undirected discretion should be avoided, since they do no favour to either judges or to litigants, nor are they likely to reduce cost and delay. In rule drafting, the provision of limits to the exercise of discretion makes the process more complex and time-consuming. It requires the rule-makers to formulate and to write down the matters the decision-maker is to take into account. This 'ain't easy', but it is essential. Below is an example of how it can be done:[42]

> The court may, on motion by a party, order production for inspection of a document that is in the possession, control or power of a person not a party and is not privileged where the court is satisfied that:
>
> a) the document is relevant to a material issue in the action; and
> b) it would be unfair to require the moving party to proceed to trial without having discovery of the document.

This rule is far from self-executing (leaving undefined, for example, what is a 'material issue' and what is 'unfair') but it at least tells the decision-maker the type of factors that should be looked at; more importantly, it directs the attention of the parties, who will have to make representations, to the matters to be considered.

New procedural code

Lord Woolf states that his new code of rules would be much shorter and simpler than existing rules.[43] This seems like a goal with which we should all agree but on reflection the question becomes, to what extent can this be achieved, given the tasks that rules have to perform? We should strive for simpler, shorter rules, but we need to be realistic. (This is not to provide support for the tortuous drafting style used in the present English rules. I am delighted to see that Lord Woolf is committed to adopting a 'simpler and plainer style of drafting'.)[44]

In the quest for simpler and shorter rules, there are two separate issues to be grappled with. The first is *coverage*. Like it or not, there are, unfortunately, a whole range of matters that have to be dealt with in the rules. Some are quite mechanical but still important, such as how to commence proceedings, how to carry out service. If the rules are to provide for disposition without trial, as obviously they must, there will have to be rules on default proceedings, summary judgment, determination of an issue before trial, discontinuance and withdrawal, and dismissal of actions for delay. There must also be rules dealing with pleadings and discovery. The latter will have to cover documentary discovery, inspection of property and medical examination of parties. If there is going to be a mechanism for enforcement of the rules, as there obviously must, this will require rules relating to interlocutory applications. Since the merits of litigation cannot be decided instantaneously at the outset, there will need to be rules relating to the preservation of rights in pending litigation, including interlocutory injunctions, appointment of receivers, certificates of pending litigation, the interim recovery of personal property and the interim preservation of property. And this list is far from complete. Making rules shorter for shortness sake may prove rather short-sighted.

Lord Woolf also suggests that the rules should be *less detailed*. But why do we have detailed rules? The answer is to instruct parties and their lawyers what to do. If you want to give this information in detail, in order to be more informative, you end up with detailed rules. Such conduct might instead be regulated by decision-maker discretion, in which case detailed rules become less necessary. Indeed detailed rules may be antithetical, since they reduce or remove discretion. However, doing this can come at a high price. Since general rules are more open-textured, their application to specific situations may be unclear, leading to the inability of the parties to fathom what is required and forcing them to resort to the court to resolve the issue, thereby increasing expense and delay. Moreover, if there are no criteria to guide the procedural judge, the exercise of his/her discretion becomes unpredictable, with two consequences. The litigants are less able to 'settle' the issue themselves and each may see a possible advantage in 'taking a kick at the can' by going before the procedural judge. In short, while shorter, simpler rules will empower judges at the expense of lawyers (which may or may not be a good thing), they are likely also to impact significantly on costs, both public and private. Since hearings to resolve issues will be more frequent, more judge time will be required to deal with procedural matters and this will necessitate more lawyer time in attending the hearings.

Where do we go from here?

We complain, quite correctly, that despite all our reform efforts we make few inroads on cost and delay. This is because we have not made dealing with these problems the major priority. In the past, we paid lip service to attacking these twin dragons, but really we have been more concerned with 'improving the system' generally, more often pursuing due process values. When we approach reform in this diffuse way, cost and delay reduction gets lost in the process and the outcome often has no real impact. Lord Woolf is genuinely concerned with combating cost and delay, but he may have fallen into the same trap as those who have gone before him (myself included).[45] His approach is unfocused. Many changes may result but, as before, there will be little or no reduction in cost and delay, indeed they may increase.[46]

What we need to do in this reform round is to be more single-minded in pursuing cost and delay reduction. Without this, it will not happen.[47] How would we go about doing this? Below I sketch the outlines of a process for civil justice reform that has this singular focus. The process has two components: rigorous analysis designed to select only reforms that will be likely to improve the cost and delay picture; and the introduction of systems to measure the actual impact of reform. To date, we have typically undertaken neither. As a result, we implement some reforms that have a little or no likelihood of reducing costs or delay. When it is all over, we have a poor, or at best an anecdotal and impressionistic, understanding of what we achieved. If we are to move ahead and obtain the admirable objectives Lord Woolf has set himself, I believe all this must change.

The first step, after generating reform proposals such as Lord Woolf's but before implementing them, is to subject them to rigorous analysis in terms of what it is they will seek to achieve, by what mechanism and at what cost. The objective is to try to weed out those proposals which at first seem attractive but have little or no chance of success in furthering the goal of reducing cost and delay. But here we have to be more specific than just talking about reduction of cost and delay. Is our goal to reduce party-related delay, court-based delay, or both? What costs and whose costs? Are we talking about private-sector costs or public-sector costs? We have to be constantly aware that the easiest way to appear to 'reduce' costs is simply to transfer or externalise them to the other sector.

Cost allocation occurs all the time in the civil justice system.[48] The issues of cost allocation and cost externalisation arise sharply in the context of shifts from orality in procedure to procedures in writing. Exchange of witness statements raises this issue (see p71). Using witness statements as evidence-in-chief saves trial time, and presumably reduces the associated private and public costs (essentially, judge time), but it may greatly increase private-sector costs. More time and money is likely to be spent on preparing written statements than it would cost to examine them orally. The same is likely true of other moves to written procedure, eg, the use of skeleton arguments, factums, briefs or whatever you want to call them. Unless such innovation leads to shorter oral hearings, there may be no saving of either public or private costs. There will be an increase in private costs because of the time taken to prepare the written material. There may be an improvement in the overall quality of the process, and of the ultimate decision, but we must always be aware of the cost implications if we are to achieve the goal of cost reduction. Moving costs between sectors may be appropriate, but we must be conscious that we are doing it.

How might this type of analysis apply to some of Lord Woolf's proposals? Court hearings may be required to settle the pleadings in many cases (with an increase in both public and private costs), suggesting this is not a good reform unless we can articulate some compensating cost or delay reduction. The practice of exchanging witness statements seems clearly to have already led to a significant increase in private costs. Consequently, it needs reforming unless we can point to other net savings in costs or delay likely associated with the present practice. While having witness statements might perform the useful function of increasing the judge's understanding of the case, it is unlikely to contribute to cost and delay reduction unless we can articulate how it will do this. The exchange of witness statements can achieve much of its objective, greater mutual knowledge and the avoidance of surprise, if it is not used in place of examination-in-chief. Thus, witness statements would not have to be polished in the same way as affidavits.[49] To reduce costs in those cases that settle, consideration should be given to making the exchange of witness statements take place later rather than earlier in the proceedings.[50] Rules that give judges general and unguided discretion are likely to increase rather than reduce costs (see above, p78).

By contrast, Lord Woolf's proposals for reforming documentary discovery and the use of expert witnesses appear promising, at least in terms of private-sector cost reduction. If the quantity of documents that have to be ploughed through and produced can be reduced, lawyers' fees incurred in the discovery process should be lower (though it is possible that this might be offset by a significant increase in interlocutory activity seeking 'extra discovery'). In his discovery proposals, Lord Woolf may have made the very type of 'trade-off' between procedural perfection and cost reduction that is essential if we are to achieve cost reductions. Reduction of the scope of documentary discovery may carry some risk that damaging documents may not surface, but this risk seems tolerable and accepting that risk is the price of cost-reduction in this context.[51] Using independent, court-appointed, experts would seem likely to reduce costs; it would no longer be necessary for the parties each to retain and prepare their own experts and to present their evidence at the trial, with a consequent saving of both private and public sector costs. Note, however, that the parties will still have to share the cost of the independent expert and where his or her opinions are contrary to the interests of one of the parties, at least that party may need to retain an expert to assist in preparing the cross-examination of the court expert.[52]

The second step in my suggested process is to implement reforms in such a way that we can measure their impact. Indeed, at our present stage of development the ability to measure a reform proposal's impact in terms of cost and delay reduction might be made a precondition to introducing the reform. There are a range of methods available for measuring reform impacts. The most rigorous, but also the most elaborate and expensive, is to run controlled experiments, using and comparing test and control conditions. However, some reforms simply do not lend themselves to controlled experimentation and will require the use of less rigorous measurements.

How might this work? An example would be to run a controlled experiment designed to measure the impact – in terms of cost and delay – of introducing case management.[53] Cases would be processed through one of two streams, either case-managed or non-case-managed.[54] As part of the project a range of variables would be measured to determine the impact of case management on cost and delay reduction, eg, time to termination, court time consumed (by interlocutory applications, trials, case management meetings), costs of the parties, party satisfaction with the process, etc. The data should be kept in such a way that it can be correlated by different types and size of cases, etc, since it may well be that the reform is cost or delay-effective in certain types of cases but not in others.[55] Similarly, controlled experimentation can be used to test the effectiveness of other reforms, eg, whether the early exchange of witness statements increases the likelihood that cases will settle earlier.

For some reforms it may be too difficult or expensive to construct a controlled experiment (eg, discovery reforms, expert witness reforms) and there it may be necessary to rely on qualitative measurements such as questionnaires administered to those who experienced the reforms and those who have not. My plea, however, is to measure the impact of reforms as best we can and to introduce no reforms without an impact measurement plan.

To do this will be expensive, which is unwelcome in this time of almost universal government austerity. But we spend money on experimentation in other government programmes,[56] and we must start doing it in the area of civil justice if we are to break the 140-year cycle of making no real inroads on cost and delay. To propose radical reforms as Lord Woolf has done is not enough: they must be closely scrutinised for likely success, and the impact of those which are chosen for implementation has to be measured, if we are truly to make headway and develop a learning curve as to what type of reform strategies work and which do not.

References

1 For example, for a similar diagnosis, see an earlier, possibly forgotten, non-governmental English report: Justice, *Going to Law: A Critique of English Civil Procedure* (Stevens & Sons, 1974).

2 *Going to Law*, note 1, also proposed radical reforms in English civil procedure. Some of the proposals it contained are similar to Woolf's. See G Watson, 'Book Review, Justice, *Going to Law: A Critique of English Civil Procedure*' (1975) 25 UTLJ 333.

3 'Christ, you know it ain't easy, you know how hard it can be,' *The Ballad of John and Yoko*, J Lennon and P McCartney, 1969.

4 Para 2.2. All paragraph numbers hereafter are, unless otherwise stated, references to Lord Woolf, *Access to Justice* (Woolf Inquiry Team, 1995).

5 From a North American perspective the style of Lord Woolf's report has some surprises. We are not used to having government reports written in the first person singular. It is also a surprise to find the report giving no reference when it is stated that a source is being relied upon (see, eg, para 1.32 and para 20.3). This detracts from the usefulness of the report. Most surprising of all is the failure to acknowledge that an idea has been borrowed from another source. Compare, for example, Lord Woolf's proposal that the pleading rules relating to the defence be changed to require the defendant to set forth his or her own version of the facts so far as they differ from those stated in the claim (p159 para 23), with the Ontario Rules of Civil Procedure, r25.07 (different version of facts to be pleaded by the defendant) and virtually

identical rules in several other provinces; the Ontario provision was borrowed from the Alberta Rules.

6 The leading articles critical of case management are Resnik, 'Managerial Judges' (1982), 96 *Harv L Rev* 374 (objecting on several grounds to the practices employed by managerial judges and that the 'managerial' decisions of these judges are largely immune from appellate review); Elliott, 'Managerial Judging and the Evolution of Procedure' (1986) 53 *U Chi L Rev* 306. See also Posner 'The Summary Jury Trial and Other Methods of Alternative Dispute Resolution: Some Cautionary Observations' (1986) 53 *U Chi L Rev* 366 (Posner is a judge). For the major judicial response to these critical commentaries see Peckham, 'A Judicial Response to the Cost of Litigation: Case Management, Two-Stage Discovery Planning and Alternative Dispute Resolution' (1985), 37 *Rutgers L Rev* 253. (Professor Resnik places the onus of responsibility for the orderly and prompt disposition of litigation with the Bar, whereas I place that responsibility equally, if not primarily, on the shoulders of the judge.)

7 See Elliott, above note 6 at 308. However, Professor Elliott's assessment of case management is not all negative. 'Both my personal experience as a litigator and the available published data convinced me that some managerial techniques are effective in reducing the amount of time and effort invested in processing a given case. There are also compelling logical arguments that managerial judging is effective in this limited sense. There is no reason to assume that lawyers are immune from Parkinson's Law that work tends to expand to fill the time available; on the contrary, the fact that many lawyers are paid by the hour suggests that our profession may be more susceptible to this principle than most.' He also argues that it is conceivable that managerial judging may improve the quality of justice, but there is no reason to be confident that judges will be able to perform this function consistently well.

8 Elliott, above note 6 at 309.

9 For small claims, the monetary limit has been raised from £1,000 to £3,000. The fast track is for cases up to £10,000. The multi-track is for cases beyond £10,000 which will be case-managed through two management hearings – one shortly after the defence is filed (usually conducted by a procedural judge – a master or district judge) and the second will be a pre-trial review (usually conducted by the trial judge).

10 Paras 6.14 and 6.22.

11 Para 4.1.

12 Para 4.4.

13 Para 20.18.

14 As noted, Lord Woolf did not recommend mandating ADR as part of the court process. Recently in Toronto mediation through a court-annexed ADR Centre has become mandatory for selected cases. Anecdotal evidence to date suggests that this is having the effect of forcing lawyers to think about, and

become engaged in mediation, and this is resulting in at least the beginnings of cultural change.

15 His documentation of the extent of delay is very brief and a little confusing: see p13 para 35 et seq. The average time from issue to setting down for trial in the High Court is 2.3 years in London and 2.8 years elsewhere. However, he then states that the time taken to settlement is very long in personal injury cases – the majority take between 4 and 6 years to settle and the average time to settle non-fatal cases was over five years: para 39. The apparent discrepancy in these figures is not explained. (Does delay in commencing the actions account for it or are there other factors at play?)

16 The figure is even lower for the county court, ie, 20 weeks. These figures are derived by calculation from data given in para 35.

17 Ontario Court of Justice and Ministry of the Attorney-General, *Civil Justice Review, First Report*, 1995. See particularly chapters 4.3 and 12. The report does not actually disclose average waiting time to trial, but indicates that at a busy centre like Toronto 61 per cent of all cases on the trial list had been there for more than 12 months (see p58). The report recommends the adoption of a goal of a waiting period for trial of six to nine months.

18 For an articulate policy justification for adopting a simplified procedure in most, if not all cases, see A A S Zuckerman, 'A Reform of Civil Procedure – rationing procedure rather than access to justice' (1995) 22 *J of Law and Society* 155. As part of the recent Ontario Civil Justice Review (see above), a simplified procedure has been adopted for cases up to $25,000 (£12,500).

19 Chapter 20.

20 Para 20.7.

21 Para 21.20.

22 Para 21.33.

23 Para 21.34.

24 Chapter 22.

25 The extent to which the possession of witness statements will empower the case-management judge (and the trial judge as case manager) cannot be overemphasised. Without such statements, a judge will know very little about the case and will constantly have to defer to counsel. By contrast, armed with such statements, a judge will be in a much better position to understand the case and hence to make a range of forceful management decisions.

26 Conversations with a very few English practitioners suggest that there is a broad range of views as to the costs associated with witness statements and their efficacy. In mega-litigation, the costs of preparing witness statements is high, but is seen as a tolerable burden, given the overall costs of such litigation. In smaller cases, costs appear to be seen as a real concern, particularly since at present it is evidently not known with any certainty in advance whether or not the witnesses will in fact be called to give their evidence-in-

chief orally. One law centre lawyer indicated that he felt that witness statements, when used in lieu of oral examination-in-chief, were a great advantage to poor, inarticulate litigants, since he could prepare a witness statement coherently setting out all of the client's information, whereas the client would have great difficulty doing this in an oral examination-in-chief. This last comment demonstrates that the use of witness statements as evidence amounts to a rejection of the evidentiary rule that leading questions are generally impermissible in examination-in-chief; such witness statements in effect constitute evidence which has been adduced largely by leading questions. Another problem with the use of witness statements as evidence is the risk that the judge will not read them or will not read them until after the cross-examination (when 'I will have a better understanding of what is really important').

27 The early exchange, however, may lead to earlier settlements – as Lord Woolf argues (see below).

28 L Fuller, 'The Adversary System' in H Berman, *Talks on American Law* 40, 1961.

29 Not Lord Woolf's words, but quoted by him in para 10. Although blunt, the words appear to coincide with his views.

30 Para 23.23.

31 Para 23.21.

32 The model for the Canadian rules is Ontario Rules of Civil Procedure, r49. For an analysis of the rule and the Canadian case law on offers to settle, see Holmested and Watson, *Ontario Civil Procedure* 49 § 3 et seq (Carswell, Toronto) or, for Ontario cases only, Watson and McGowan, *Ontario Civil Practice 1996*, r49 (Carswell, Toronto).

33 The leading case establishing this principle in Ontario is *Niagara Structural Steel (St Catherines) Ltd v WD Laflamme Ltd* (1987) 58 Ontario Reports (2d) 773 (Ont CA). Lord Woolf discusses this point, at pp197–8, paras 18 and 19, concluding that while under payment into court the cost consequences are automatic, under the new regime this will not be so and the exercise of discretion will be necessary. I doubt that this will in fact happen for the same reason as it has not happened with payment into court in the UK or with offers to settle in Ontario.

34 Paras 7.16–20.

35 Para 7.17.

36 For a historical example, see Holdsworth, *The New Rules of Pleading of the Hilary Term 1834* (1923) 1 Camb LJ 261.

37 Chapter 17.

38 Para 16.24.

39 Elliott, above note 6 at 316–317, referring to the potential for arbitrariness inherent in managerial judging, describes a judicial workshop at which sitting judges were asked to propose approaches for managing the same

hypothetical case. Dramatically different solutions were revealed. He concedes that the various judges' reactions might also have differed had they been asked to rule on a point of law, but at least 'when judges make *legal* decisions, the parties have an opportunity to marshall arguments based on an established body of principles, judges are required to state reasons to justify their decisions, and appellate review is available. None of these safeguards is available when judges make *managerial* decisions.'

40 Para 22.5.

41 Paras 22.13–21.

42 Rule 30 of the Ontario Rules of Civil Procedure, which I had a hand in drafting.

43 See para 20.20 and chapter 26.

44 Para 26.25.

45 I am personally guilty of this. I was counsel to the committee which prepared the new Ontario Rules of Civil Procedure in 1985 and I had a substantial role in drafting the rules. As rules reformers, we set as one of our goals combating cost and delay. However, the resulting rules, though a 'great improvement', had virtually no impact on reducing cost or delay; indeed, they almost certainly increased the cost of litigation.

46 Professor Judith Resnik has observed that 'the history of procedure is a series of attempts to solve the problems created by the preceding generation's procedural reforms'. Resnik, 'Precluding Appeals' (1985) *70 Cornell L Rev 603*, 624 .

47 That proposed reforms seem likely to reduce costs and delay is, I suggest, a necessary condition for introducing them. However, it is not a sufficient condition. Reforms which seem to have a real likelihood of reducing cost and delay also need to be otherwise acceptable in terms of due process values, fairness, etc. But if we are to reduce cost and delay, we will have to broaden our notions of what is acceptable in terms of due process, etc.

48 Take as a mundane example the 'issuing' of the originating process 'by the court'. As we know, nearly all the work involved in this step is in fact done by the plaintiff, who prepares all the papers and does all the leg-work, with the court being involved in minor, largely administrative, acts. It certainly seems more efficient to have a party, motivated by self-interest, doing these tasks but it does represent a cost allocation between sectors.

49 Preparing and exchanging *summaries of the evidence* that a witness could give, which would not be used in lieu of examination-in-chief, would add to private costs (without directly reducing trial time) but may provide real cost and delay benefits in terms of permitting judges to be more effective case managers. The exchange of *full witness statements* to be used in lieu of examination-in-chief requires a close comparison of the private costs involved in preparing such statements (which is generally considered to be substantial) against the private costs saved through reduced trial time.

50 This issue presents an interesting question of a 'trade-off' between reducing cost and reducing delay. Postponing witness statement exchange will have the overall effect of reducing the private sector costs incurred in those cases that settle early. However, as Woolf anticipates, the early exchange of witness statements may lead more cases to settle early. What will be the actual impact, in practice, we do not know. This would be the type of question that could be explored through controlled experimentation that I discuss below.

51 Compare Elliott, note 6 above at 321: 'We cannot afford to decide every case based on the fullest possible information. Nourishing the fiction that justice is a pearl beyond price has its own price.' (Footnote omitted). He adds the warning that the 'attempt to escape the necessity of making *explicit* cost-benefit judgments about procedure merely leads to basic techniques like managerial judging that invite judges to narrow issues in an ad hoc fashion without safeguards.' Whether the risk referred to in the text is in fact a tolerable one is arguable. Relieving a party of the obligation for having to 'trawl through' all of its documents may be an open invitation to parties never to turn up the 'smoking gun' that favours the opponent's case. It can be further argued that Lord Woolf's notion that a party does not have to read through all its own documents really assumes that documents somehow come pre-arranged in the four categories that he articulates. Since this is obviously not so, I query whether it is in fact wise to relieve a party of the obligation of reading all its own potentially relevant documents. I have reservations about my statement that the 'trade-off' referred to in the text is a reasonable one.

52 Here I am speaking only to the question of whether Lord Woolf's reform might be capable of reducing costs. In terms of truth-finding and party satisfaction I have reservations: see above.

53 Elliott, note 6 above at p326, observes that '[o]ne of the crying research needs in civil procedure is for empirical studies of how managerial judging actually works in practice'. He further observes that '[c]ritics of managerial judging, such as Professor Resnik and Judge Posner, rightly point out that we lack sufficient data to evaluate conclusively whether, on balance (after the costs of managerial judging are taken into account), managerial judging creates net benefits by increasing the overall efficiency of civil litigation as a mechanism for resolving disputes.'

54 To make the experiment more informative, the non-case-managed stream might itself be an experimental condition, ie, a 'minimal intervention stream'. In this stream, immediately after the filing of the last defence, cases would be administratively assigned a fixed trial date ('for the month of') and a general rule would be that there would be no adjournment of the trial, or any other hearing along the way, without the personal attendance request of the parties and a request from one of them.

55 The research design can be further refined to examine other variables. Some

would argue that case management by a team of judges is too diffuse and that, to be really effective, case management has to be carried out in any given case by one person. This is the pattern in the United States, where 'individual calendars' are in use. This variable could be introduced into the experiment by having some cases managed by teams and some managed by individual judges. However, there are limits to these types of refinements: unless case volumes are huge, adding further variables may mean it takes too long to generate statistically significant results.

56 In Canada much less money (virtually none) is spent on research into the operations of civil justice than is spent on research in such areas as health, education and corrections. Is the situation similar in the UK?

Will managed care give us access to justice?[1]

CARRIE MENKEL-MEADOW

Carrie Menkel-Meadow is professor of law and director of the Center for Conflict Resolution at the University of California, Los Angeles.

Introduction

It is somewhat ironic that a country which chose to have socialised medicine and government-supported legal aid comes so late to the notion of active case management by its judicial officials. In the United States, where socialised medicine and law have largely been anathema, judicial and administrative management of cases has been common for close to 20 years.[2] Whether this has increased or decreased access to justice remains a highly controversial question.[3] My brief is to sound a cautionary note from comparative experience. 'Managed care' of the legal system is unlikely to be a panacea for the costs and delays of modern civil legal systems.

The causes of inadequate access to justice are many: so, therefore, must be the solutions. Lord Woolf's report seeks to address only some of the relevant issues: he ignores others. Effective implementation of his proposals should await a more thorough analysis of how managed courts might work in practice. In addition, we must consider the relationship of courts to other social and legal institutions, such as legal aid and out-of-court advice schemes, tribunals, private institutions and providers of mediation and other dispute-resolution devices such as international arbitration.[4] A variety of legal rules, customs and practices (including those relating to costs and even the criminal justice system) influence cost and delay in civil cases but have remained unreviewed by Lord Woolf. It is a difficult task to disentangle, and deal with, all the variables.

89

Deeply embedded in Lord Woolf's report and in my own approach is, and must be, a recognition of the complexity of legal culture in two different ways. First, it is difficult to change our common Anglo-American adversarial approach.[5] Second, there are hazards to cross-cultural comparisons of legal institutions with different supporting legal, constitutional and social structures.

This chapter deals with three general aspects of Lord Woolf's report that bear upon the question of 'access to justice' and one requirement of effective reform. Thus, it deals with four issues: case management; the transformation of the adversarial culture of Anglo-American legal procedure and practice (or the assimilation of case management into it); the role of settlement and ADR in achieving justice; and a final cautionary concern[6] that rigorous empirical research will be necessary to track the consequences of proposed changes and innovations.

Much of the Woolf report relies on assertions regarded as self-evident, for example, that the passage of simplified rules and the introduction of multi-track case management *will* result in reduction of cost and delay. Yet no data or even predictive estimates are offered for the bases of these causal statements, not to mention of what additional resources or costs might be incurred by the suggested proposals. If legal sociology or (as we now call it) socio-legal studies has taught us anything, it is that legal change may often produce both intended and unintended results.[7] Indeed, the specific reforms suggested by Lord Woolf in the forms of increased judicial case management, 'simplified' rules of pleading, discovery and evidence, and offers of settlement, have all produced unexpected consequences and costs when introduced in the United States.[8]

I am concerned with 'access' and 'justice', both concepts with a certain degree of elasticity and imprecision in both legal philosophy and practical law. Stated as the goals of modern legal systems, 'access' and 'justice' may sometimes be in competition with each other with both too much (overloaded, 'over-lawyered' and unnecessarily complex cases) and not enough (barriers of cost preventing a majority of claimants of few means from participating) provision of 'accessible justice'. I am concerned too with the factors placed together (ironically) in my title. Is management (of courts, of 'value for money' in legal aid) consistent with care?[9] Will there be enough consideration for the individual needs of people who have problems requiring some intervention of the legal system?

Justice or access?

Behind any proposal for change, we must ask who is suggesting or supporting change. Who is resisting it and with what expected effects for particular constituencies? In the United States, active adversarialists have learnt to take advantage of, or deform, new rules or process reforms that they initially resisted.[10] Many different parties may have an interest in proposed reforms but the interests of judges, barristers, solicitors, lay 'legal personnel' and clients (whether individuals or entities, rich, middle-class or poor) may be decidedly different from each other.

Unacknowledged contradictory or competing purposes are apparent in Lord Woolf's report on civil justice and the green paper on legal aid. The first appears nobly motivated by a desire to reduce cost and delay in the civil justice system. By contrast, the second is clearly concerned with reducing the costs of legal aid and adopting an approach of 'capped' or budgeted funds more familiar to North Americans. Indeed, the proposals for 'value for money', franchising and quality assurance in legal aid go much farther in controlling provision than has ever been accomplished in the United States. This is perhaps a consequence of the higher expenditure per head of population.[11] There are many proposals in the two reports that should be cross-related but, for the most part, they are not. It might have been preferable to have published them one after the other rather than at the same time.[12]

Lord Woolf proposes, among other things, a uniform set of rules for the High Court and county courts which should simplify the costs of practice, except that it is matched to a 'multi-track' programme of case management that would divide cases into three categories, small claims under £3,000, a fast-track for claims under £10,000 and a multiple track for more complex cases (defined by their monetary value). Are there no cases of legal or factual complexity at lower monetary levels requiring some form of case management? To the extent that this tracking subjects cases to different rules, some injustices might develop. If discovery is more limited in the lower-value cases, it will prejudice cases in which the defendant is likely to have more information or better access to information and may cause particular harm to poorer litigants who may require discovery in order to prove their cases.[13] In the United States, the move toward ADR began, in part, by labelling some cases 'minor' cases (defined by low monetary value or case types, such as neighbour disputes)[14] and resulted in widespread opposition to ADR by both legal services activists and academic critics, who saw a 'multi-classed' justice as inherently unfair.[15]

Lord Woolf recommends that cases are to be actively managed by a new cadre of retrained 'procedural judges' working in teams. Other proposed reforms are aimed at increasing the simplicity and responsiveness of pleadings (see p68). Lord Woolf wants increased use of witness statements (with greater emphasis on written rather than oral presentation) (see p71); court control of expert witnesses (see p72); and increased incentives for settlement in offers to settle (by both plaintiffs and defendants) (see p73). ADR is to be recommended to the parties in litigation but there is little endorsement of court-sponsored (or, more importantly, court-funded) ADR programmes.

With the exception of Lord Woolf's mention of the need for some legal aid funds to be allocated to ADR use, there is little effort in these reports to examine the effects of the proposed reforms on legally aided clients. If ADR is to remain essentially a private service proposed by counsel or by judges at a management conference but not analysed by reference to the likely decreased funding available for legal aid, how can ADR or other reforms possibly increase access to justice? It may be hoped that the greater diversion of cases into the small claims procedure may result in cases being handled promptly and perhaps without lawyers. As a result, there could be additional funds available for other purposes, such as legal aid and ADR. Yet examination of the Woolf report and the green paper on legal aid indicates that the goals of access and justice have not been considered together.

More significantly, although the goals of the Woolf report are to reduce delay and cost with increased judicial management and by increased 'policing' of adversarial lawyer behaviour, it has been our experience in the United States that increased case management has often meant more meetings with judges and case managers (with increased hourly fees for the lawyers). Thus reforms which were intended to cut costs often leave the lawyers smiling like the Cheshire cat in *Alice in Wonderland*. What are the likely implications for legally aided clients if it turns out that conferences with judges increase, rather than decrease, costs?

The implicit theme of Lord Woolf's report is that the lawyers must be 'tamed' to cut costs and delay and the judges are the ones to do it. Is it too cynical to suggest that he considers increased access to justice more likely as the result of an accretion of powers to the bench (even with few additional resources) than the provision of more resources for legal aid or more fora for the pursuit of justice?

Finally, the reports can be read together to form a theme of increased 'bureaucratised justice' as law takes its place alongside the 'managed care' of medicine and the cost and quality control of business management. Although Lord Woolf does not aim to dismantle completely the adversarial system that we know and love, the effect of his proposals would be to move the legal system ever so much closer to the continental European inquisitorial-bureaucratic justice scheme of more judicial control over case presentation and investigation.[16] Lord Woolf's failure to recommend court-sponsored forms of 'appropriate dispute resolution' (the newer term for ADR) moves the English system closer to its European neighbours and further away from its North American cousins.[17] Coupled with increased cost-monitoring, franchising and quality control standards[18] in legal aid, the provision of legal services and justice is heading down a more bureaucratic-administrative path. There appears to be a relatively unbounded faith in the ability to frame and cabin cases and people in categories (monetary value of case, cases of greatest need or urgency or merit), regardless of complexity. This allows the process, so it is claimed, to be rationalised; to be made cheaper and faster; and to provide greater access.[19]

I am not opposed to all the individual proposals but, like others, I am less sure that such major legal cultural change can be legislated or brought into effect by a single, if well-intentioned, inquiry and report.[20] Legal culture is far more complex and powerful than we might imagine. Despite the initial welcome to Lord Woolf's ideas, I predict more controversy ahead.[21]

Case management

The thrust of Lord Woolf's report echoes a theme familiar to North Americans. Litigation has become too expensive, too cumbersome and too time-consuming (for the clients, if not the hourly billing lawyers).

We must begin with the question of baseline measures. What is cheap, simple, fast and efficient in an ideal world? By comparison with North American practice, reaching trial within 80 weeks of issue seems most reasonable (see p67). Costs, of course, are more difficult to compare because, as a general rule, US courts do not have the same cost-shifting rules (each side generally meets only its own costs),[22] nor are costs and fees as likely to be subsidised by the government.[23] Yet it seems clear from the research of Professor Genn[24] that costs are too large as a proportion of the total award to litigants and cases are taking a long time to settle (often four to six years). Thus, Lord Woolf seeks to establish 'cost controls' on litigation (like 'cost controls' on legal aid) by requiring judicial control of the process by two stages of judicial intervention, at a case management conference early in the case and at a pre-trial review shortly before trial, of at least those cases in the third tier of 'multi-track' cases (those with values above £10,000). These case management conferences are accompanied by a requirement that solicitors brief their clients about costs and inform both clients and the court about fees and costs at key times in the case. Lord Woolf hopes that transparency will render costs more reasonable by subjecting them to some element of both market competition and judicial monitoring.

Procedural judging

Because cases in England and Wales are not assigned initially to single judges, as is common in United States federal, if not state, systems, Lord Woolf proposes that teams of judges will be assigned the judicial management and procedural monitoring functions. Settlement will also be encouraged by suggesting, if not requiring, ADR, and by the use of written offers of settlement. Lord Woolf believes that increased court attention to cases at earlier stages will help establish an 'equality of arms' between the parties; will encourage earlier settlements; and will allow more efficient deployment of the limited resources available to the system as well as to the litigants.

We are beginning to learn in the United States that the effects of cost reduction, case management and settlement practices do not necessarily all redound to the equal benefit of all involved. Savings to the parties are often balanced by increased costs to the system or courts.[25] Greater court administration of cases requires additional costs in staff and court personnel. Lord Woolf glosses over, or attempts to finesse, this issue by suggesting that judges educated to try cases will step voluntarily into new roles (at least after some further training) and undertake more and different work without necessarily any more resources.

Alternatively, a separate class of 'managerial judges' will be created with a different defined role from the traditional judicial one. Such procedural judges would face issues about both cost and status. They may lack equivalent authority if not perceived as the equivalent of adjudicating judges. The United States has spawned an active jurisprudence on the question of the appropriate judicial role, partly from academics and partly from judges themselves. There is argument as to whether judges should remain 'passive' or be more active in adjudicating cases.[26] Most American federal judges now engage in case management, through the requirements imposed by rules of procedure for pre-trial conferences much like those contemplated by Lord Woolf. On the other hand, some courts with high caseloads have sought to separate the management function from the judicial function. They do this by utilising magistrate judges (not appointed under the full rigours of the constitution) or even private lawyers (as happens in the Northern District of California)[27] who volunteer to help provide early evaluation of cases (see p45 and p50), facilitate settlement or set discovery schedules.

The 'tracking' of judicial functions potentially has both positive and negative effects. Those who serve as procedural or managerial judges may actually prefer this work or be better equipped to do it. Thus, either with the training contemplated by Lord Woolf or by dint of personal preference or accumulated experience and expertise, a cadre of 'procedural judges' may emerge who are good at managing cases.[28] In the United States, the Federal Rules of Civil Procedure even provide for the formal appointment of a Special Master to assist the court in such case-management functions as discovery, investigative and settlement co-ordination in particular cases.[29] Training, experience and expertise are helpful to this process, but particularly so, where, as in the United States, the case-management function is often combined with a settlement function. Managing, settling and deciding cases (fact-finding and law interpretation) draw on quite different skills which do not come easy to all.

On the other hand, not all good judges will take readily to the new managerial task if judging in the traditional sense remains the highest status occupation of the court. It is likely that an increased hierarchy in the judiciary will emerge, augmented by the dependence on deputy judges to hear cases. Procedural judges without the full status and authority of High Court or other judicial officers may have difficulty in controlling and policing the case-management function. Thus the expertise and specialisation required for case management might also lead to greater hierarchies on the bench and at the Bar. For case management conferences to be successful, it matters who attends. Will this be solicitors, clerks, senior or junior counsel? Will attendance at such conferences drive up the fees for both private and legally aided litigants? Will clients be required to attend, as is the case in many United States jurisdictions where settlement is in issue?

Finally, it is difficult to imagine how the necessary staff co-ordination required to keep track of 'teams' of case managers can possibly reduce the cost of judicial administration. At the very least, team members will have to keep each other appraised, either orally, in the English tradition, or by computer or written docket entries, of the status of cases following conferences, submissions and orders. The American experience has been that case management, while often effective at monitoring case flow (especially when coupled with modern technology and computerisation) and aggregate case administration, may, at least at the outset, result in increased costs of judicial management and administration. Indeed, greater judicial administration, in the form of court clerks, ADR directors and other administrators, has led to new career paths and offices. All this has happened in the name of efficiency but it has required a great initial outlay of resources.[30] New layers of administration and modern management, even when well intentioned, can result in more stages, increased complexity, more documents to be filed, more co-ordination and more staff. So where then is the cost and delay reduction?[31]

Conferences

For all its potential difficulties, good case management can streamline case presentation; reward efforts to speed up cases; and lower costs. It is, however, extremely important to consider the goals, conduct and content of case-management conferences. I differ from Lord Woolf's conception of these in a way which has some bearing on how the 'counter-adversarial-spirit of co-operation' training of judges and lawyers should be structured.

Lord Woolf suggests that the specific objectives of case management are to encourage early settlement; diversion, where appropriate, to alternative forms of dispute resolution; encouragement of a spirit of co-operation between lawyers and parties; avoidance of unnecessary combativeness, identification; *reduction* (my italics) of issues as a basis of case preparation; and finally, where settlement is unlikely, speeding cases to trial. All of these goals have implications for both judicial and attorney training (and 'reculturation', as discussed below) and affect understanding of the process of a case-management conference.

Goals of settlement and trial management may be different. To make these conferences effective in the United States, parties (through their counsel) are often asked to prepare conference memoranda indicating their discovery schedule, the issues and the likely witnesses (especially experts). Like many of his American brothers and sisters, Lord Woolf thinks that negotiation and settlement will be facilitated by narrowing and reducing issues. Here is my evidence of the need for completely revamped training and reculturation of the entire legal profession. Modern negotiation theory tells us that settlement may often be more likely when there are more issues, rather than fewer. If there are numerous issues at stake, parties' complementary, and not necessarily competing, needs and interests can be traded off to increase the number of potential settlements in 'Pareto-optimal' terms, ie, parties explore a number of possibilities until no one can be made better off without some harm to the other side.[32]

By contrast, the legal process narrows disputes and makes them harder to resolve. The legal process monetises disputes by taking a variety of issues (such as the desire for an apology, rehabilitation, medical costs, lost wages, loss of consortium, pain and suffering) and converting them all to monetary awards or damages. Thus, if judges and lawyers are to use the case management conference for exploration of settlement, they may act differently than if they were preparing for trial.

Conferences may need to be divided into two parts: consideration, on the one hand, of what might be necessary for settlement through examining the interests of the parties and discussion, on the other, of issues relevant to trial, such as timetables, witness statements and experts. Narrowing the issues may assist presentation at trial but be unhelpful to settlement.

Judges will clearly have to learn about their new roles and the substance of their recommendations. They will have to understand the differences between various processes such as arbitration, mediation and various forms of private hybrids if they are to advise parties and their lawyers on diverting cases to appropriate forms of dispute resolution.

This chapter does not consider the issue of advice schemes, but it is an absolutely essential function of any court that promises access to justice to provide information about its own procedures and what else might solve litigants' problems. I remain concerned about quality control, both of lay advisers and of judges, who may be helping to manage cases or divert to ADR without fully understanding what they are doing. Different forms of ADR are quite varied in terms of party control, third-party neutral functions and the possible structure and content of outcomes.

ADR and judges

Judicial referral to ADR presents additional challenges in the British context. Since Lord Woolf has not supported the notion of court-annexed ADR, now common in both federal and state courts in the United States, judges will be both 'educating' litigants about, and 'recommending' them to, services from other agencies, both public and private, outside the existing court structure. In the United States, we are just beginning to grapple with the difficult issues of formal court referrals and recommendations to providers of dispute resolution services outside of the courts. What should be the appropriate quality standards? Who is liable in the event of error or malpractice? What confidentiality and accountability is required?[33] How are 'procedural judges' to educate themselves about available ADR options that they might recommend and their effects? How 'coercive' will a judicial suggestion seem to a party?

I have spent much of the last year and a half training judges at both the federal and state level about ADR. A surprising amount of ignorance persists, even in the United States with its vast assortment of programmes. Training must cover not only the content of ADR but give some understanding of the experience of how it works and what the effects of a judicial referral will be. Related to this issue is the question of how much 'procedural judges' will themselves become involved in attempting to settle cases: or will they just 'encourage' parties to do so? How will they facilitate party settlement? By scheduling negotiation sessions? Controlling preparation of witness statements and discovery? In the United States, the issue of the role of the judge in participating in settlement discussions has been very controversial and, in my view, requires special training.[34]

Cost

If there are to be no court-supported ADR programmes, who will pay for the 'diversion' of cases to appropriate dispute resolution? Legal aid funds are not currently available for representation, or presence at, mediation or arbitration. Will this system create another form of 'classed' justice, where some will be able to pay for some alternatives but others will not? Both the recent green paper on legal aid and the government's proposals for divorce and mediation suggest the diversion of some legal aid funds to ADR. This is essential for any claim to access to justice for all. Contrary to much prejudice that only lower-value cases would be diverted to ADR in the United States, in fact the biggest users of private schemes are major corporations involved in highly complex and very expensive lawsuits who can afford to buy 'private justice'.[35]

Research in the United States demonstrates that increased case management and settlement activity may in fact slow case-processing time[36] because it takes judges away from judging and involves them in other activities that may or may not shorten the trial process or queue. As others have pointed out (see p71), some of the cost and delay reduction reforms will push legal expenses to the beginning of cases. This may 'front-load' rather than eliminate expense by, for example, requiring earlier preparation and revision of witness statements or attendance at case-management conferences. Several studies demonstrate that the one way to ensure quick case processing and earlier settlements is to set a firm trial date and keep to it. This is less possible in the US system than in England and Wales, because the same courtrooms tend to be tied up with criminal matters and cannot predictably be assigned in advance to civil cases.[37]

Case management works best when parties are called to account for timetables and punctual submissions of discovery and other stages in the case. Calling the parties to conferences causes them to focus on a case and that, in itself, often produces settlements or clarification of issues. Nevertheless, case management is itself time-consuming and has some costs. What is more, without some settlement-seeking and guiding activity, it becomes just another routinised, bureaucratic step or layer on the way to more fees. If not used effectively, it will not provide the cost and delay reduction Lord Woolf contemplates.

Those contemplating Lord Woolf's reforms must consider the possibility that litigation delay actually reflects an equilibrium point. As argued by the legal economist, George Priest, litigation rates have a tendency to stabilise over time. If case management, ADR or settlement actually reduces delay, more cases may go to trial. Decreased delay reduces one of the incentives for settlement. Thus, when cases can be quickly tried, more cases will be attracted to the trial process. When the queue becomes too long again, parties will settle until delay is reduced to the equilibrium level. Priest thus argues that any attempt to reduce delay will simply eventually result in more trials and fewer settlements until the system reaches its natural equilibrium point.[38] In my view, the use of case management and increased settlement incentives and ADR will have some initial effects in changing the equilibrium level to allow for greater access. If more cases can be processed with increased management, diversion or negotiation, then more cases will come into the system. This means, at least initially, that more people will have access to some form of justice. With increased use of ADR or other forms of case-processing, the 'new' equilibrium point for the number of cases solved in one way or another could be much greater than now. This is indeed increased access to justice.

Transformation of the adversary culture

If greater management will not solve all the problems of cost and delay and lack of access to justice, can these advances be achieved by greater 'care'? Lord Woolf seeks to reduce the culture of adversarialism and hopes that increased co-operation between the parties will reduce some of the wear, tear and cost of civil justice.

Having spent much of my professional life complaining about the costs, inefficiencies and human injuries caused by the adversary system,[39] I am sympathetic to Lord Woolf's desire to make the litigation process more co-operative or (perhaps a better expression) collaborative. Much cost and delay is attributable to the rancour and harsh competitiveness with which modern litigation is conducted.[40] Competition between adversaries has the effect of maintaining the number of billable hours. In some civil disputes, say with government or employers about public benefits and jobs, very crucial and life-threatening issues may be involved. In these kinds of case, a degree of competitiveness may be acceptable when it is not in others. I support the ideal of introducing more collaboration into the process but the reality will be hard to achieve. Cultural change of the sort envisioned by Lord Woolf cannot be legislated, reported, 'green or white papered' or probably even changed too much by court orders and sanctions. At least, this has been the experience of that most adversarial of groups, the aggressively competitive lawyers of the United States.

Distortion and manipulation of reforms

Efforts to mandate 'co-operative' behaviour are often distorted or manipulated by lawyers who seek to remain adversarial and who have a very robust legal culture to support them. It is possible that British civility and traditions can be harnessed to make change more effective than in the United States, but I rather doubt it. As in the United States, the English legal profession, thankfully, can no longer claim that homogeneity of 'polite gentlemen' who all belong to the same club. Heterogeneity of lawyers, clients, judges and other legal actors makes for diversity, and diversity sparks some competition over values. Thus, the larger culture must also be considered when one seeks to change the legal culture which is embedded in other social realities.

Lord Woolf raises two basic objections to the adversarial model: parties (really their lawyers) control litigation, and practice has 'degenerated into an environment in which the civil litigation process is too often seen as a battlefield where no rules apply'.[41] Thus he suggests that the courts should take control of the process and the rules should be changed, simplified and clarified so that responsibilities are clear; information is exchanged earlier; and there is more flexibility with respect to some issues (supplementation of witness statements) but less on others (one expert for both sides). Judges will control this process, though they will have less power to discipline recalcitrant parties than currently exists in the United States, where sanctions in the form of monetary penalties, as well as other procedural orders, are authorised by rules of procedure. Thus, judges are to be 'enforcers' of a new co-operative approach to case preparation, though it remains unclear how lawyers are to learn their 'new attitude' and craft.

A United States Federal rule requires lawyers, in essence, to vouch for their assertions and pleadings. Sanctions may be awarded against those who fail adequately to investigate claims or turn over discovery. This has led to an era of increased litigation about the meaning of the rules.[42] Even with the recognition that English and Welsh lawyers may behave themselves better than Americans, it will be interesting to see if rule and practice changes will be sufficient to secure full co-operation in litigation. I hope it works, but our experience has been that innovations and rule changes are often distorted so as to meet the almost insatiable desire to retain the adversarial fight.

For example, court-sponsored arbitration programmes have been cynically used by some parties for discovery purposes in expectation of an appeal for a retrial. This is now leading to examination of the question of what it means legally to engage in 'good faith participation' in a court-ordered programme.[43] Equivalent attempts in the United States to require earlier and more honest disclosure of case facts and witnesses[44] have resulted in most Federal district courts opting out of the new rules' requirements for early and 'voluntary' disclosure. This is, in part, due to active lobbying by the Bar to preserve their old ways and also in response to arguments that the new rules will lead to costly litigation about their meaning. It is possible that the culture of British lawyers may be different from their American cousins' because of the weaker constitutional force of 'due process' or the lack of oral examinations before trial. Certainly, litigators in the United States would never willingly relinquish their 'due process' rights to stage the battle of experts that characterises their adversarial litigation on anything involving a question beyond the ken of ordinary people.[45]

New rules have often provoked more, not less, adversarial behaviour. They may change the conduct, but so far not much of the game, of litigation.[46] What is more, rule changes may have unintended consequences and varying effects on different classes of cases. Restricting discovery in some cases may harm particular classes of litigants, such as those suing for discrimination, where only the defendant may possess the relevant evidence.

'Re-culturation' and re-education

The solution is not more, or even more simplified, rules[47] but effective methods for 're-culturation' or education. The culture will be changed only when innovations appear to be effective. Thus, lawyers must be taught to think about handling cases differently. Only when they are successful at this will the culture become more collaborative and co-operative. This re-education process must proceed simultaneously on all levels: in the universities, in all law courses, in apprenticeships, in continuing education for solicitors, barristers and judges. To the extent that other professions seem to have encouraged other ways to solve legal problems (like mediation in the family law context) more readily than lawyers, we can expect some 'cultural competition'. Perhaps only when clients make it clear that they prefer the services offered by those who do not engage in such unproductive adversarial conduct and can still solve the problem will lawyers respond.

To the extent that adversarialism is not only culturally, but economically, based, there will have to be financial incentives for more 'co-operative' behaviour. Attorneys still believe that more discovery, more preparation of witness statements and more motions are a good thing because they will produce greater fees. In the United States, there is some evidence that clients, like large corporations, who are strong enough to control the fee structure[48] are now reversing fee patterns and rewarding early settlement with bonuses and penalising trials by paying reduced hourly fees. To change the culture, lawyers and judges must see economic rewards for so doing. In this, they may have different economic and other interests.[49] Aside from clients beginning to recognise and demand less costly and wasteful lawyers, some lawyers have come to realise that it is in their economic interest as well as that of their reputations to create efficient solutions and to be seen as 'co-operative agents' in their clients' behaviour and relationships.[50] Lawyers must be re-educated so that they are perceived as true 'problem-solvers'. To do this, co-operative behaviour must be reinforced by economic reward.

Recent research in a number of fields outside the law has demonstrated just how inefficient adversarial behaviour is. Social and cognitive psychologists have demonstrated that a variety of distortions of the reasoning process result from adversarial approaches to problems. Thus we often devalue or cannot hear the validity of claims made by opponents in litigation, simply because they are opponents. This is called reactive devaluation.[51] It is often helpfully corrected by a third-party neutral, like a mediator, who can explore the validity of claims detached from their proponents. Similarly, and most crucially for the settlement of civil litigation, proponents of a case or argument often overvalue their case, simply because it is theirs and they are overconfident in both their legal and economic evaluation.[52] Other distortions of reasoning include letting the first (primacy) or last (recency) argument advanced govern one's views; letting the fear of losing some advantage control evaluation of what could be gained from someone regarded as an opponent (loss aversion and risk aversion dominating investment in contingencies); and continuing to fight a losing battle for fear of acknowledging weakness (the escalation of conflict in adversarial activity). Thus to change the culture may require some explicit teaching and learning about just how 'costly' (as well as painful) adversarial thinking can be. This teaching needs to be focused on modern negotiation theory, incorporating an understanding of social and cognitive psychology, economics and communication theory.

Other research is beginning to focus on the other side of the coin: the advantages of co-operative behaviour. In a much-touted computer tournament, the political scientist Robert Axelrod demonstrated that the most robust and most successful program for 'winning' many repeats of a computerised prisoner's dilemma game (a standard games theory problem allowing a judgment of strategic behaviour) was a program that co-operated until it was 'defected against', then it retaliated only once ('tit for tat').[53] Thus, the program was co-operative but reactive and forgiving. Lawyers, biologists and game theorists are now busily exploring the ramifications of this work to explain the value of co-operation in sustaining human life and producing better legal results. Such decisions as whether or not to co-operate in discovery or other aspects of litigation are obvious applications.[54] Other political scientists have begun to explore the various motivations that explain under what conditions people can be made to act other than in their unenlightened self-interest (voting, collaborative problem-solving, international diplomacy, rescuing or helping behaviour and so on)[55] and employ 'mixed motives' combining self-interest and other goals.

There is not enough space here to explore all of this exciting new work which attempts to explain why people (and lawyers) behave adversarially or not. The point is simply that human and legal behaviour is too complex to be changed by decree or report. We will need very sophisticated educational and informational programmes to counter behaviour patterns which are rigidly held by a very entrenched and narrowly educated profession.

Thus, to make the transition to my third major area of inquiry, I am seriously troubled that Lord Woolf does not do more to 'require' or attach ADR-consciousness to the courts in his bid for procedural and cultural reform. It is my own (personal and perhaps American) experience that the major source of cultural change in combating adversarialism is to educate people through the concrete tasks and experiences of specific ADR applications to legal problem-solving.[56] ADR is the educative tool by which the adversarial system is most likely to be tamed, rather than through rule-making or case management (unless it focuses on settlement and ADR, as well as case processing and scheduling). Lawyers must be taught to appreciate other forms of behaving and legal problem-solving,[57] because so many do not really know how to negotiate except by employing conventional adversarial means. ADR, in certain forms, including integrative negotiation, is exactly the kind of potentially transformative process that educates and can make cultural change in the process of solving concrete problems. Lord Woolf leaves that process to outside providers by reference from the courts. In my view, if Lord Woolf's proposals are to have any success, the courts and the legal profession must be more actively engaged in various ADR and settlement procedures.

The role of settlement and ADR in access to justice

Even if we accept Lord Woolf's assumptions that access to justice will best be served by reducing cost and delay, he has not devoted enough explicit attention to the underlying processes of negotiation, settlement and appropriate dispute resolution in fulfilling these goals. More important, justice itself will be better served if cases are settled better or are directed to processes that may be more responsive to the problem at hand.

Settlement or ADR cannot be regarded as a panacea for all the justice system's troubles, nor will ADR create social and economic equity where there was none before. Settlement or ADR should only be employed when it would make the parties better off than if they were to litigate. There are clearly limits as to when ADR should be used; this is demonstrated by the vigorous debate in the United States about the inappropriateness of some of its forms where there are power imbalances, such as with women in divorce mediation[58] and with ethnic or racial minorities when dealing with dominant groups.[59] These limitations should be considered properly before mediation becomes mandated or relegated to particular kinds of disputes, like divorce. Yet settlement clearly serves some purpose if it reduces costs, emotional distress, or business, economic and emotional risks; enhances relationships; creates better and more durable solutions; and deals with the basic conflict underlying a particular dispute into which it may have crystallised. When used in the best ways possible, ADR and good settlement procedures provide the parties with an experience of greater participation in their cases and sometimes, if not always, with a higher quality solution to their problems.[60] If Lord Woolf seeks to provide access to justice, and if he wants sincerely to remove unproductive adversarial behaviour from our systems, then settlement activity and ADR should more explicitly be on the public agenda of court and procedural reform (with appropriate resources as well).

Appropriate dispute resolution: the promise

The theory behind ADR offers us a wide range of rules and processes for arriving at the best possible outcomes for a wide variety of disputes. Thus, in one sense, advocating greater use of ADR runs counter to Lord Woolf's search for simplified procedures that reduce cost and delay. Indeed, given the modern world's greater complexity, the increased likelihood of conflict being generated from our more heterogenous societies and the increased occurrence of multi-party actions, a simplified, trans-substantive rule system may not work. In other contexts, notably mass torts in America, I have recently argued that the increasing complexity of cases, lawyers, types of parties and injuries make our system of trans-substantive procedural and ethical rules inadequate to the tasks at hand.[61] ADR permits the selection of a process that may be tailored to the needs of the parties in a particular dispute. It allows them to choose together a process that may emphasise fact-finding, precedent-development (litigation), or more multi-party participation and tailored and contingent solutions with a focus on the future, rather than the past. Thus rules and agendas can be adapted to particular problems (as long as the parties agree) and sometimes particular expertise may be sought out for decision-making. Thus, rather than Lord Woolf's one expert for the litigation, an expert with knowledge of the particular scientific or other issues in the case might be a mediator facilitating a solution or an arbitrator making a well-informed ruling.

ADR and settlement encouragement cannot occur in their optimal state without appropriate education and training. Intellectual and informative presentations may provide cognitive understanding of how legal problems might be solved differently, but judges and lawyers will also need experiential training if they are to learn how to negotiate or conduct themselves in other settings like mediation. The National Institute for Trial Advocacy has flourished in North America for over 20 years. We now assume that trial lawyers must learn their skills with practice. The same cannot yet be said of negotiating and settling cases. As the barriers between solicitors and barristers begin to fall, both sets of English lawyers will need to learn new skills. The role of a representative in a court is different from in an arbitration or a mediation, as is that of a third-party neutral from a judge. The different roles call on a different understanding of the part being played[62] as well as different performance skills.[63] Even Lord Woolf's 'procedural judges' will be performing roles more akin to mediators or managers, closer to ADR than traditional adjudication. As he recognises, they will need training for these new roles.

To transform our adversarial culture, advocates will have to learn to devote as much attention to conceptualising and achieving good settlements[64] as to preparing for trial. Lord Woolf places some emphasis on the use of offers of settlement as another tool of delay and cost reduction (see p73). To incorporate this, structured negotiation and ADR devices are essential. Lord Woolf's treatment demonstrates clearly how monetised our conceptions of settlement have become. The offer of settlement and subsequent taxation of costs has been very controversial in the United States.[65] Recent research suggests that parties often want things in addition to, or instead of, money (for example, the 'cathartic' effects of a hearing, an apology, future medical expenses or medical monitoring). Thus thinking about how to settle cases may require more than the 'Lloyd's of London' formula of splitting the economic difference between two opening monetary bids. Creative negotiation skills require thought about ways to 'expand the pie' (or increase or change the *res*, the thing about which the parties are arguing) before we have to divide it (creating, as well as claiming, value).[66] In a time of shrinking public funds, we may need to think about other kinds of creative settlements in order to achieve justice, not just to dismiss cases.

An increase in the kinds of available proceedings and in the number of possible creative solutions in resolving legal and social problems is as effective a way of improving access to justice as many of the means chosen by Lord Woolf. Official court support of other types of proceedings would seem inevitably to lead to more access, with the possibility of more routes to justice. One must ask, therefore, why Lord Woolf resisted two forms of American use of ADR: some compulsory referrals and processes and official court approval and provision of services.

The answers will lead me conveniently to my last subject: the need for rigorous and well-resourced research. It is clear that Lord Woolf seeks to accomplish his reforms with a minimum of increased resources being allocated to the legal system, either to the courts or to the legal aid scheme. This is a time of 'cost-containment' on both sides of the Atlantic. He is fearful that the courts neither have, nor could obtain, large increments of budgetary support for new programmes.

Lord Woolf, though seeking to reduce adversarialism, is still a product of his own training and experience, the traditions of the British courts. The various ADR processes are often frightening to traditional lawyers and judges because they are so various, informal, untidy, not rule-bound, and fraught with interpersonal conflict and psychological, as well as legal, issues. They call for a focus on business decisions and the future, not only on fact-finding and investigation of the past. They require some synthetic and creative skills as well as the more familiar analytic and deductive skills of legal practice and adjudication. Such fear is not solely a British phenomenon. I have encountered it among my colleagues at the bench and Bar in the United States. But, in this time of increasing competition with other professions and scarcity of economic resources for fees, more traditional lawyers should note the entrepreneurial spirit of younger lawyers and the competition from social workers, psychologists and accountants[67] in this field. These rivals may be more responsive to client needs and changes in the economic marketplace.

Finally, I suspect Lord Woolf was concerned and affected by the confusions and wide varieties of views he found on ADR in his consultations with American judges, lawyers, academics and others. The empirical success of ADR has yet to be conclusively demonstrated and the debate remains somewhat fierce in some quarters.[68] We await the results of two important empirical evaluations of whether cost and delay plans, pursuant to our Civil Justice Reform Act, have accomplished their goals, including the use of court-sponsored ADR programmes. Some have suggested that ADR should be relegated to the private sphere or used only when two private parties seek resolution of their private disputes: the court system should be left to more 'public' or complex cases. However, in the United States we have had difficulty in defining what those cases would be[69] and have determined that some public intervention and recommendation of ADR processes is at least worth an experiment.

Rigorous evaluation and research

Lord Woolf's inquiry into the reduction of cost and delay in search of access to justice replicates the concerns of many modern legal systems. There is more demand on the system than we can meet. Our procedures have become complex and, in some cases, unresponsive to the demands of modern litigation. We know that large numbers of poor and middle-class people cannot afford to use the present system. So we all seek solutions to these problems.

Lord Woolf's solutions may, however, not be radical enough to solve all the problems. Access to justice may require the expenditure of more funds on translation services or education programmes to advise the public of its legal rights and how to realise them. It may require us to break the legal monopoly and allow a wide variety of other providers of services to offer legal and quasi-legal services such as advice, tribunal representation, mediation and document preparation.[70] More people may get fewer or more limited services through routinised, high-volume, computer-driven services or as the result of restrictions on what contracted, budgeted and quality-controlled legal services can provide.

Simplified rules may make things somewhat easier for the lawyers and judges. Yet, unless the small claims procedures operate differently from the way they have in most countries, where they have become 'collection of debt' courts for corporate creditors of individuals, procedural reform will not necessarily redound to the automatic benefit of all consumers of the legal system. If discovery is limited, in some cases early settlement may actually be discouraged, since parties need a certain minimum amount of information to settle their cases. Simplified rules will work in an era in which cases are becoming, if anything, more complex, requiring extra management and additional guidelines, often suited to the particularities of case type. Case management offers the potential of setting up someone other than the lawyers or parties to be responsible for ensuring due progress (see p16 and p65). This effort to take some control away from busy lawyers is probably a good idea, even if judicial attitudes toward this new role still need to be ascertained. Nevertheless, case management may produce some costs of its own and some of the more legalistic reforms will undoubtedly be cleverly manipulated as lawyers, judges and some parties vie for control of the litigation process.

The key to access to justice remains adequate resources and consideration of more radical ways to deliver justice. Our concept of justice may be transformed by how we achieve it. Thus, when conducted well, mediation of multiple parties in complex and even some public disputes offers the potential for more democratic and collaborative participation in legal[71] and governmental affairs. Thandi Orleyn from South Africa recounts in LAG's publication *Shaping the Future*[72] that, in her country, there was some hope that mediation would create more responsive and finely textured resolutions to complex property disputes in the new regime in South Africa.[73] Indira Jaising's contribution to the same book told us that in India, with vast numbers of people affected by private and governmental action, new forms of legal action, such as class actions and direct actions, vested in the Supreme Court and directed towards law reform, were being created to adapt to another modern state's different needs.[74] Thus, access to justice will mean different things in different contexts. What may work to bring governmental and state agencies to account may not be what is required to bring corporate wrongdoers to book.

Even at the individual party-to-party level, mediation offers the possibility of transforming relations; uncovering the underlying conflict which caused the dispute; and providing for arrangements of the future rather than adjudication of the past through the blunt instrument provided by awards of damages. It will not be suitable for all cases. Some cases require definitive rulings, mandatory injunctions or the termination rather than the continuation of relationships. Yet, if one of the goals of legal reform is to make users of the legal system feel comfortable with it, 'justice' may come in more than one form. Different consumers of the system may have different requirements.

Thus, whatever reforms are undertaken, they must be monitored and studied so that there is little doubt about what the effects of particular reforms are. An Australian contribution to *Shaping the Future* reported that, in studying court delay in New South Wales, the New South Wales Civil Justice Research Centre learned that it was the parties themselves who were mostly responsible for delay through failure to provide each other with adequate information.[75] Thus a particular policy initiative, such as mandatory disclosure rules, might fix the problem. It is however rare for rigorous research to precede rather than follow policy initiatives. As we await the results of studies conducted by RAND and the Federal Judicial Center on the effects of the Civil Justice Reform Act in the United States (see p43), I have no doubt that we will find mixed results. This is evaluation research after a wide variety of policy initiatives. Different regions of the country are likely to find different solutions to the cost and delay problem. In districts where there is not much delay (in some, trial is possible within nine months), there may be other goals of the justice system to be achieved, such as innovative ways to handle prisoners' habeas corpus or civil rights claims, or earlier and better settlements of particular kinds of cases. At the national level, we may learn that mass torts affecting hundreds of thousands of people may require their own rules, procedural, substantive and ethical.[76] Different processes used in different contexts produce different results. We know that case types, lawyer personalities, resources available, client needs and local and national legal culture all affect rates and dispositions of disputes and litigation behaviour.[77]

Summary

The reforms suggested by Lord Woolf will have, if implemented, both intended and unintended consequences. I would have focused more on adding other processes to the mix of adjudication, as well as his proposals to promote case management and rule simplification. But, whatever the final results of the inquiry into the civil justice system of England and Wales may be, surely we (more particularly, you) should try to learn what is working where and for what reasons. As students of procedural justice in the United States have been surprised to learn, disputants do not always value the same things as regular members of the legal institutions (judges and lawyers) or even the researchers![78] To return to my earliest theme: who is managing and caring for whom in the legal system is far from obvious. Who will benefit from legal system reforms requires careful monitoring and study.

References

1 'Managed care' is the current term associated with administrative and competitive cost control of medical care in the United States within a regime of mostly privately funded insurance reimbursement for medical care. The government pays for health care of the elderly in the federally funded Medicare programme and subsidises the medically indigent through the Medicaid programme which is administered through the states. Both are currently under siege, with proposals for massive cuts by the Republican-controlled Congress.

2 J Resnik, 'Managerial Judges' 96 *Harvard L Rev* 376 (1982); R Peckham, 'A Judicial Response to the Costs of Litigation: Two-Stage discovery planning and alternative dispute resolution' 37 *Rutgers L Rev* 253 (1985).

3 See, eg, C Menkel-Meadow, 'Pursuing Settlement in an Adversary Culture' 19 *Fla St L Rev* 1 (1991); Owen Fiss, 'Against Settlement' 93 *Yale L Rev* 1545 (1982); Stephen Yeazell, 'The Misunderstood Consequences of Modern Civil Process' (1994) *Wisc L Rev* 630.

4 See, eg, *Legal Aid – Targeting Need* (HMSO, 1995); *Looking to the Future: Mediation and the ground for divorce* (HMSO, 1995) (white paper).

5 See C Menkel-Meadow, 'The Trouble With the Adversary System in a Post-Modern, Multi-cultural World', Hoftstra University, conference on legal ethics, 1996.

6 This has already been suggested in British reactions to the Woolf report; see Michael Zander, 'Are There Any Clothes for The Emperor to Wear?' 145 *New Law Journal* 154 (1995).

7 See C Menkel-Meadow, 'Durkheimian Epiphanies: The importance of engaged social science in legal studies' 18 *Fla St L Rev* (1990). Zander reviews some of the American literature pointing to increased delay following the use of case-management conferences or increased judicial participation in settlement; see, eg, T Church et al, 'Justice Delayed: The pace of litigation in urban trial courts' Federal Judicial Center (1978). For my own review of this literature see C Menkel-Meadow, 'For and Against Settlement: The uses and abuses of the mandatory settlement conference' 33 *UCLA L Rev* 485 (1995); see also M Galanter and M Cahill, 'Most Cases Settle: Judicial promotion and regulation of settlements' 46 *Stan L Rev* 1139.

8 See J Resnik, note 2 above; Richard Marcus, 'Of Babies and Bathwater: The prospects for procedural progress' 59 *Brooklyn L Rev* 761 (1993); Charles Sorenson, 'Disclosure Under the Federal Rules of Civil Procedure 26(a) — "Much Ado About Nothing"' 46 *Hastings L J* 679 (1995); C Menkel-Meadow, 'Pursuing Settlement in an Adversary Culture: A tale of innovation co-opted or the law of ADR', 19 *Fla St L Rev* 1 (1991).

9 C Menkel-Meadow, 'What's Gender Got to Do With It? The morality and politics of an ethic of care' 22 *NYU J of Law and Soc Change* (1995).

10 Examples include the aggressive use of motions to disqualify lawyers for conflicts of interests under ethical rules, demands for sanctions and litigation under Rule 11 for recalcitrant lawyer behaviour, contestation over the meaning of words in rules requiring disclosure (of documents, basis for claims, expert witnesses, etc).

11 At the time of writing, the Legal Services Corporation in the United States might be eliminated altogether, with funds transferred to the states for 'block grants' where funding for legal services will compete with a variety of other social welfare programs. See G Singsen, 'Reality Bites: The US Legal Services Corporation' in R Smith (ed.) *Shaping the Future: New directions in legal services* (LAG, 1995) for an optimistic view.

12 In contrast, the 1995 British white paper on divorce reform and mediation expressly claims to be consistent with the goals of the Woolf report for cost and delay reduction, rule simplification and greater access to justice. There is acknowledgement in this report that some reforms will require government resources—for instance, the provision of some legal aid funds for family mediation if it is to be made available to all.

13 See C Glasser, 'Civil Procedure: A time for change' at p210 in *Shaping the Future* (note 11 above).

14 The early out-of-court, but government-funded, ADR centres were called 'Neighborhood Justice Centers'. I have written about the contradictory goals of the ADR movement (access and participation v efficiency and docket-clearing) elsewhere; see C Menkel-Meadow, 'Review Essay: Dispute resolution: The periphery becomes the core', 69 *Judicature* 300 (1986).

15 See, eg, R Abel, 'Informalism: A tactical equivalent to law?', 19 *Clearinghouse Review* 383 (1985); R Delgado et. al, 'Fairness and Formality: Minimizing the risk of prejudice in alternative dispute resolution' (1985) *Wisc L Rev* 1359; R Abel, *The Politics of Informal Justice* (Academic Press, 1982); R Hofrichter, 'Neighborhood Justice and the Social Control Problems of American Capitalism', in Abel, ibid.; Lazerson, 'Justice in the Halls', in Abel, ibid. Recently, legal services advocates have taken a more 'mediated' approach to ADR, recognising that it might increase access to justice in some cases and be more appropriate for disputes of certain kinds; see L Singer, M Lewis, A Houseman, and E Singer, 'Alternative Dispute Resolution and the Poor, Parts I and II', 26 *Clearinghouse Review* 2 (May/June, 1992).

16 See, eg, J Langbein, 'The German Advantage in Civil Procedure', 52 *U Chi L Rev* 823.

17 I realise this is something of a controversial statement. The English legal system hardly resembles the European model (though Lord Woolf clearly likes some of the practices on the Continent, including German billing procedures; see Annex V of the Report), and many North Americans would contest the claim that the United States and Canada have fully embraced ADR in the courts; see 7 *FJC Directions* Alternative Dispute Resolution Issue (December 1994); D Stiensta and T Willging, *Alternatives to Litigation: Do they have a place in the Federal Courts?* (Federal Judicial Center, 1995); J Resnik, 'Many Doors? Closing Doors? Alternative Dispute Resolution and Adjudication', 10 *Ohio St J on Disp Res* 211 (1995).

18 Legal Aid Board monitoring of quality control could easily become the bureaucratic equivalent of 'managed care' in the United States, where doctors now complain they are controlled by non-medical personnel who do not understand their medical protocols or the sensitivities of the individual doctor-patient relationship. On the other hand, 'total quality management' was clearly the buzz word of private corporate accountability for the 1980s. The new legal aid scheme contemplates competition in bidding and services by non-solicitors in advice, representation in tribunals and in mediation, thus broadening the possibility of types of services and enlarging what we might consider to be appropriate measures of 'legal quality'.

19 These reports are testaments to the continuing faith in the rationalised and instrumentalist bureaucracy of Max Weber, despite growing concerns in modern scholarship and in practice that the regulatory state has some problems of its own in the tensions between discretion and rules and efficiency. I am mindful of my first research project in which I evaluated the quality and efficiency of an American Bar Association-sponsored legal clinic. Despite the attempt to create a routinised and efficient practice with modern technology and the use of computerised case types, the lawyers reported to me that 'the cases just kept falling off the assembly line'; C Menkel-Meadow, *The 59th Street Clinic: Evaluation of an experiment* (American Bar Association Press, 1979).

20 Indeed, in other contexts I have expressed scepticism about our ability to allocate cases for treatment based on case typologies; see, eg, S Goldberg and F Sander, 'Fitting the Forum to the Fuss', 10 *Neg J* 49 (1994); C Menkel-Meadow, 'Legal Negotiation: A study of strategies in search of a theory', 1983 *ABF Res J* 905.

21 Other reforms of the English legal system, such as elimination of the conveyancing monopoly and rights of audience for solicitors, were certainly not accomplished without controversy and great debate.

22 Losers do pay attorneys' fees and costs by statute in a limited number of actions, including civil rights claims, some environmental, consumer and

corporate securities claims and other such claims where the theory is that the plaintiff's lawyer has performed a semi-public function by prosecuting or policing an important public policy, as well as suing for a private wrong.

23 The American Legal Services Corporation, which is likely to lose most of its funds or be wound up (see note 11 above), provides a relatively small staff and a legal aid programme for only the most indigent litigants. If such litigants have claims that will result in monetary gain (personal injury actions, for example), they must find private counsel (usually on a contingency fee basis).

24 See Interim Research Report, Annex 3 that costs do consume large proportions of the awards made to litigants, and likely have an adverse impact on the rate of claiming. We know from other research that the rate of claiming is substantially lower in the United Kingdom than in the US. See, eg, H Kritzer, 'A Comparative Perspective on Settlement and Bargaining in Personal Injury Cases' 14 *Law & Soc Inquiry* 167 (1989); H Genn, *Hard Bargaining* (Oxford University Press, 1988).

25 See, eg, S Shavell, 'Alternative Dispute Resolution: An economic analysis', 24 (1) *J of Leg Stud* (1995), suggesting that system and aggregate costs are not co-extensive with costs and assessment values for individual litigants. Indeed, costs and other economic assessments (settlement value of the case) are often not the same for litigants and their lawyers.

26 For a sampling see A Chayes, 'The Role of the Judge in Public Law Litigation', 89 *Harvard L Rev* 1281 (1976); F Lacey, *The Judge's Role in the Settlement of Civil Suits* (Federal Judicial Center, 1977); R Peckham, 'The Federal Judge as Case Manager: The new role in guiding a case from filing to disposition', 69 *Calif L Rev* 770 (1981); see also J Resnik, note 17 above; C Menkel-Meadow, note 20 above.

27 For descriptions and empirical evaluations of this programme see J Rosenberg and J Folberg, 'Alternative Dispute Resolution: An empirical analysis' 46 *Stan L Rev* 1487 (1994).

28 In the United States, several federal judges have gained a national reputation for their ability to manage large, complex cases in mass torts, bankruptcy, consumer and securities class actions and civil rights cases. Some judges have reputations as managers and others as settlers.

29 See Fed R Civ Proc r53.

30 I recently heard Judge Richard Arnold, a Federal Circuit Court of Appeals judge, describe the Federal judiciary's efforts to secure its appropriation from the Federal government this past year. The Federal courts in the United States enjoy a budget level of about $3 billion (£2 billion) (with over 27,000 employees, of which only a small percentage comprise the judiciary and its salaries). Address to American College of Trial Lawyers, 21 September 1995.

31 Consider, if you will, the analogy that we can draw from computerisation

and other forms of modern technology. We all thought that computers and faxes and modems would reduce the need for paper files and help us destroy fewer trees. Why then do all of us feel we have more paper (drafts more easily generated, copies in various forms – we still need 'hard' copies) than before?

32 See for example, Fisher and Ury, *Getting To Yes* (Penguin, 1981); C Menkel-Meadow, 'Toward Another View of Legal Negotiation: The structure of problem solving', 31 *UCLA L Rev* 754 (1984); K Arrow, et al, *Barriers to Conflict Resolution* (Norton, 1995); H Raiffa, 'Post-Settlement Settlements in Negotiation Theory and Practice', in W Breslin and J Rubin, eds, *Program on Negotiation* (Harvard University, 1991); Idem, *The Art and Science of Negotiation* (Harvard/Belknap, 1982).

33 C Menkel-Meadow, 'Judicial Referral to ADR: Issues and problems faced by judges', 7 *FJC Directions* 8 (1994).

34 See, eg, M Galanter, 'A Settlement Judge, Not a Trial Judge? Judicial Mediation in the United States', 12 *J of Law & Soc* 1 (1985); C Menkel-Meadow, note 33 above and 'Judges and Settlement', 21 *Trial* 24 (1985); H Kritzer, 'The Judge's Role in Pretrial Case Processing: Assessing the Need for Change', 66 *Judicature* 28 (1982).

35 See membership of Center for Public Resources Institute for Dispute Resolution; B Garth, 'Privatization and the New Market for Disputes: A Framework for Analysis and a Preliminary Assessment', 12 *Stud in L, Pol and Society* 367 (1992).

36 M Rosenberg, *The Pre-Trial Conference and Effective Justice* (Columbia University, 1964). Though this study is old, we still await more modern replications. We will have new data and results from two ongoing studies authorised by the Civil Justice Reform Act; one by the RAND Corporation and the other by the Federal Judicial Center. These studies are intended to evaluate the effects of 15 different cost and delay reduction plans in Federal district courts.

37 In big cities in the United States lawyers in civil cases are given electronic beepers when their cases have been set down for trial, and they are 'on call' to appear when a courtroom becomes available.

38 G Priest, 'Private Litigants and the Court Congestion Problem', 69 *BU L Rev* 527 (1989).

39 See C Menkel-Meadow, 'Toward Another View', note 32 above; C Menkel-Meadow, 'Is Altruism Possible in Lawyering?' 8 *Ga St L Rev* 385 (1992); C Menkel-Meadow, 'The Trouble With the Adversary System in a Post-Modern, Multi-cultural World', Hofstra University, Conference on Legal Ethics, 1996.

40 When does 'modern litigation' begin? See C Dickens, *Bleak House.*

41 Para 3.4.

42 S Burbank, 'The Transformation of American Civil Procedure: The Example of Rule 11', 137 *U Pa L Rev* 1925 (1989); Marcus, note 8 above.

43 E Sherman, 'Court Mandated Alternative Dispute Resolution: What form of participation should be required', 46 *SMU L Rev* 2079 (1993).

44 Judge Schwarzer, former Director of the Federal Judicial Center, began the impetus to change the rules and reduce the gamesmanship of adversarial discovery practice. See Schwarzer, 'Slaying the Monsters of Cost and Delay: Would disclosure be more effective than discovery?' *Judicature* Dec–Jan 1990 at 178, and W Brazil, 'The Adversary Character of Civil Discovery: A critique and proposals for change', 31 *Vanderbilt L Rev* 1295 (1978).

45 Indeed, in several recent large and complex cases, judges have either requested or agreed to expert witnesses who have testified about contested questions of law such as legal ethics; see, eg, *Georgine v Amchem Products*, 157 FRD 246 (1994).

46 M Galanter has gone further to suggest that negotiation is part of the same adversarial game of 'litigation': M Galanter, 'Worlds of Deals: Using negotiation to teach about legal process', 34 *J of Leg Ed* 268 (1984).

47 Like Garry Watson (see p78), I fear that more simplified rules will either mean more judicial discretion because the rules can't possibly cover every situation, or that there will be increased litigation about what the rules mean or how they should be applied (which has been our experience in the US).

48 See R Litan and S Salop, *More Value for the Legal Dollar: A new look at attorney fees and relationships,* 1992.

49 See J Macey, 'Judicial Preferences, Public Choices and the Rules of Procedure', 23 *J Leg Studies* 627 (1994); J Cooper, 'Judges' Self-Interest and Procedural Rules: Comment on Macey', 23 *J Leg Studies* 647 (1994).

50 See R Gilson and R Mnookin, 'Disputing Through Agents: Cooperation and conflict between lawyers in litigation', 94 *Columbia L Rev* 509 (1994).

51 See L Ross, 'Reactive Devaluation in Negotiation and Conflict Resolution' in Kenneth Arrow et al, *Barriers to Conflict Resolution,* 1995.

52 R Mnookin, 'Why Negotiations Fail: An exploration of the barriers to the resolution of conflict', 8(2) *Ohio St J Disp Res* 235 (1993); C Menkel-Meadow, 'Lawyer Negotiations: Theories and realities – what we learn from mediation', 56 *Mod L Rev* 361 (1993).

53 R Axelrod, *The Evolution of Cooperation* (1984).

54 See, eg, J Setear, 'The Barrister and the Bomb: The dynamics of cooperation, Nuclear deterrence and discovery abuse', 69 *BU L Rev* 569 (1989).

55 J Mansbridge (ed.) *Beyond Self-Interest,* 1991.

56 See C Menkel-Meadow 'To Solve Problems, Not Make Them: Integrating ADR in the law school curriculum', 46 *SMU L Rev* 1995 (1993).

57 R Fisher and W Jackson, 'Teaching the Skills of Settlement', 46 *SMU L Rev* 1985 (1993).

58 T Grillo, 'The Mediation Alternative: Process dangers for women', 100 *Yale L J* 1545 (1991).

59 See, eg, R Delgado et al, 'Fairness and Formality: Minimizing the risk of

prejudice in alternative dispute resolution', 1985 *Wisc L Rev* 1359. A recent empirical study of small claims court mediation in the state of New Mexico confirms some but not all of the claims of how disempowered people fare in mediation. Minorities did less well in (in monetary assessments) than majority group litigants but were more satisfied with mediation than litigation, while women fared better in mediation but were more critical of it than conventional litigation. Assessments of party satisfaction with processes depended on whether the third-party neutrals matched the litigants in racial, ethnic and gender composition. See M Herman et al, *MetroCourt Study: An assessment of race and gender prejudice in mediation*, 1993.

60 See C Menkel-Meadow, 'Whose Dispute Is It Anyway? A philosophical and democratic defense of settlement (in some cases)', 83 *Geo L J* (1995).

61 C Menkel-Meadow, 'The Ethics of Mass Tort Settlements: When the rules meet the road', 80 *Cornell L Rev* (1995).

62 See, eg, R Fisher, 'What About Negotiation as A Specialty?' 69 *ABAJ* 1221 (1983); M Millhauser, 'Gladiators and Conciliators – ADR a law firm staple', *Bar Leader* (Sept–Oct 1988) at 20.

63 Have these different performance skills been made part of the quality performance standards in legal aid franchising?

64 By this I mean settlements that meet the parties' needs, leave no economic or other 'waste' on the table, have efficient transaction costs, are fair to the parties and are more attractive to the parties than what the court might order. For my evaluative criteria of a good settlement, see my article at note 20 above and see also Fisher and Ury, *Getting to Yes* (Penguin, 1981).

65 See Fed R Civ Proc r68 amendments and controversy.

66 See D Lax and J Sebenius, *The Manager as Negotiator: Bargaining for cooperation and competitive gain* (Free Press, 1986).

67 In the last year, I have been retained to teach and train about ADR to two of the Big Six accounting firms in the States. These firms expect to offer 'expert' ADR services as adjuncts to their business and litigation management consulting services.

68 See, eg, Judge T Eisele, 'Differing Visions, Differing Values', 46 *SMU L Rev* 1935 (1993).

69 For my own views on how difficult it is to separate 'private' from 'public' or 'public-interest cases' see C Menkel-Meadow, 'Whose Dispute Is It Anyway?' note 60 above.

70 The American Bar Association has recently recognised that paralegals will provide some legal services and has become involved in drafting standards, rather than losing control altogether.

71 See C Menkel-Meadow, 'The Many Ways of Mediation: The Transformation of Traditions, Ideologies, Paradigms and Practices', 11 *Negotiation J* 271 (1995).

72 R Smith (ed), (LAG, 1995).

73 Nuffield Foundation Seminar on ADR, London, November 1994.

74 I Jaising, 'Public-Interest Litigation: The Lessons From India' in *Shaping the Future: New directions in legal services* (note 72 above) pp175–187.

75 T Purcell and G McAllister, 'Filling the Void in Civil Litigation Disputes – A role for empirical research' in ibid, pp257–272.

76 See Symposium, 'Mass Torts: Just Desserts?' 80 *Cornell L Rev* (1995).

77 See Kritzer, Genn, op cit note 24 above.

78 A Lind and T Tyler, *The Social Psychology of Procedural Justice* (Plenum Press, 1988).

CHAPTER 5

Multi-option justice at the Middlesex Multi-Door Courthouse

BARBARA EPSTEIN STEDMAN

Barbara Stedman is director of the Middlesex Multi-Door Court-house, Cambridge, Massachusetts. In this chapter, she describes its work.

> The courts of this country should not be places where the resolution of disputes begin. They should be places where disputes end after all means of resolving disputes have been considered and tried. – Justice Sandra Day O'Connor

The expansion of innovative approaches to resolving legal disputes is providing new opportunities to courts throughout the United States. Collectively referred to as alternative dispute resolution (ADR), these offer alternatives to the traditional litigation process and are challenging established approaches to the delivery of justice. The motivation for change comes from the judiciary, the Bar and the public. The chief reasons for dissatisfaction with the present system include the emotional and financial costs to parties of protracted litigation; the increased number of cases being handled by an already over-burdened court system; and a perception that traditional litigation is a rigid system that focuses on legal liability and damages rather than one that seeks to solve problems. ADR techniques such as mediation, case evaluation, arbitration and complex case management provide more efficient, flexible, creative, satisfying and less costly ways to resolve conflicts than the traditional litigation process (see pp127–129). In response to the growing need for these services, there has been a dramatic increase in the number of private providers and public ADR programs.

The Middlesex Multi-Door Courthouse (MMDC) is a court-annexed[1] ADR programme in Massachusetts which provides a comprehensive approach to dispute resolution within the administrative structure of a trial court. It was established in 1989 with the overall

119

goal of improving the administration of justice through more timely resolution of disputes, greater cost-effectiveness for the courts and the consumers, and increased public satisfaction with process and outcome. The programme delivers a wide variety of dispute resolution services through a single coordinating entity.

The model

The multi-door courthouse is based on a model first articulated by Professor Frank Sander of Harvard Law School in 1976 at an American Bar Association conference on public dissatisfaction with the justice system.[2] He provided a plan for institutionalising systematic ADR referral within the public sector. Sander's ideal courthouse of the future is a dispute resolution centre that offers both intake and dispute-resolution services. The intake (or screening) unit diagnoses the dispute and refers the parties to one of a variety of dispute resolution processes. This matching of the needs of a case and its parties to an appropriate ADR process is the key to the multi-door programme. Each 'door' of the multi-door courthouse represents one option in resolving disputes. Litigation becomes only one choice among others. The idea is based upon the central premise that there may be advantages or disadvantages in any specific case to using one or another dispute-resolution process.

Multi-door programmes, established after Professor Sander's vision, vary in the sophistication of their intake process and the variety of dispute-resolution mechanisms available. The Middlesex programme is the only one that provides an individual case-screening conference. Most other systems divide cases into different types and then refer all those in one category to one process, for example, all motor vehicle torts will be sent to case evaluation or all construction cases to mediation. By contrast, the Middlesex programme ensures that each case is individually assessed and referred to a process on the basis of its particular characteristics. As a result, the participants in a case may select case evaluation, mediation, complex case management or arbitration depending on the number of parties, the complexity of the issues, and the relationship between parties and/or their lawyers.

The background

The original planning for the multi-door courthouse was initiated outside the court system by a small group of private citizens who developed a demonstration project and raised most of the money for its implementation. Although the impetus did not originally come from the judiciary, court leaders were encouraging and supportive. From the beginning, the multi-door courthouse was planned as a court-annexed programme and organised on the understanding that, if successful, it would be formally integrated within the Massachusetts Trial Court.

Judicial commitment was reinforced with the final report of a Massachusetts Futures Commission (see p35). The commission consisted of a distinguished group of judges, lawyers, court administrators, business and community leaders, and academics. Their task was to look ahead three decades to the future of the Massachusetts courts, to envision a preferred judicial system and to identify ways to achieve it. They determined that 'access to justice' means more than simply access to courts, lawyers and the judicial process. The report stated, 'The presence of an attorney or the existence of a judicial forum do not themselves assure that justice will be done. Providing access to justice means providing the opportunity for a just result.'[3] It concluded that adjudication alone would not be adequate to accommodate the next century's wide range of disputes and disputants. It advocated a system in which consumers of the public justice system would have convenient access to a wide variety of methods for resolving their disputes. Some of those remain adjudicatory in nature, such as trials and arbitration. Others rely on agreement between the parties, like mediation, case evaluation, and various forms of facilitated but non-binding settlement processes. The report further noted that the courts would take an active role by assisting the parties in choosing the most appropriate method. The system would be characterised not only by a wide range of dispute resolution methods but by a respect for consumer choice.[4] The MMDC embodies these principles.

The multi-door courthouse opened its doors to cases in 1990 in the Middlesex (Cambridge) Superior Court, situated just outside Boston. The Middlesex court was selected because of its demographics and the fact that it has the most active civil case load in Massachusetts.[5] Cases are randomly selected for screening from the court's civil case list. In addition, they can be referred by the judiciary or the parties. The programme has now provided services to more than 6,000 cases. In 1994, 1,200 cases went through individual case-screening conferences.[6] Four per cent settled at the screening or before a follow-up. Forty per cent opted out of a referral to one of the multi-door courthouse's doors. Some of these elected to go to a private ADR provider, some that the case could be settled without additional intervention, and others that judicial intervention was unnecessary (a few of these cases also will re-enter the programme at a later date). Altogether, approximately 56 per cent of the screened cases elected to go forward with one of the multi-door courthouse's dispute resolution options. Of these, 71 percent settled at or within 60 days. Many of the rest had partial settlements or would otherwise settle before the trial date. Follow-up reports on the cases indicate that almost all participants felt that the process had been highly beneficial, even if it did not result in immediate settlement.

The programme

> The Multi-Door Courthouse may well be one of those ideas that is easy to describe but difficult to implement. – Frank E A Sander

A multi-door courthouse is built from five essential building blocks: intake (screening) and referral; the composition of its panels of neutrals; the selection and qualification of neutrals; ADR options; and programme evaluation.

Intake

The first step in developing an ADR programme is to determine case types and intake procedures. The multi door courthouse handles the full spectrum of civil cases. In addition to standard tort and contract cases, it has had particular success with cases involving commercial disputes, construction matters, real estate transactions, legal and other malpractice suits, product liability, business and partnership dissolutions, employment disputes (including wrongful termination, discrimination, harassment, covenants not to compete and other related issues), land use and other equitable matters. The recent introduction by the court of a mandatory non-binding conciliation programme for motor vehicle torts has removed these from the programme unless complications require more individualised attention.

Cases are still randomly selected from the court docket. However, increasingly cases are referred by the judge or lawyers involved. This reflects the increased acceptance of ADR in general and the multi-door courthouse concept in particular. Judicial referrals generally arise from status conferences, pre-trial hearings or attempts by the parties to seek equitable relief by way of injunctions or temporary restraining orders. A few cases have been sent in the middle of trial for the purpose of resolving a discrete issue or, occassionally, the entire case. In such circumstances and if a screener is available, the case is handled on a walk-in basis. Otherwise, referral occurs by way of a mandatory screening order sent out by the court. Although cases are taken randomly off the docket, they are reviewed to determine their suitability before the actual order is sent.[7]

The best time at which to intervene is hard to predict. Some cases need a measure of discovery before lawyers have enough information to negotiate a settlement. Others need to be brought in at the earliest possible stage, before positions are entrenched. While some cases are referred by lawyers even before the case is filed, the majority come in at some stage of the discovery process. In these, the screening conference can also serve as a case management tool by resolving discovery or other procedural disputes. Sometimes, the screening conference is the first meeting between counsel and provides a convenient opportunity to reach agreement on the scope and scheduling of the discovery process. Parties willing to limit their discovery to what is necessary for settlement discussions have the reward of containing costs and thus reducing antagonism. Prospective cost savings can even be incorproated in settlement negotiations.

Costs can become the driving force of litigation and a major impediment to its settlement. For example, one plaintiff, from outside the state, was suing for 'speculative' damages in the amount of $1 million for a failed business deal. He had incurred expenses of $300,000 (about £200,000) and his two defendants together $500,000 (about £330,000). Unsurprisingly, this hefty financial investment was impeding settlement. The parties might well have felt completely differently if they had entered dispute resolution at an earlier stage. The longer litigation continues, the more entrenched the parties become in their positions. The extent of their liability for costs exacerbates the situation.

An individual screening conference is set up for appropriate cases. This provides a unique opportunity for individual case needs assessment and litigation/ADR management. This is the hallmark of the Middlesex programme. It is conducted by an experienced multi-door courthouse staff lawyer. It is confidential, with no report made on the court file or to the judge assigned to the case. This confidentiality is protected by statute and promotes frank discussion of both the legal and non-legal issues. The tone of a screening conference usually differs substantially from status or pre-trial conferences in court. In these, participants tend to be less candid and to maintain their adversarial posture by developing, building and maintaining their positions. The screening conference, on the other hand, is directed towards information exchange with the goal of problem-solving and dispute resolution. The process is designed to involve the participants in assessing their case needs from a practical perspective. There are four fundamental components: introduction to the programme and education of the participants in dispute-resolution processes; the gathering of information, including the case facts, procedural history, legal issues, and the subjective factors that may impact on the case; the identification of impediments to resolution; and matching the case with an appropriate ADR process and neutral.

Introduction and education

The educational component continues to play an important role in identifying how different processes may be useful in a particular case, although many lawyers have become much more sophisticated about ADR and have greater understanding of its importance. For those unfamiliar with the multi-door courthouse, the screening process begins with an explanation of the programme and a review of the protocol including confidentiality.

Information gathering

The screener then gathers information relevant to an understanding of the nature and dynamics of the case. The parties make a short, informal presentation of their perspectives on the legal foundation of the case; the status of discovery and other procedural matters; legal damages or equitable relief sought; and any previous settlement discussions. In this non-adversarial setting, the parties are usually able to hear each other's perspectives in a less defensive way than in court. Sometimes, common ground and the basis for further settlement discussions is established at this time. In addition, the screener tries to elicit information about the subjective, non-legal issues. These can be more elusive to discover.

Identification and examination of impediments

A skilful screener helps to uncover the underlying concerns of the parties and to identify what is necessary to resolve the matter. Some cases are straightforward, with standard liability and/or damages issues, but substantial numbers are complicated by concerns which are harder to determine. Often the parties are not fully aware of the impact of hidden emotions and resentments. Obstacles to resolution can include diverse factors such as lack or failure of communication, poor preparation, no demand or unrealistic expectations, no offer, client control issues, related cases in other courts, discovery delays, contentious relations between the parties and/or attorneys, and underlying issues of power and control. Some of these barriers can be removed simply by identifying them. Others require concrete steps such as hiring an appraiser or delivering documents. Once barriers are removed, the litigation process and/or settlement negotiations can proceed. In some cases the resolution of discovery issues will lead to a mediated settlement. In others, litigation proceeds to trial. The effective screener becomes intuitive with experience. Frequently, a well-placed question or observation provides the catalyst for bringing the parties to the settlement table.

A recent multi-door courthosue case involved the dissolution of a legal partnership between two brothers. Each brother was separately represented. Both lawyers, accompanied by one of the parties, came to the screening conference. The case had been referred by a judge at a very early stage. It soon became apparent that the litigation reflected considerable emotional dispute between the brothers. The elder brother had been in practice with his father for several years. He felt that, on his father's retirement, he had been generous in offering a partnership to his less experienced younger brother and was surprised when, two years later, his brother wanted to leave. They had, however, worked out an agreement covering the relevant matters to be decided. The agreement fell apart and for another two years they tried unsuccessfully and bitterly to resolve the matter before the younger brother began litigation. Both parties seemed committed to their positions and indisposed to participate in settlement negotiations. The older brother felt he had not been appreciated and the younger one felt he had not received a fair share. Each had a large emotional investment in proving the other wrong.

Their intransigence was broken by questioning about the impact of this battle on their family. The brother present at the screening immediately acknowledged that the dispute had created a terrible rift and was very uncomfortable for the members of the family. When asked if a resolution of the matter would make it easier for everyone at the next family function, his attitude changed and he indicated a strong interest in proceeding. His brother's lawyer needed to check with his client, but mediation was agreed the next day. It took only two sessions for a full resolution of the case.

Referral

Having examined the dynamics of the case and impediments to its settlement, the screener helps the parties to determine the most appropriate type of intervention. Parties may choose to leave the programme or to continue with one of the available options.

A wide range of factors are relevant in choosing the most appropriate ADR process. These include: the nature of the case (for example, debt, employment and complex environmental cases require different treatment); the number of participants (a two-party 'slip and fall' is very different from a multi-party construction case); the relationships between the parties and/or their lawyers (which will be on a spectrum between contentious to conciliatory); the nature of the relationships between the opposing parties (whether there is an ongoing relationship between them or the case arises from a one-time deal); and the procedural status of the litigation (whether discovery is complete or trial is distant, imminent or simultaneous). If the parties are not yet ready to select an ADR process, the programme continues to work with the case through follow-up telephone calls.

After a mutual assessment of the case, the screener reviews the full range of dispute resolution options available; discusses the fee arrangement and scheduling procedures and makes a recommendation. The litigants and their counsel, however, make the final decision about whether they want to use ADR and, if so, which process they want. A dispute resolution date can then be scheduled and a neutral assigned. Neutrals are assigned from the multi-door courthouse panels and are selected on the basis of their specific expertise, availability and personal suitability, given the dynamics of the case. The parties are sent a confirmation notice and the neutral's biographical data. They must approve the selection.

The screener also helps the parties to establish parameters for the ADR process they have selected. Agreement may be reached on who will attend; the number of sessions to be scheduled, whether any discovery or settlement proposals will be exchanged before the session; and whether the parties will submit any exhibits or written arguments to the neutral in advance. Most importantly, the screener works to set the tone for genuine participation in the process and to establish whatever common ground may exist. On some occasions, this may be limited to an indication that all parties want to resolve the conflict and are willing to negotiate in good faith to do so.

Some cases benefit from a progression of techniques. For example, one party in a complex business case needed a 'reality check', to assess the strength of its position. In consequence, case evaluation was chosen for the limited purpose of getting an impartial assessment of a particular legal argument. Once that issue was resolved, more comprehensive settlement of the entire matter through mediation became possible. On other occasions, a neutral has been deployed to undertake complex case management in order to manage the discovery process and then changed role to mediate the entire dispute or been replaced by someone else to do so.

The key to effective use of the programme is to identify the needs and status of the case progressively and fashion the best approach to remove obstacles to resolution. For example, in a personal injury case, the defendant's wife was one of the plaintiffs and had a viable claim which became an impediment to settlement when divorce proceedings became nasty. Although agreement was reached with the insured on liability and damages, the case could not be fully resolved without the wife's co-operation. Since there was so much hostility between the parties, it was decided that only a binding process would bring closure to the matter. After discussion, the parties agreed to arbitrate the allocation of damages between the husband and wife.

The 'doors' of the courthouse

Although most cases can benefit from using an ADR process, the parties must share a common interest in using the selected process effectively. There are circumstances in which ADR is usually inappropriate. These include cases which present a novel question of statutory interpretation and one party wants to make new law; when one of the parties is committed to the dispute and is unwilling to let it go; and where one or both of the parties is not negotiating in good faith or is not open to changing their position.

The multi-door courthouse uses an evaluative model that provides a way to clarify and prioritise interests; assess strengths and weaknesses of the legal positions; address personal concerns; and examine a variety of settlement options. Below are short descriptions of the most frequently used ADR options.

Mediation

Mediation is a voluntary process in which a neutral third party assists the participants in resolving their dispute through a series of joint and private sessions. Although it may not be universally effective, mediation is particularly well suited to business and employment cases where there may be a blend of legal, business and personal or emotional issues. It is often also appropriate for cases with multiple parties or which are complex or where the parties have, or have had, an extended business or personal relationship. Mediation is confidential and allows the parties full participation in the process. It represents the most commonly used form of ADR in the multi-door courthouse.

Case evaluation

This is a procedure in which the parties or their lawyers present a summary of their case to a neutral third party for an independent determination of its strengths and weaknesses. The evaluator will assist the parties in settlement negotiations. If the parties wish, the evaluator will give an oral advisory opinion as to settlement value and/or issues of law. Although case evaluation is used primarily in tort cases, it can offer a focused neutral determination of liability and value in business or employment cases. Like mediation, it is confidential and non-binding.

Complex case management

Complex case management provides the parties with a neutral who may operate with the authority of a special master and the flexibility of a facilitator, case evaluator or mediator. It is recommended when there are ongoing problems in the case management of discovery and interlocutory motions. The role of the complex case manager is determined by the specific needs of the case. The neutral may mediate procedural disputes or, if the parties so request, may have the authority to make final decisions. It is useful in multi-party, multi-issue, or hotly contested cases. The procedure may be wholly, or partly, confidential.

Arbitration

Arbitration is a form of adjudication which is more private and less formal than trial. The participants can present legal arguments and offer evidence. Unless otherwise agreed, the arbitrator makes a binding decision on liability, damages or both which can be entered as a judgment and enforced accordingly. The parties also can reduce risk by setting high and low parameters.

Arbitration/mediation ('med-arb') is an excellent compromise when both sides are willing to mediate but one or both sides want to be assured of a final conclusion to the case. The protocol calls for a standard arbitration with a written binding award. Without revealing the award to the parties, the arbitrator then works with the parties to mediate a settlement. If the parties can reach a negotiated settlement, the case is settled on those terms. If not, the arbitrator presents the award to conclude the case. The process is well suited to motor vehicle cases, small claims, or small business, commercial or employment cases.

Summary jury trial

The summary jury trial is an abbreviated trial with a non-binding jury decision. A six-person panel is drawn from the regular jury pool. Each side makes an informal presentation to the jury in the form of an opening or closing statement. The appointed neutral then instructs the jury as to the applicable law and the jury deliberates privately for about 30 minutes. The attorneys and parties can then speak with the jurors about their reaction to the case, probable verdict and judgment. If the parties wish, the neutral can then assist them in negotiating a settlement. The appeal of the summary jury trial is access to jurors. It is recommended when there is a great disparity in positions and jury reaction is a critical factor. It works especially well where documents submitted to the jury are more determinative than the credibility of the witnesses.

Other

Other processes, including a hybrid of any of the above, may be fashioned to suit the particular needs of a case.

Examples of mediation at work

ADR processes, particularly mediation, provide a wider array of settlement options than those traditionally available from the court. Some of the settlement terms reached through the multi-door courthouse include: rehabilitation of an employment relationship, outplacement opportunities, renegotiating terms of a covenant not to compete, apologies, agreement to provide sensitivity training, dividing businesses into two separate entities, providing easements or rental agreements, and a variety of other solutions. Below are details of some examples that illustrate some of multi-door courthouse's ADR processes.

Clarification of underlying interests through mediation

Two partners had purchased a large tract of land and sold a portion for a small residential development. Division of the remaining portion, which had an unusual shape, was the source of a dispute which had soured the business relationship. Each partner wanted to own the part of the land which contained the access road. Mediation allowed the parties to clarify their interests. One partner wanted lake frontage in order to build a house, which was impossible without the road. The other wanted to build a small commercial mall next to the residential development. He too felt he needed the road. Once the disparate interests were realised, the participants brainstormed a way to use to use the land beneficially for both. The final resolution included an easement through one partner's property to enable the other to create the access road to the proposed mall.

Resolution of a dispute through arbitration/mediation

A dentist hired an employment agency to recruit an associate to work with him in his practice. As part of its services, the agency drew up a contract for the associate with a clause restricting the right to set up practice in competition. After a few months, the associate left and set up his own dental practice nearby to which, according to his former employer, he took several patients. On seeking to exercise his rights against the associate under the 'no competition' agreement, the dentist learned that the agreement was legally invalid because such clauses are prohibited in the medical field. He then sued the agency for providing him with an illegal contract, which had left him vulnerable to competition from his former employee. He claimed that this competition crippled his practice. He was frustrated and needed to tell his story. He was willing to go to mediation. The owner of the agency, however, wanted to end the litigation and was not willing to participate in a non-binding process.

After discussion with the screener, the parties agreed to an arbitration/mediation. They presented their case in a standard arbitration format and the neutral made a written award which he did not reveal to the parties. In mediation, the parties worked out a formula for a structured settlement. The arbitration award was, thus, never revealed.

Lender liability resolved at mediation

Borrowers took out a mortgage from a bank for a three-family house which they operated as a rental property. They fell behind in their mortgage payments and the bank started a foreclosure action. Although both parties agreed on a payment plan to forestall the foreclosure, the bank neglected to inform its agent, who went ahead and repossessed the property. The agent informed the tenants who were in occupation that the property was foreclosed upon and that the rent should be paid to the bank. As a result, the tenants wasted the property, causing substantial damage, and refused to pay any rent to the borrowers even after they explained the bank's mistake. Eventually, the tenants left and the borrowers were able to replace them. After the wrongful foreclosure, the borrowers made no mortgage payments. The bank sued them for the balance owing and the borrowers counterclaimed for rescission of the mortgage based on the alleged breach of contract.

At the time of the multi-door courthouse screening conference, the loan had been in default for over three years. The case went to mediation and was resolved with an agreement. This included a new contract between the borrowers and the bank with terms that reflected, on the one hand, payment by the bank of damages and, on the other, payment by the borrowers of some of the back mortgage payments. It was significant that the parties agreed to continue their relationship with this new agreement rather than simply agreeing to a final pay-off.

Multi-party claim managed by complex case management though mediation fails

Intervention is not always successful. Adoptive parents, a former priest and a former nun, sought relief from an adoption agency and numerous social service agencies for alleged negligence in preparing them for the potential problems of adopting three older children from an extremely troubled family. The claim was based on inter-sibling sexual abuse which the adoptive parents felt that they could have prevented if they had been placed on notice that it might occur. They had been told about the children's background but not about behaviour patterns that they should anticipate or the steps that they should have taken to ensure the children's safety and prevent some of their destructive behaviour, which had exacerbated their emotional problems. They were seeking damages to pay for future therapy and likely institutionalisation for two of the children.

The initial claim was for damages of $18 million (about £12 million). The adoption agency had insurance only up to $1 million and the other 11 defendants had small policies and/or limited personal resources. Approximately ten depositions had been already taken and the adoption agency was requesting 30–40 more.

The initial screening conference took four hours. All lawyers were present and agreed to participate in complex case management (CCM) for the discovery process. Through CCM, all parties agreed to split discovery and move into mediation with the same neutral. A few essential depositions were taken with the taking of the rest suspended until the mediation was completed.

Since dealing with so many participants was cumbersome, all parties agreed that the parents and adoption agency would go to mediation and the other defendants would contribute or supplement the settlement in later sessions. One of the original stumbling blocks was removed when the parents agreed to reduce their demand for settlement purposes to the agency's policy limit. The parents felt that this was a major concession and believed that this would provide a 'ballpark' settlement amount.

In the first private session with the agency, the neutral reviewed the legal positions, discussed the possible impact on the jury, discussed risk, fashioned a risk analysis and asked them to come up with a counter-offer. The adoption agency came up with a $120,000 (£80,000) offer and made it clear that it would not budge. The neutral hesitatingly went back to the parents who felt that they had been tricked into lowering their original demand and were unwilling to bid against themselves. The agency refused to increase their offer and indicated that they were only interested in having the neutral convince the parents that their case had no merit. The agency resisted the neutral's assessment of their legal position and likely jury response. They ended the session and rescheduled the depositions. The case is still in litigation and the costs are enormous.

Contract dispute resolved by mediation

A business had a contract to package rubber tubing. The packer had a manufacturer design an automated packaging system in order to meet contractual obligations. The manufacturer delivered some of the machinery and the packer began to use it. The packer claimed that the machinery did not work properly and, as a result, it had to use its older machinery with additional labour costs. In total, the packer claimed damages based on the increased cost plus the amount paid for the defective machinery. The manufacturer counterclaimed for the balance of the contract price unpaid by the packer. Some of the machinery was never delivered because of the overdue balance. The manufacturer claimed it could not mitigate its loss because the machinery was specifically designed to meet the packer's unique needs and could not be sold to anyone else. The packer offered to settle at a reduced amount because it realised that the manufacturer's financial position precluded the former from receiving the full sum demanded in any circumstances. In response, the manufacturer offered to pay an even smaller amount and threatened to file bankruptcy if pressed for more.

Through mediation, the parties agreed on a structured settlement over time with an agreement for judgment to be held in reserve until payment was completed. The settlement included provision for non-disclosure and penalty payments if the manufacturer was late in making payments. The manufacturer also accepted the return of the machinery with a plan to retool or melt it down.

Neutral panels

The multi-door courthouse maintains its own panels of highly quali-fied neutrals, including mediators, case evaluators and arbitrators. The initial policies and procedures were developed by the multi-door courthouse steering committee. The programme has always been attentive to the composition of its panels. Although most court-connected ADR programmes maintain open panels – where inclusion is based solely on objective criteria and cases are assigned to neutrals in order – the individual nature of the multi-door courthouse pro-gramme requires a smaller and more managed list. By limiting the numbers to 30–40 on each panel, the screeners learn the specialities and facilitative skills of each neutral. The selection process combines objective and subjective criteria.

In 1994, a newly revised system for neutral qualification and selec-tion was implemented. A special committee, working with the pro-gramme staff, devised a system for the continuous evaluation of the panels and selection of new panellists. The committee established a two-step process.

During the first stage, applicants were reviewed for four basic qualifications: adequate time availability for case assignments; will-ingness to accept some multi-door courthouse cases *pro bono* or at a reduced fee; expertise in subject areas relevant to multi-door courthouse needs; and professional training and dispute resolution experience. Mediator requirements also include completion of an approved mediation skills training course or apprentice programme (minimum 30 hours), extensive experience as a mediator and experience of or specialisation in one or more areas covered by the multi-door courthouse case-load. Case evaluators must have, among other qualifications, ten years' experience at the Bar, seven years' trial experience in civil cases and 20 per cent of their trial experience in an area of specialisation. The arbitrator panel is comprised of recognised experts with specialisms in particular areas of work. It includes some non-lawyers. There is no separate complex case management or summary jury panel.

During the second stage of the selection process, the subjective criteria are considered. Multi-door courthouse staff observe the selected applicants to assess their competence as neutrals. Final appointment is based on these observations and evaluations.

The selection committee meets periodically to review the applications and makes selections based on the numbers of neutrals needed for each panel. Selections are based on content area expertise, reputation within the legal community and ability to work with legal and interpersonal issues. The interest of qualified applicants eager to affiliate with the multi-door courthouse has required the development of a policy to rotate panel membership. The committee is in the process of implementing a policy in which individuals who have served as members of a panel for more than four years may be asked to assume senior status. They will be called upon on a more limited basis and asked to lend the benefit of their experience to newer panel members. This policy will involve a larger cross-section of the ADR community and provide professional opportunities for a greater number of people. For complex case management or summary jury trials the multi-door courthouse will sometimes go outside its panels to meet the special needs or requests of parties.

The multi-door courthouse also sponsors informal 'brown bag lunches' (so called after the colour and nature of the packaging in which participants bring their food) to bring neutrals together to share ideas, strategies and special interests. Some recent topics have included such issues as confidentiality, 'the ones that got away' – how other mediators might have handled a tricky problem – or ways in which the screeners might improve the readiness of parties at the mediation session. These are well attended and help to create a collaborative feeling within the programme.

Programme evaluation

The multi-door courthouse informally monitors the operation of its programmes through exit questionnaires, direct observations and random follow-up phone calls. The exit questions cover the dispute resolution process selected; the manner of dealing with the legal and non-legal issues; the process of structuring the outcome; the suitability and competence of the neutral with special regard to knowledge of the subject and law, neutrality and lack of bias, and skill in structuring the outcome; and the general effectiveness of the programme with regard to the particular case and the goals of the parties. These play an important role in the ongoing assessment.

The State Justice Institute conducted an independent evaluation of the multi-door courthouse and a full report was published in 1992.[8] The evaluation focused on three substantive areas: case processing time, litigant and court costs, and participant satisfaction. The study also assessed case-screening procedures. Cases processed through the multi-door courthouse were compared with cases using traditional court processes. 94 per cent of respondents who had used the multi-door courthouse reported that they would voluntarily bring another case for screening. More than 90 per cent said they would consider using the dispute resolution process again and all reported that would use the same neutral. Although both the traditional trial process and the multi-door courthouse received high marks, the parties using the multi-door courthouse reported greater satisfaction with the manner of case presentation; the process in which both legal and non-legal matters were addressed; the opportunity to participate in structuring the outcome of the case; and the fairness of the process.

Technical assistance

The multi-door courthouse offers assistance to other trial courts in the design and implementation of dispute resolution programmes. The multi-door concept is flexible and can be adapted to a variety of settings. It is important to be sensitive to the particular culture of a court, since this tends to be firmly entrenched. The challenge is to find a credible way to present new ideas and approaches without threatening the very institution on which people rely. The best means of doing so is, of course, to use the people who are already working there. The first step, therefore, is to identify the organisations or people who should be involved in the planning stage. Each of the multi-door courthouse satellite programmes has engaged the assistance of the local Bar associations, other interested organisations and key court personnel. Once local people are involved in the design and implementation, they have a greater investment in the programme's success. A more realistic and acceptable programme can be developed with input from those who know their court and constituencies. The basic components – screening, matching and referral, neutral panel development, ADR options, and evaluation procedures – can then be modified to suit particular needs. This approach to programme development is demonstrated in the fortunes of the multi-door courthouse's satellite programmes in the Probate and Family Courts and in the Worcester, Massachusetts Superior Court, 50 miles outside Boston.

The Probate and Family Courts programme had to be developed in two phases. In the first, court personnel were interviewed but not directly involved in the programme design. They were presented with a fully designed programme which was to be implemented with little room for modification. The programme languished because of disinterest and apparent resentment within the court and was phased out in six months with little success. In the second revitalised phase, key court personnel were involved in all phases of the design. Initially, weekly meetings were held in the offices of the Chief Justice of the Probate and Family Court. Representatives from the multi-door courthouse, the court administration and the Family Service officers reviewed all details together.

Several sessions were spent in refining the paperwork. For example, in reviewing the judicial notices for screening conferences, the technical term 'case caption' was replaced by 'case name' to be more understandable to the large numbers of litigants in person in this jurisdiction. While this example may seem trivial, it is quite representative of the detailed engagement that gave court staff an investment in the programme. By incorporating their ideas, a partnership was formed. The final programme design was well suited to the court and provided a model for a collegial working relationship between court personnel, the project director from the multi-door courthouse and new ADR people. The programme is operating with great success, due in large measure to the commitment of the relevant staff.

Every new programme has initially been greeted with resistance and scepticism. Forging trust between the planners, the community and the court played a critical role in the success of the Worcester Superior Court programme. The first challenge was the winning of the trust of the Bar in Worcester, a rural community west of Boston.

It has a reputation for distinguishing itself from its nearby city. Worcester lawyers still conclude deals by handshake. Any ideas originating from Boston are immediately questioned. Multi-door courthouse planners began meeting members of the Worcester Bar. It took a full year until the programme was ready to be implemented but, once the Bar was committed, its members took the front line in engaging with a highly resistant court.

In each programme, there are a variety of modifications. For example, the probate and family mediators also provide screening services. The multi-door courthouse provided special training in screening techniques. All the probate and family mediators are required to have training in special divorce and general mediation. In Worcester, the court's resistance to change and limited physical space necessitated a modification of the procedures. The screening conference was incorporated into a regularly scheduled pre-trial conference in order to reduce the amount of change in the clerk's office. Although this brought in the cases at a later date in the litigation process, it provided an opportunity to educate the Worcester community about the programme and benefits of ADR. A substantial number of cases are now entering earlier as self-referrals from people who are familiar with the programme. The court community is also now accepting the programme and is bringing the cases in at an earlier stage.

This basic building block strategy for programme design provides a firm foundation, with flexibility to meet the particular needs of the court and community. This approach is consistent with ADR theory and practice and has been effective in the programmes developed from the multi-door courthouse model.

Institutionalising ADR programmes in courts

The experience of the Middlesex Multi-Door Courthouse is that certain fundamental issues need to be addressed before undertaking the effort of bringing ADR into the courts. Key decisions need to be made about goals, design, the nature and type of rules, the providers, and the structure and authority of the administration. It may be instructive to set out the lessons that we have learnt.

Needs assessment and preliminary plan

The design of each ADR programme requires an initial assessment of the court's needs and resources to identify the problem or condition which the programme will target. The goals may vary considerably. Some courts may be motivated by an operational need to reduce backlog because of limited court resources. Others, particularly family and probate, may begin with the premise that mediation is most suitable in child custody and access cases, irrespective of backlog issues.

The first step for the programme planners is to meet identified interest groups in order to establish a well represented steering committee. At this stage the committee should outline a preliminary timeframe, with realistic short-term and long-term goals.

Programme design

The steering committee should begin with a review of current court procedures, identify court resources (personnel, space, funding) and begin work on the programme design. Research on new and established programmes in other courts should be undertaken. Older programmes can provide useful tips based on experience, while newer programmes are confronting the present problems of implementation. The ADR field is very collaborative and programme operators and designers generally are pleased to share information and experience.

Some of the questions that need to be answered are set out below.

Who will sponsor the programme?

Sponsors might include Bar associations, the courts, independent non-profit, government or private dispute-resolution programmes or others.

What types of cases should the programme handle?

The spectrum of cases will affect the design and scope of the programme. For example, a programme that only handles motor vehicle torts will look different from one that deals with the full range of civil cases, even if the caseload is identical. The intake process, the ADR options offered and the composition of the neutral panels will all need to be different.

Which ADR options should be provided?

The number and nature of ADR mechanisms offered is also related to the type of cases handled. While arbitration and/or case evaluation may be the preferred option(s) for small personal injury claims, a broader range is necessary for other types of cases, such as domestic relations or complex litigation.

Under what authority will the programme operate?

ADR programmes in the courts may be authorised by legislation or by rules of the Supreme or local court. If there is no explicit authorisation, programme planners can play an active role in drafting legislation or developing strategies for gaining support from the necessary authority.

Should the programme be free or charge a fee for service?

The income base may affect the range of options offered as well as access to the programme. A free programme may be offered, at least initially, to a smaller range or number of cases. Or perhaps only mediation services would be offered free and not other ADR options. For example, a court docket with a heavy percentage of indigent or low-income parties may not be able to sustain fees for ADR services. It may be in the court's interest to subsidise ADR, at least while the mediation component of the programme develops and demand for its services grows. Over time, additional options, such as case evaluation, may be added. Some ADR providers and programme administrators believe that participants in an ADR process should pay something, however minimal, in order to feel involved in the process.

Are the goals of the programme limited to ADR services?

While the programme's primary goal may be to offer ADR services, other purposes may also be accomplished. For example, if the programme includes a screening conference, case management may be enhanced by reaching agreement on discovery and other pre-trial preparation. By minimising the traditional scope and duration of discovery, the parties may reach an earlier settlement, even without further intervention.

How are the neutral panels selected and supervised?

There should be some protocol for the selection of neutrals, preferably by a committee independent of the administrators of the programme. The local legal culture will influence the selection of panel members.

Is it important that panel members have subject-matter expertise in the matters which fall within the jurisdiction of the court? The answer to that question may vary according to the different types of

ADR offered. For example, content expertise may matter for case evaluation but not for mediation.

The quality of the panel should also be overseen, so that any concerns about particular members or general protocol can be addressed in a timely way. The programme should seek evaluations of the process and the neutrals from its consumers, the parties and their lawyers. Also, the programme should provide educational opportunities and opportunities for neutrals to collaborate with each other, perhaps through formal training sessions as well as informal gatherings, such as a brown bag lunch.

Finally, any programme should have a certain amount of flexibility so that it can respond to changing needs on a daily basis and adapt to the long-term growth of the ADR field and the dynamic needs of the courts.

Conclusion

The proliferation of ADR options and methods of delivery create both a challenge and an opportunity to judicial systems seeking to expand their services. The multi-door courthouse design provides a comprehensive model that can be adapted to meet a variety of programme goals.

References

1 'Court-annexed' refers to programmes integrated into the court procedures. Court-annexed ADR programmes may be staffed by court-supervised personnel or independent agencies. The MMDC operates within the trial court, receives partial funding from the trial court, and operates within the administrative structure of the court, but remains an independent entity.

2 Frank E A Sander, 'Varieties of Dispute Resolution Processes' *70 FRD 79* (1976).

3 *Reinventing Justice*, p64.

4 Ibid, pp17–21.

5 The Massachusetts Trial Court comprises seven court departments which operate independently from each other but under the authority of a Chief Justice for Administration and Management. The court departments include probate and family, housing, juvenile, district, municipal, land and superior. The Superior Court has joint jurisdiction with some of the other courts. Each court department and the individual courthouses under its jurisdiction has its own character and culture.

6 Barbara E Stedman, *Middlesex Multi-Door Courthouse Annual Report 1994.*

7 Authority for the mandatory order comes through r16 providing judicial authority for managing cases. In Massachusetts a 'time standards' rule plays a prominent role in case management. Pre-established deadlines are set for various events in the litigation process. Depending on the claims, cases either have a 6-month (accelerated), 14-month (fast) or 36-month (average) wait before trial. The majority of cases are on the fast track and are ordered into the screening conference around 10 months after filing. Usually discovery is still in progress.

8 *Final Report* (State Justice Institute Grant No SJI–90–03C–E–046).

CHAPTER 6

Challenges in the evolution of ADR in the UK: the CEDR experience

KARL MACKIE

Professor Mackie is chief executive of CEDR, the Centre for Dispute Resolution, and special professor at the University of Birmingham.

The 1990s have witnessed a remarkable transformation in attitudes to ADR among opinion leaders in the legal systems of the UK. Initially it attracted lawyers' total scepticism, but ADR is now being increasingly adopted as one of the important elements in the system overhaul that is now underway. Most recently, this has been illustrated by support for its development both in Lord Woolf's interim report and the Labour Party.[1]

There is a sense now that ADR is likely to be a mainstream part of legal practice and dispute resolution, though one should not underestimate the ignorance, scepticism, resistance and, perhaps most of all, inertia concerning ADR that still exists in the legal profession. Proactive practitioners are now busy exploring how to exploit this development; defensive practitioners are still working on an assumption that court reforms may make ADR go away. The bulk of practitioners are somewhere in between and are waiting to be told what to do by pressure of events or otherwise. The debate on ADR is now shifting from consciousness-raising to more detailed questions of how and where to link ADR into the system and how to manage its introduction and implementation.

This chapter is a reflection on the experience of the Centre for Dispute Resolution (CEDR). CEDR has played a significant role in assisting this change of attitude, and is developing its thinking and its strategy for the next phase. The paper outlines, first, the pre-1990 position and the rationale behind CEDR's launch and structure, second, the various dimensions of the transformation that has since taken place, and third, some thoughts on the prospects for ADR based on CEDR experience: it does not consider the question of forms of, or justification for, ADR.[2]

ADR in the UK before 1990

One of the principal reasons for CEDR's launch was the apparent failure of ADR to make any real impact on the legal systems within the UK and Europe despite, on the one hand, the accumulation of evidence of its growing importance in the USA and, on the other, the growing pressures to reform the English civil legal system. Of course, a number of events that occurred before 1990 have an important place in drawing a full picture of ADR's history and practice, including the establishment of the Advisory, Conciliation and Arbitration Service (ACAS) and the Forum for Initiatives in Reparation and Mediation (FIRM) (see Marian Liebmann's chapter 7).

By 1990, Mediation UK had become the umbrella organisation for neighbourhood and other community mediation schemes throughout the UK. In the family field, two organisations were especially active, the Family Mediators' Association and what is now National Family Mediation, a confederation of local family conciliation services.[3] Finally one might refer to the growth of ombudsman schemes as part of a search for 'alternatives'. These developments were not initially associated with the push for integrating ADR into the mainstream of non-family civil legal practice, though later, as the ADR debate grew and became increasingly focused on the theme of how to promote mediation in civil litigation, Mediation UK and the family mediation organisations were able both to reinforce the growth of ADR and to draw additional momentum themselves from it. ACAS was less directly involved in this phase of ADR development.[4]

Early efforts to transplant ADR directly from the US were relatively limited. One of the US private ADR organisations in the late 1980s had a British company undertake market research into the potential for ADR in England and decided there was little prospect for a business in the field. In 1989, however, a commercial provider, IDR (Europe), launched operations on the basis of a link to another US ADR group, and has continued, albeit with a change of name (ADR Group). Finally, a group of twenty City law firms explored the idea in the late 1980s of forming an ADR network amongst themselves but this failed to attract sufficient financial support.

The core reasons for resistance to the adoption of ADR in UK civil litigation practice probably parallel early US reactions of scepticism towards the notion that mediators (or other new kinds of neutral) add value to what courts or lawyers already do. The growth of ADR in the

US was not seen as evidence of a need to examine its potential. Rather, it was an excuse for UK practitioners to suggest that it reflected deep flaws in US litigation practice such as the impact of juries in civil trials, contingency fees, non-recovery of costs, excessive discovery and witness procedures. Now that CEDR is increasingly active in mainland Europe, similar arguments are heard from civil lawyers there to explain away the rise of ADR in the UK compared to continental Europe. Adversarial common law procedures are said to necessitate balancing mechanisms for better dispute resolution in a way that Roman law civil procedures do not.

Of course, there is some truth in such perceptions. Apart from the USA being a much larger jurisdiction, its problems are increased by an 'adversarial industry' approach to lawyering and litigation practice. However, while problems in the UK and in Europe may be less pronounced, they are still present. As a result, ADR still offers potential benefits to clients not only of earlier and more cost-effective settlements, but also of more appropriate processes and 'justice' in many cases. And, importantly, the need for general reform of the civil justice system has now become more acceptable to the English judiciary than it was in the late 1980s. This can be seen by the initiation of Lord Woolf's review and increasing support for the Lord Chancellor's statements that government legal policy should reflect a sense of what is 'appropriate' dispute resolution in terms of process, remedies and costs to the public purse.

CEDR

One of the sources propelling ADR growth in the US was increasing corporate concern at the rising level of legal costs and the frequency and cost of litigation. By the mid to late 1980s, similar concerns were frequently expressed in the UK. The Confederation of British Industry in fact organised a conference on ADR and managing legal costs, although little specific emerged from it. At the same time growing numbers of lawyers had become increasingly aware of the real benefits of US ADR procedures while conscious of the increasing level of dissatisfaction amongst English litigants with the costs, delays and unsatisfactory outcomes of litigation proceedings.

An informal series of discussions amongst a group of such lawyers, including myself, led to the view that ADR developments would not make any progress without the launch of an independent organisation to act as a flagship for ADR. This led to the decision to launch

CEDR and also to a number of key decisions on the form of organisation which would best ensure that ADR moved from being a fringe concern to a mainstream activity, mainly within the UK's legal system but also at a European level.

This strategic approach determined the main features of CEDR and the actions taken by the original steering committee, namely to launch CEDR as:

- non-profit making, funded initially by membership subscription (similar organisations in other jurisdictions have largely been started by government funding);
- an organisation that was 'blue-chip' in character;
- supported by the CBI and industry, including appointment of a senior business figure as chairman;
- a 'flagship' in ADR promotion, training and ADR services;
- involving as members of the steering committee not only lawyers in private practice but also lawyers from industry and senior accountants as a message that ADR was something for all professions and clients, not just 'another lawyers' game'.

The organisation was designed, in other words, to show that industry and other professions would and did support ADR, thus sending a strong message to the legal profession and senior figures in the government and legal system that ADR needed to be taken seriously.

The launch of CEDR and its subsequent activities has had the intended impact, and has eased the way for others to develop their contributions to the growth of ADR interest, training and practice.

The evolution of ADR: the acceptance phase

The period since 1990 has therefore been a phase primarily concerned with 'winning hearts and minds' – establishing the credibility of ADR at an intellectual and professional level both within the legal profession and in the client community. To some extent this has only been achieved alongside proof that the practice of ADR is developing, but the real challenges for ADR practice fall within the next phase of development.

Below are some of the significant developments between 1990 and 1995 which demonstrate the increasing acceptance of ADR and particularly mediation as a concept. This acceptance springs from a number of sources – the work of CEDR and others in education and lobbying on ADR, the evidence of initial practice successes, the growth of ADR support and practice around the common-law world and not only in the US. As highlights rather than the whole story of growth during the five years from 1990, these advances described speak for themselves in terms of the speed of transformation from ADR being seen as an inconsequential fringe interest to being seen as one of the important tools of reform of the legal system.

Highlights of 1990–95

CEDR

– Membership has grown to over 300, including leading private and public-sector companies, law firms and other professional firms, trade, industry and professional associations, with the beginnings of European law firm membership.
– 75 of the top 100 English law firms have joined, and a significant number of major Scottish law firms.
– The Law Society of England and Wales and the London Common Law and Commercial Bar Association have joined as affiliate members.
– The Treasury's Central Unit on Procurement has joined as an affiliate member.
– Over 800 cases from a range of sectors, UK and international, have been referred for ADR advice to a value of over £1.5 billion (see below).
– CEDR has received a grant from the European Commission to review ADR developments in the European Union.

The legal profession

Reports from the professional bodies have consistently supported in principle the concept of ADR and its further use by lawyers. Since 1990 there have been reports on ADR by Henry Brown for a Law Society Working Party, by a committee under Lord Justice Beldam (the Beldam Committee), and as part of a report on civil justice by a joint committee of the Law Society and Bar Council (the Heilbron-Hodge Committee). The last two reports called for pilot schemes to test court-annexed ADR. A similar request to the Lord Chancellor was put forward by Bristol Law Society. Its rejection by the Lord Chancellor's Department (LCD) led to the launch of a self-standing Bristol Law Society scheme.

The Law Society of England and Wales has encouraged lawyers to undertake training in ADR. The Law Societies of Scotland and Northern Ireland have also done so, in addition to launching their own schemes. The Faculty of Advocates in Scotland has also launched an ADR scheme.

Outside the professional associations, many firms of solicitors have demonstrated an apparent enthusiasm for ADR training on mediation with CEDR or other bodies such as the Academy of Experts and IDR (Europe), or taking up membership of CEDR or of a lawyers' network such as ADR Net. Other firms have launched ADR specialists or units, and a large number of brochures on ADR have been produced.

The final accolade for ADR in 1995 was the inclusion of ADR as a new category within the *Encyclopaedia of Forms and Precedents*.

Lord Chancellor's Department and the judiciary

At first sight, ADR developments would appear to fit especially well with the thinking of a Lord Chancellor in a government determined to break down professional tradition and monopoly and encourage saving on legal costs. Indeed, the Lord Chancellor has spoken repeatedly in favour of ADR and taken a broad approach to rethinking litigation as only one of a range of potentially appropriate methods of resolving disputes. However, the LCD until recently resisted practical support for ADR or any suggestion that ADR should be incorporated into court-annexed schemes or even pilot schemes. This resistance has been strong despite the trend in other jurisdictions towards court-annexed ADR as one instrument of reform of litigation practice (in the US, Canada and Australia) and despite calls for pilot schemes from the Beldam and Heilbron Committees and from a National Consumer Council review of ADR.

The source of this resistance, despite the apparent match between ADR and the general philosophy driving LCD reforms, has never been fully articulated. It appears to be based partly on earlier family mediation research which suggested court-annexed schemes may be less effective than free-standing ones; and partly on a desire not to put further financial or administrative burdens on the courts and thus go down a state-regulated route rather than a free market route to dispute resolution. Unfortunately, a more public debate on these issues has not taken place, but a review of them is important for the future of ADR (see below).

Recent LCD policy has been more explicit on the need for reform of the wider legal system, particularly in the context of attempts to win control over the growing legal aid burden on the Treasury. A green paper on legal aid has proposed new structures for legal aid which would redirect some of the current funds into ADR options and even allow mediation groups to apply directly for legal aid funding. In the field of family mediation, a white paper on divorce has proposed making mediation the favoured approach to management of divorce arrangements, subject to an initial filtering scheme of information and advice. The paper rightly suggests that in the divorce field, mediation is particularly appropriate, compared to lawyer-bound adversarialism. Mediation is also, conveniently, much cheaper.

In the meantime, the judges have also taken their own steps to promote ADR. One of the earliest innovations was in the Official Referees' Court where one of the referees, Judge Fox-Andrews, introduced a practice direction to stay proceedings while parties attempted ADR in appropriate cases. Judge Fox-Andrews' approach was perhaps regarded by his brother judges as somewhat maverick and was not extended in the court. However, by December 1993 the Commercial Court had issued a practice note declaring that it would expect solicitors and counsel to consult their client and the other side on the appropriateness of ADR in their cases. The clerk to the court retained a list of individuals and organisations who could provide such services.

Subsequently, in January 1995 the High Court issued a practice note on efficient case management which again formally referred to ADR.[5] A pre-trial checklist, to be lodged with the court at least two months before trial, required a declaration that ADR had been considered with the client and the other side. The practice note interestingly mooted the possibility that ADR might be suitable not only to resolve the case but also to clarify or streamline the issues to be tried.

These initiatives have been followed by Lord Woolf's interim report on access to justice. Lord Woolf took the opportunity to address the question of ADR. His report provided yet more support in principle for the concept. However, rather in keeping with LCD policies, he avoided any calls for more robust court-annexed ADR procedures, limiting his proposals to measures such as better judicial and public education, to encouragement of judges to consider referral to ADR when they adopt the active procedural management envisaged in the report, and to support for some funding for bodies like Mediation UK in community work.

Lord Woolf argued that it was inappropriate to go further towards a mandatory scheme, partly because his report would already pose enough new challenges to the courts, and partly on the grounds that there was still limited evidence for ADR's contribution to cost-saving or to case management in the context of English courts compared to the US.

Other government and public-sector initiatives

CEDR's strategy towards ADR has always been a bi-polar one. On the one hand, it was important to persuade the legal profession and the courts of the value of ADR in improving client services and access to justice. On the other, given the traditionalism of lawyers – perhaps reinforced in this instance by the unpleasant logic of ADR that if you save costs you may be cutting lawyer fees – it was important to build up a momentum of support for ADR among the clients and representative client organisations. CEDR has also therefore campaigned for ADR amongst business and public-sector bodies, and a number of these developments are worth outlining to show the scale of progress towards acceptance of ADR in principle.

Perhaps the most significant measure of ADR's impact is in the range of government departments where some ADR support has now been expressed:

- support for ADR as contributing to industry efficiency, particularly small businesses, in the Department of Trade and Industry (DTI) White Paper on Competitiveness;
- DTI agreement to promote ADR through its new national network of 'one-stop shops' for business, the 'Business Link' schemes;
- support for ADR practice in management of government contracts with the publication of a Guidance Note on Dispute Resolution by the Central Unit on Procurement of HM Treasury (1995, No 50);
- a Department of Environment review of adversarialism in contract practice in the construction industry recommends an adjudication form of ADR (the Latham Report);
- a Department of Environment consultation paper on neighbours and noise suggests the benefits of mediation;
- Ministry of Agriculture, Fisheries and Food's use of an ADR clause in construction contracts;
- Department of Health announcement in 1995 of support for pilot schemes in three health regions using mediation for clinical negligence claims.

These developments are echoed, although less strongly, in other parts of the public sector:

- first tenders for mediation services for medical complaints procedures;
- tender for mediation service for the Housing Corporation Housing Ombudsman in housing association tenancy cases;
- use of ADR proposed in the post-privatised railway system for disputes between the various companies in the industry;
- support for mediation clause in local authorities' Guidelines on Model Community Care Contracts;
- pilot scheme on ADR between CEDR and Citizens' Advice Scotland

At the level of the European Union, conciliation procedures have been encouraged in new public procurement directives, while CEDR received support for a review of European ADR and small and medium-sized enterprises across Europe.

The business community

Many of CEDR's members are now drawn from household-name companies in addition to important backing from the Confederation of British Industry, which has hosted a number of industry conferences. In addition, a large number of trade, industry and professional associations have joined CEDR. A number of trade association ADR schemes have been launched since 1990 – the Glass and Glazing Federation, Building Employers' Confederation, Heating and Ventilating Contractors' Association, PACT (independent film producers), Royal Institute of Chartered Surveyors.

In the construction industry, the Latham Report recommended the use of a form of ADR – adjudication (a binding decision during contract performance) – as a core contractual procedure. Interest in the pensions industry in ADR was further heightened when the fall-out from Robert Maxwell's death led to settlement by mediation of the major litigation actions undertaken to secure compensation for Maxwell company pensioners.

Apart from these developments and individual cases referred to ADR, there have been numerous contracts now adapted to include ADR procedures, both industry-standard forms (Institution of Civil Engineers, Electrical Contractors' Association, National Association of Steel Stockholders and others) and individual contracts. The head of Standard Chartered Bank's legal department announced publicly that his bank's preferred option in any case was to use ADR rather than litigation, although individual British companies have to date generally taken a lower profile on ADR use than some of their US counterparts.

Education and training

ADR has now been formally adopted, albeit in limited form, as part of the professional training of solicitors and barristers. In addition, the Judicial Studies Board has held at least one seminar on ADR for senior judges. Less information is available nationally on the extent of growth in coverage of ADR in undergraduate law teaching, though it is certainly included in courses at the Universities of Birmingham and Dundee and at the London School of Economics. The number of student requests for assistance received by CEDR suggests that many dissertations are being written on the topic. It appears that it is litigation practice rather than ADR which is seriously under-researched. Outside law, ADR as a form of dispute resolution is now being regularly taught in courses for architects, surveyors and other construction professionals.

There are at least six British textbooks now available, which is an improvement on the earlier dearth of literature compared to US material.[6]

Within the field of ADR, a range of organisations now offer training courses in mediation. ADR is in the classic position of most emerging disciplines and professions: the market is fragmented, models of approach do not necessarily match, organisations compete for credibility and resources. Undoubtedly, if more ADR was actually practised, there would be more debate on questions of the quality and sufficiency of training. However, the inherent difficulties of generating practice in this discipline mean that this issue has not yet been confronted. The major exception is in family mediation, where mediation is likely to become a mainstream practice if the Lord Chancellor's divorce reform proposals are enacted.

Despite this background, or perhaps because ADR organisations have had the space to concentrate on training, some of the mediator training programmes are very good, and may rank alongside the best international courses available. The major question mark has been the length of programme available. Given that an ADR career is not yet an option for many professionals, there is a limit to the time and money which potential trainees will devote to developing their skills. Also, mediators' real education comes with practice, after the foundation stage. Mediation work has not been readily available to most trained mediators, although the most enthusiastic will often seek to extend their experience by working voluntarily in local neighbourhood schemes or other contexts where they can.

There is, finally, a question as to who mediators ought to be. The issue has arisen in the family field, where there has been something of a gentle professional 'turf' battle between lawyers and non-lawyers on who should be involved in the field. The issue is also relevant if and when court-annexed schemes develop, that is to say, whether mediators for actions in court should themselves be lawyers, a suggestion of the Beldam committee.

CEDR has, as a matter of policy, believed from the outset that the field should be multi-disciplinary. Access to its training and panels is, therefore, open to all and has been taken up by many professional groups as well as lawyers. There are, however, two provisos. First, the field of dispute resolution tends to be more central to the concerns of the legal profession than others. One would expect it to be of more interest to them. In consequence, over 60 per cent of those accredited in CEDR training are lawyers. Second, lawyers and parties, particularly in commercial cases, tend to want someone as a mediator who understands the technical issues and context. In construction cases, this may be a surveyor; in a major piece of commercial litigation, a lawyer. Thus, it is CEDR policy to appoint mediators with a relevant background where we can, for reasons of credibility with the parties and speed of understanding the issues, while acknowledging that mediation skills are themselves transferable across dispute types.

ADR practice

While ADR practice has been slower to develop than the debate on ADR, and is likely to remain so (see below), there have been sufficient cases to testify to ADR's potential, even taking CEDR's work alone. We have been referred in five years to over 800 cases with a claims value of over £1.5 billion. The majority of these have not proceeded to formal ADR, either through a refusal of one party to participate or because the cases settle in the course of the parties considering ADR. Currently around a quarter proceed to formal ADR.

What is most impressive, however, is the range of cases where ADR has been seen as potentially appropriate or has worked as a process.

This variety can be expressed in a number of ways – in the **sectors** from which cases have come – commercial, construction, personal injury, insurance (professional indemnity, Lloyd's market, policy-holder, third-party claims), financial services, pensions, partnerships, family businesses, education, charities, joint ventures, venture capital, local government, international commercial, consumer; in the **values** of claims mediated, from issues with a few thousand pounds at stake or no financial element at all to a £200 million claim and many over £20 million; the **stages of litigation** when the action is referred, from pre-litigation to shortly before trial (or appeal); in the **nature of the outcome,** from new commercial contracts to payment of compensation; in the **representation** involved, non-lawyers, solicitors, solicitors and counsel; and finally in the **forms of ADR** used – case appraisal, executive tribunal (mini-trial), mediation, procedural review, med-arb, adjudication, facilitation and consensus-building.

This range is a fair indication of the potential scope for ADR in the future. However, it is only right to add that, to date, the typical case would be one in litigation, with parties represented by solicitors, where the outcome is not a continued business relationship but a settlement of the litigation by payment of a sum of money before mediated negotiation around case merits and litigation risk analysis. ADR promotion has therefore been most successful amongst litigation lawyers and undoubtedly helped improve the **timing of settlement** of cases. Most civil actions settle out of court, shortly before trial, but in cases coming to CEDR the parties are a little way short of the steps of the court and previous negotiating attempts will have failed.

Apart from one-shot cases, there are also a number of attempts at dispute schemes covering a more regular flow of cases – schemes with insurance companies or trade associations or such as the Bristol Law Society's launch of a local scheme. These schemes may help accelerate pre-litigation case referrals. In the smaller-value cases, there is the added difficulty of effectively funding training and practice, so far largely met by either low-fee or *pro bono* work undertaken by CEDR or other ADR or community mediation organisations.

ADR's future in the UK

'Promotion' of ADR in the UK and internationally has been effective enough to tilt the balance of opinion amongst opinion leaders in the UK legal system and government towards support for alternatives to litigation. The recent Labour Party policy statement on the justice system confirms that ADR will also be seen as an important tool of reform of the legal system if the opposition is elected to government. A similar shift of opinion is predictable across the European Union within the next five years. There is now a core mediation track record in commercial, family and non-family civil litigation. We have therefore now entered what is in many ways a more complex phase of determining how the potential benefits of ADR, particularly mediation, can best be realised across and beyond the current justice system.

This is an enormous yet exciting challenge for policymakers, ADR organisations and other 'stakeholders' in the justice system. The Legal Action Group conferences on this theme bring a welcome opportunity to review the options available and domestic and international experience. Having worked in this field as a practitioner, academic and CEDR director, I attempt to set out below what I see as some of the major issues in the ADR field that we need to address for the future.

The management of diversity

The legal profession and legal system, including legal educators and researchers, are already struggling to break out of Dickensian ideology and structures to accommodate the complexity of social life and transactions, and disputes in the late twentieth century. An overarching theme for the justice system is the accommodation of diversity. The essential intellectual thrust of ADR is to argue for *appropriate* dispute resolution – what approaches achieve the best balance of justice and cost-effectiveness for particular kinds of case? And what is the appropriate definition of justice and cost-effectiveness in any particular context?

As a general principle, any future structures should emphasise flexibility rather than create tendencies to certainty and rigidity. We should be wary of any calls for this field to be regulated or 'professionalised' earlier than it needs to be or risk a repetition of the current problems of the legal profession and legal system. In 1991, I argued that the Council on Tribunals or some other institution should have its jurisdiction extended to oversee the ADR field.[7] This proposal has now been taken up by the Labour Party in a policy paper on access to justice.[8] If such a development comes about, the role of such a body should be 'enabling' rather than 'regulatory'.

Working towards a level playing field

I admit to a degree of frustration when critics sometimes point to low case numbers as evidence of the shortcomings or slow progress of ADR. There is an overwhelming imbalance in the societal resources and public subsidy dedicated to lawyers, courts and adversarial education and practice compared to those committed to ADR. The government has at least conceded some recognition of this in that the green paper on legal aid talks of some re-allocation of legal aid funding. However, the British government and institutions have failed to invest in justice and in the future by supporting ADR organisations. The achievements of ADR organisations in the UK are hugely impressive when one compares the British attitude to the support given by governments, foundations and companies in the US, Australia and elsewhere.

Legal aid could only partly meet the needs of the field. Payment on a case-by-case basis does not in itself necessarily support the infrastructure of ADR organisations. This is required, particularly in the early years, to support activities such as promotion of ADR as a concept, education and training, research and development and in the management of the quality in practice within and across organisations. This would not involve large expenditure in comparison with the £1.25 billion currently spent on legal aid alone, leaving aside other subsidies that support the traditional systems.

Now that there is much clearer support in principle for ADR from government, it is important that government and ADR organisations address the issue of how best to achieve a more level playing field in terms of public funding. In fact, even getting on to the field would help us achieve a fairer test match against the traditional alternatives than we can at present.

Industry structure, professionalism, quality and effectiveness

ADR scholars devote their time to ADR theory, practitioners to finding and managing cases, politicians to ensuring effective management of the public purse and public opinion. Not enough time is devoted to thinking through what form of 'industry' we should be seeking to establish for ADR. Unfortunately, socio-legal scholars and jurists tend to come from a theoretical background where such a concept is often an 'alien' theoretical category. Yet it is a fundamental issue for the whole field of ADR. What sort of service or business is the ADR field and what professional, business or statutory structures should manage and deliver it to the diverse communities it addresses?

If we do not articulate, debate and guide the choices in this field, then we will nevertheless be making choices, but guided by implicit theories and short-term or sectional interests. Already the debate amongst family mediators and elsewhere is shifting towards 'accreditation' as a beacon of quality. The Labour Party is also attracted to a national accreditation scheme.

The need for training is clear. CEDR endeavours to set a leading standard in its accreditation (and recently won an award for its training). However, it seems questionable to make individual accreditation the major focus for ADR service quality. The assumptions underlying the proposal need to be debated. It is not the only, or even necessarily the best way to ensure growth and quality in the field. We already have well-established national systems for accrediting solicitors and barristers which have not prevented us from finding ourselves with a legal system that is not delivering what our community needs. In addition, the expansion of organisations and individuals offering ADR services may simply add to public confusion.

There is a real need to debate other models of industry structure. For example, there is a powerful case in family, consumer or small claims cases for a statutory or quasi-public service on the model of ACAS in employment disputes. Failure to debate the structure of the ADR industry prevents us thinking in more radical ways about the future for ADR or how to ensure best provision.

Lawyers and ADR

The question of industry structure also bears on the issue of how and where lawyers play a role in ADR. There has been a long-running tension in the ADR field regarding lawyer involvement, particularly as to family or small claim cases. Do we need the lawyers? In commercial ADR and higher-value cases, the legal profession will undoubtedly remain centrally involved, although a 'looser' regime may emerge if the profession of 'mediator' becomes sufficiently well-established to make less relevant the question of mediators' professional origins. Lawyers have major opportunities to extend their work and job satisfaction through more active involvement in ADR, and can deliver a valuable client service by participating. They can best do so if more effectively educated than they are at present about ADR practice and its contrasts with adversarial proceedings.

The greatest problem arises in family and small claims cases. Part of the controversy may be a question of lawyer mindset, but it is also again a problem of resources. Lawyer involvement typically raises costs as against dispute resolution processes managed by less well-paid professionals or volunteers. Set against this, if lawyers are not involved, what is the real danger in using ADR of an erosion of parties' rights, especially among weaker or less well-informed clients?

There is unlikely to be any easy answer to the dilemmas in this situation other than by reducing lawyers' fees (by the various mechanisms currently proposed or happening), or by finding other ways to inform clients of rights. Finally one might rethink the role of mediator in these cases towards greater acceptance of 'evaluative' mediation or quasi-ombudsman ADR methods, in order to remove the need for party representation. Perhaps we come back full circle to small claims courts, but with a different orientation and training.

Finally, we must remember that lawyer reward systems are part of the issue as to how we achieve a level playing field for ADR within the system. The major incentive for lawyers to use ADR at present is that it can achieve a better client service. A satisfied client may come back or recommend others to do so. However, this 'marketing' view of service may clash with the fact that ADR, in any one case, may reduce legal fees. Lawyers have therefore little immediate financial incentive to use ADR, a situation formally intensified by the policy of the Legal Aid Board that mediation proceedings do not attract legal aid funding. Conditional fees may improve this situation a little, but other mechanisms are needed to ensure that lawyers are motivated by case outcome rather than case duration.

Court-annexed ADR

One of the major arguments for this development is that it is likely, as in the US, to increase the number of referrals to ADR. In addition to any financial disincentive lawyers might have to use ADR, there is often a tactical problem in adversarial proceedings. To suggest a dialogue with the other side may be interpreted as a sign of weakness (and in any case be seen as an extra burden when lawyers and clients have other day-to-day pressures on them).

The High Court and Commercial Court practice directions represent a tentative step towards a court-annexed system. Lord Woolf has also indicated that judges should in the future take more active steps to propose ADR or take into account failure to use it. A major issue for the ADR field will be how to add more weight to this court role. The Lord Chancellor's department, in some respects quite justifiably, is cautious about how far to entangle ADR with the court system. This should not, however, prevent a fuller debate and pilot schemes to test how to ensure that negotiating tactics work in favour of early ADR adoption rather than against it as at present. Otherwise cases will still drift into litigation that need not do so and the justice system will also lose the wider benefits of ADR.

Client, legal and mediator education

While there has been a shift in favour of ADR amongst opinion leaders, there is still a major educational challenge beyond that. CEDR will certainly be giving even greater attention to client education in the next phase of development. Informed clients will encourage lawyer activism. It is, of course, equally vital that ADR is fully incorporated into legal education and training. In this respect, there remains a special challenge because much of the real education in ADR lies in experience of the process rather than in the more familiar territory of case-law and statutory interpretation.

Finally, education of the 'neutrals' in ADR procedures needs to be more fully developed to match the theory with effective practice. For this to happen, there needs to be careful monitoring of how well existing practices are working (and against what criteria) and further experimentation with ADR procedures and pilot schemes. In saying this, we should not neglect the need to research more effectively litigation practice now or as reformed, in order better to compare ADR with the alternative models for delivery of justice. As US researchers have discovered, this is no easy task.

Conclusion

If there is one overwhelming lesson from practical case-work in the ADR field, it has been the strengthening of my conviction that there are literally thousands of disputes in our society which would benefit, in terms of process and outcome, from greater use of ADR. We are too cautious about its potential. Whether this can be achieved and at the same time meet political objectives of cutting public expenditure, is a more complex question. Certainly, before the launch of CEDR, we were told frequently that ADR would not work for our system of civil litigation or for complex commercial cases. We have proved that it can and does work and that it also has extensive potential for cases pre-litigation or in those that are inappropriate for litigation.

ADR is not some kind of magic potion or panacea. It works for solid reasons which can be articulated and researched in order to improve future practice. And there are many cases, occasions and times when it is not entirely appropriate (though in my view, ADR is partially appropriate for most disputes at some stage of their life cycle). It also will only work well if there are well-trained mediators supported by an effective infrastructure of ADR organisations, and this should include a clear and widely recognised interchange system between the ADR systems and court or tribunal procedures. The potential for ADR calls for more radical thinking, innovation and investment rather than the caution traditionally associated with the legal profession and British institutions. None of us can predict what will be the exact outcome of this upsurge in ADR interest ten years from now. As regards the civil justice system, we are however in the classic situation of many litigants. We have a deep sense that there must be a better way but somehow, without ADR, it has eluded us as each interest group fights its corner rather than faces the future. Perhaps if we had found a way to incorporate skilled mediation into the decision-making process of the Lord Chancellor's Department and elsewhere, we would have achieved an earlier and better civil justice 'settlement' than we can currently foresee.

References

1 *Access to Justice: Labour's proposals for reforming the civil justice system* (Labour Party, 1995).

2 This has been extensively covered elsewhere by myself and others.

3 The switch in the latter's name from 'conciliation' to 'mediation' itself is an interesting illustration of the significance of US ADR influence on terminology in the field.

4 One of the remarkable aspects of ADR's growth internationally is how disassociated its development has been from well-established national labour relations systems that in effect use ADR practices. Indeed I believe I was the first person to inform ACAS that it was really an ADR organisation.

5 *Practice Note (civil litigation: case management)* [1995] 1 All ER 385, Lord Taylor CJ, pre-trial checklist, paras 10–12.

6 See especially Andrew Ackland, *Resolving Disputes Without Going to Court: A consumer guide to alternative dispute resolution* (Century, 1995) and Karl Mackie (ed), *A Handbook of Dispute Resolution* (Routledge, 2nd edn

1995). See also A Bevan, *Alternative Dispute Resolution* (Sweet & Maxwell, 1992), Brown and Marriott, *ADR Principles and Practice* (Sweet & Maxwell, 1993), Mackie, Miles and Marsh, *Commercial Dispute Resolution* (Butterworth, 1995) and Rutherford and Simms, *Dispute Resolution: Arbitration and ADR* (Financial Times Law and Tax, 1995).

7 See further K Mackie, 'Conclusion: Dispute resolution futures' in K Mackie (ed), *A Handbook of Dispute Resolution: ADR in action* (Routledge and Sweet & Maxwell, 1991) p281.

8 Op cit, note 1 p5.

CHAPTER 7

The future of community mediation

MARIAN LIEBMANN

Marian Liebmann is projects adviser with Mediation UK and was its director between 1991 and 1995.

Mediation is a process by which an impartial third party helps two or more disputants to work out how to resolve a conflict. The people concerned, not the mediators, decide the terms of any agreement reached. Mediation usually focuses on future rather than past behaviour. It differs from negotiation by using a third party to help the process and from arbitration in that it does not usually result in a binding decision. Mediation therefore leaves all other legal remedies available if they are needed.

The growth of mediation in the UK

Although mediation is a traditional method of resolving conflict in Asia and Africa, the influences on current mediation practice in the UK came mainly from North America and Australia. Early developments took place in the UK in the 1980s, starting with victim/offender schemes and moving on to community mediation. Parallel to these developments were similar initiatives in the field of family mediation and commercial mediation. These resulted in similar networks of mediation services and experienced mediators. In addition, the Advisory, Conciliation and Arbitration Service (ACAS), set up by the government in 1974 to help resolve conflict between employers and employees, had a continuing influence.

The Forum for Initiatives in Reparation and Mediation (FIRM) was started in 1984 to bring together all those involved in victim/offender and community mediation. Later, schools conflict resolution work also joined the list. A magazine and newsletter were among the

161

first methods used by FIRM to disseminate information and increase the flow of ideas. A membership scheme enabled those with a general interest to become involved. In 1991, FIRM changed its name to Mediation UK, to explain its purpose more clearly.

Mediation UK now consists of a large network of projects, organisations and individuals interested in mediation and other constructive forms of handling conflict. It provides general information and advice on mediation and also specialises in the areas of community, victim/offender and schools mediation. One of its main activities is to help set up new mediation services, and ensure that high standards are developed and maintained.[1] It also organises many events, including a large annual conference. It currently has a membership of about 400, of which 100 are organisations and 300 are individual members. Eighty of the organisations are mediation services, of which 50 are community/neighbourhood mediation services, 25 are victim/offender mediation services, and 20 are concerned with conflict resolution work and mediation in schools (some services operate in more than one area).

Less than ten community mediation services existed in 1987. Why the increase? To some extent, the growth in community mediation services has followed the rise in neighbour disputes as perceived by the public, local authorities and other agencies. In 1992–93 there were 3,137 domestic noise complaints per million of the population,[2] amounting to over 150,000 incidents in one year. This was a 20 per cent increase over the previous year, and nearly double the number of complaints seven years before, in 1985–86.[3] There are many reasons which may account for this.[4] Among these may be included lifestyle clashes (especially between generations), increased shortage of housing (leading to difficulties in moving or inappropriate allocations of tenancies), more people spending time at home due to unemployment, the increase in noise-making equipment, and the general increase in stress and poverty, which often makes difficulties with neighbours seem like the 'last straw'.

Local authorities are interested in mediation for a variety of reasons. The expense and often failure of legal remedies to deal with neighbour conflict leads to a need to provide an alternative to existing methods of resolving disputes. There is also a growing conviction that mediation is more appropriate for certain types of disputes, and has a real potential for rebuilding communities. Council departments, particularly those dealing with housing and environmental health, have come to see community mediation services as cost-effective ways of dealing with neighbour nuisance. This means that they are often willing to fund or part-fund (either by grant or contract) mediation services, so that they can be enabled to do this work and relieve local authorities of an increasing burden which they feel they do not have the time or expertise to undertake. In 1994, this process led the Department of Environment to produce, with help from Mediation UK, a booklet entitled *Mediation: Benefits and Practice* which encourages local authorities to look seriously at the possibility of providing funds to help initiate mediation services.

Whereas the first community mediation services were almost all to be found in very urban areas, some of the newer ones are based in small towns and rural areas. Some of the rise in neighbour disputes is undoubtedly due to the stresses of urban living but problems such as boundary and noise disputes are found in all communities. Some types of problem, such as those involving 'travellers' cause particular problems for rural areas. In more remote areas of the country, there may be friction between long-standing residents and 'incomers'.

Some general community mediation services act as a base for other, more specialist, provision, such as elder mediation for problems involving older people, particularly but by no means exclusively, in institutions. Medical mediation, environmental mediation, organisational mediation, public services mediation are all areas which are beginning to grow. Many form links with, or are developed from, existing community mediation services.

Why and when does mediation work?

There are several reasons why mediation may work better than traditional legal processes, especially for interpersonal disputes:

a) Instead of polarising parties into two enemy camps, mediation encourages them to focus on the problem between them and not on each other. Parties are encouraged to look at their needs and feelings in a particular situation. Mediators do not have to spend time looking at flaws in the arguments of either side, but instead focus on common ground between the disputants and the way forward.

b) Mediation gives both parties an opportunity to tell their version of events fully and to hear what the other party has to say. There are always two sides to the story, and both sides will have legitimate concerns and grievances. People are more likely to change their actions if they hear about how their behaviour is affecting the other person, than if they are simply told not to do something.

c) Disputing parties are more likely to keep to a solution that they have been involved in, rather than one imposed by an outside person. A solution imposed by the court generally makes one party a winner and the other party a loser. Mediators believe in the idea that both sides can win – that there is likely to be a solution which will meet most of the needs of those involved.

d) People are able to reach agreements that are appropriate to their particular situation; their needs might be quite different from the requirements of others with a similar type of dispute.

e) Mediators ask people what they want. In many cases, this is simply an apology from the other person for the distress that they have caused. Once they have taken the matter to a solicitor, they find themselves on a rollercoaster ride they cannot stop.

f) Mediation is a confidential process. This enables people to say whatever they want without the fear that it will be taken down and used in evidence against them. The Court of Appeal has decided that admissions or conciliatory gestures made during mediation are not admissible if the mediation is unsuccessful and comes to court, except in the rare case where someone indicates that s/he has, or is likely to have, caused severe harm to a child.[5] Thus, mediation allows people to express their emotions and also provides a safe place for people to vent their anger.

g) Mediation is more likely to get to the root of the problem, particularly in neighbour disputes, where one incident may often have been the cause of a long-running neighbour dispute. The resolution of the conflict may depend on finding out the real cause, which can easily be lost in an involved legal history. Cases which have been thrown out of court when it was deemed that the dispute was caused by 'six of one and half a dozen of the other' have subsequently been successfully solved by mediation.

h) Disputes have many strands or aspects to them but courts can only deal with matters of law. In many cases, courts cannot deal with the whole picture.

i) Although mediation looks at the past, its focus is on the future. How do the parties want the situation to be from now on? This is important because neighbours who take each other to court usually have to return home and carry on living next door to each other.

It is important to know when mediation is appropriate and when it is not. There are several indications which may help to determine this:

a) Mediation can help when both parties want to preserve their relationships, when there is good will on both sides, and when it is in both parties' interests to sort things out. It can also help when the law is not clear – and when both parties are tired of the dispute.

b) Mediation is not appropriate if either party is unwilling, or it is not really in one party's interest to settle.

c) Mediation is also not viable if there are threats or fear of violence, and police action may be indicated; or where the dispute needs a public judgment.

Community mediation services

Several different options have been tried in the UK, and there are advantages and disadvantages to each. Broadly speaking, there is now a consensus that the independently organised community mediation service best fulfils the needs for independence of operation and community involvement. Most of the 50 existing community mediation services operate this model.

In most cases, the local mediation service is set up as a separate organisation, usually a registered charity, with an independent management committee. This oversees the general running of the service and the work of a co-ordinator in managing a group of mediators, usually volunteers from the local community. As a model, this has several advantages. First, the service is seen as independent and impartial. Many different agencies can, thus, refer cases to it in the expectation of saving the time of their officials. The management committee, volunteer mediators and the referral network help the organisation to become a genuine community service. The training of volunteers helps to spread mediation skills more widely through the community.

A disadvantage of this model is its vulnerability to funding pressures. With no statutory organisation to undertake long-term funding of a community mediation service, much effort has to be put into raising funds, often from charitable trusts and businesses, as well as from statutory sources. On the other hand, drawing funds from many sources may sometimes be a source of strength as opposed to over-reliance on one source of funding. New services often attract start-up resources for six months to three years from national or local government special project funding for urban areas, crime prevention or environmental action (noise). Some government funds, such as the Single Regeneration Budget, now require a three-way partnership between voluntary organisations, local government and local business.

Community mediation services may also attract ongoing local

government revenue funds, especially from housing and environmental health departments, which are the ones which usually have the greatest need for mediation resources. Until recently, most of such funding was given in the form of a local government agency grant, for a period of one to three years. Now many local authorities are being required to purchase services by way of local contracts, and more recently still, by compulsory competitive tendering. The advantage of contract-based funding is that it is more secure. The disadvantages include the serious implications of failing to complete the contract and the greater number of conditions that the local authority may require. Also, different departments may have different contract requirements. For example, a council's housing department may limit a contract to disputes concerning local authority housing tenants and the environmental health department to those relating to noise, leaving other kinds of neighbour disputes unfunded. However, several local authorities have co-ordinated their efforts towards funding a community mediation service for all the citizens in a particular area. A recent development, especially since housing associations have taken over the provision of social housing from local authorities in some areas, is that housing associations may also have contracts with local community mediation services.

Most community mediation services receive some funding from the charitable sector. However, this funding tends to concentrate on innovative work. Most charitable trusts are not willing to pay for a community mediation service *ad infinitum* – both because they do not have the resources, and also because they feel that the government, in some form, should be footing the bill.

Mediation case studies

Two cases taken from Mediation UK's Annual Report 1994–95 illustrate circumstances where mediation probably achieved more than legal action might have done.

Mediation unblocks multiple agency log jam

The relationship between two large families went rapidly downhill when one of the teenage boys from one fell out with the girl from next door. They had been going out with each other for a few months. Respective brothers and sisters took sides and started swearing at each other, calling one another names and throwing stones at each other's houses. One party had threatened 'to torch' the other's house and things had reached the point where the police had been contacted. Everyone was getting more and more stressed. A series of professionals, including the local police, community and social workers, educational psychologists, teachers, housing workers and solicitors, became involved. None was making much progress.

Mediators visited both the parties several times and explored options for getting round this log jam. From a list of basic requests, compiled with the help of mediators, there emerged the bones and then the flesh of an agreement between all the parties concerned. A face-to-face meeting was planned but had to be put off because of a bereavement in one family. However, the mediators 'shuttled' between the houses to get the agreement in place before a rapidly approaching Christmas.

The mediators said that they would be in touch after a couple of months to see how things were going. On their return, everything had calmed down. The neighbours were talking to each other. Everyone was keeping to the agreement.

Neighbours and food smells

Maria, a widow in her seventies, was greatly distressed by the smells which she said were coming from a food stall underneath her window and which aggravated her asthma. Ruth, a young woman, and her husband lived next door. They made their living by selling health food from the stall. Maria said that she had tried to take legal action but that the couple had got 800 signatures from local people saying that they could smell nothing. Ruth said that Maria had a commercial interest in the restaurant below her flat, which she had once owned, and felt that the stall was competitive.

At the mediation, the neighbours' mutual distress was ventilated and all of the issues discussed. The couple said that the council had approved their stall and that it had an extractor to deal with the smells. They said that they were starting a food business, as Maria had once done, and thought that car pollution might have affected her asthma as she lived on a busy road. They offered to demonstrate the extractor filter to her and change it every month instead of every three months (as required by law) if Maria would stop her legal action. She said that she would try to find an alternative and acceptable site for them and talk about any further problems rather than writing letters. Both said that they would be willing to mediate any further problems.

Both these cases illustrate typical situations where expensive litigation, environmental health actions or even criminal proceedings might arise from disputes which can be successfully mediated. It is unlikely that any alternatives to mediation would have produced good and lasting solutions.

The future

Legal remedies have become very expensive in both time and money, and legal action is almost always more expensive than mediation. There are many stories of neighbour disputes which have cost thousands of pounds. Mediation could have helped in most of these cases. For instance, a couple from Buckinghamshire began litigation to prevent cricket balls from a neighbouring village green coming into their garden. They lost their case and were faced with an unexpectedly large legal bill for £12,000.[6] Another case, in which two families sued each other concerning a whole host of complaints, including noise, dogs, rubbish, verbal abuse and much more, cost a total of £50,000 for an 11-day court hearing. The legal bill for one of the disputants, £27,000, was covered by legal aid, and thus ended up as a cost to the taxpayer.[7] This is also true for court cases brought by environmental health departments, such as one which cost £100,000 in all. It concerned noise from budgerigars, which the neighbours said was completely intolerable. The environmental health department took the budgerigar breeder to court, but lost the case, and had to pay £60,000 from local council funds. The defendant's costs of £40,000 were paid by legal aid. Much of the cost might have been avoided with mediation.[8]

The court process is an adversarial one, so that even when a neighbour wins a court case against another neighbour, the resentment built up does nothing for neighbourly relations, and in many cases makes things worse. Given the advantages of informality, speed and ability to take both parties' interests into account, it makes obvious sense for mediation to replace legal solutions where possible. A recent survey carried out by the National Consumer Council showed that about three-quarters of those who had experienced a serious dispute consider that the present legal system is too slow, too complicated, too easy to twist if you know the rules, needs bringing up-to-date, and is off-putting for ordinary people.[9] All those who had experienced a dispute were then given three alternative ways in which the case could be resolved and asked which they preferred. Only eight per cent preferred 'a full trial in court'. Twenty-three per cent opted for 'sitting round a table with an independent expert who makes the decision'. The majority, 53 per cent, chose 'sitting round a table with an independent expert who helps you to reach an agreement between yourselves'. Those with recent experience of going to court made similar choices.

Nevertheless, there are some caveats to simply replacing all legal processes by mediation. Mediation may simply result in the less powerful party agreeing to the demands of the other, more powerful party, because they 'fear the worst' outside the mediation setting. There is also anecdotal evidence from the US that mediation can be in danger of being used as 'cheap justice'. Poorer citizens may be diverted to mediation, because it is cheaper on the public purse, while citizens who can afford a lawyer have the choice whether to go to mediation or to go to law. There is also the point that compulsory mediation can result in parties just 'going through the motions' when they have been directed to mediation rather than choosing it voluntarily. Most mediators feel that mediation has to be a voluntary process to stand a chance of working properly.

The increasing costs of civil litigation and the length of time taken to deal with cases have led to the Woolf inquiry on civil justice. Mediation UK arranged for local mediation services to attend regional seminars. Its written submission[10] emphasises the safeguards needed to ensure that mediation is a just process. Mediation must be voluntary so that people choose to take part and can leave at any time. Mediators need to assess whether or not a case is suitable for mediation, screening out cases where there is fear or intimidation. Ground rules must be agreed at the outset by all parties. Mediators can help to ensure power is not misused and should stop a mediation if there is danger of intimidation.

Mediation is not a legally binding process. Agreements are made in good faith. Using mediation does not affect a person's legal rights. Mediators have no power to make judgments, enforce decisions or agreements. Mediation UK recommends that mediation should be freely available to all people in dispute as their first method of trying to find a solution with litigation as a last resort. Unless people are offered an alternative, they have no choice but to take legal action. The development of independent community mediation centres in all local authority areas is necessary to ensure that cases are kept out of the court system. In addition, systems are needed to divert appropriate civil court cases to community mediation services. Training of the judiciary and barristers in the principles of mediation would help them to be aware of the benefits and make suitable referrals, and solicitors would need to outline all the options available to their clients, and, if appropriate, refer them to mediation speedily. Finally, Mediation UK asks for funding to continue to develop its work on accreditation of mediators and services to ensure high standards.

In his interim report, Lord Woolf highlighted the benefits of alternative dispute resolution and especially mediation:

> A number of organisations, including Mediation UK and schemes run by local authorities, provide mediation services which are designed primarily to resolve and defuse disputes between neighbours. These have made a considerable contribution to the resolution of disputes, resulting in a significant saving to the court system. Almost without exception the bodies who provide these mediation services are underfunded. This is not in the interest of their clients or of the Court Service. I recommend they are funded more appropriately. I would very much hope in any review of legal aid the need of bodies of this nature will be taken into account. In many situations, they provide the only way that the citizen can obtain access to justice, and in any event they may offer a better and less confrontational way of dealing with disputes between neighbours, where a continuing relationship is often important.[11]

Court-annexed or independent mediation?

In Australia and the USA there are several places where mediation is available in a court setting, as part of 'a multi-door courthouse'. The advantages of this arrangement are that disputants – or usually the first complainant – can come to the court and have a range of processes explained, and make a sensible choice. It means that many cases which might otherwise end up in court can be diverted on the spot. The disadvantage, however, is that sometimes this can lead to a very truncated process, where the mediation is very much 'settlement-driven' rather than 'process-driven', that is, focused on getting a settlement as quickly as possible, sometimes without consideration of all the issues. Sometimes, too, the formality of the court setting leads to mediation becoming just another formal process, even if it is not as formal as the full court hearing.

Another approach is to start from the other end, assuming the primacy of mediation in the community and legal action as an unfortunate necessity for the very few cases which cannot be resolved through mediation or which require a public judgment. This would presuppose a multi-purpose mediation and conflict resolution centre, based in the community, with trained mediators able to handle cases in all the different areas: community, family, victim/offender, consumer, environmental and so on. This scenario is included in one of the most recently published books on resolving disputes, in which the author points out the far-reaching social effects of such a switch from adversarial to co-operative values in resolving disputes.[12] There would, however, always be a role for a certain minimum of law, to lay down standards of right and wrong.

The advantage of independent mediation services is that they can preserve mediation as a process which can be adapted to the disputants and can take place in their own community. However, they may miss out on cases from the court which might otherwise come their way, because they are not attached to the courts. Lord Woolf opposes the institution of court-annexed ADR largely because independent mediation is already quite widely available.[13] Mediation UK agrees. Also, once the legal process has commenced, people feel that they have little option but to continue.

Similar discussions have taken place in the context of victim/offender mediation and of family mediation for some years. In the latter setting, there are often two agencies, one in-court mediation and the other an out-of-court independent family mediation service. The argument continues over the rival merits of court-based and independent mediation. Court-based mediation is available on the spot and, as a result, attracts referrals, but the process is often rushed and far from ideal. Independent mediation is a more considered process, but may miss out on referrals because of distance and being 'outside the system'. There is a place for both.

Future funding

Community mediation impinges on so many different local authority and national government departments that it has not been clear who should take responsibility. The result has been buck-passing between the Home Office (crime prevention, community safety), the Lord Chancellor's Department (legal aid, the courts) and the Department of the Environment (domestic noise). In addition, both the Department of Social Security and the Department of Health have also been approached for funding.

Two new developments offer ways forward.

Cost-effectiveness

It seems self-evident that mediation must save time and money but it is another matter to prove that this is the case, especially for neighbour disputes. Neighbour disputes can circulate through so many different departments that it is very difficult to put a figure on the time and money saved. For instance, the same neighbour dispute in various guises can surface through a complaint to the housing department, the environmental health department, the police, the local race equality council, the citizens advice bureau, or end up in the local magistrates' court or county court. It can also lead to disputes between different local authority departments, such as the housing department (which may want to evict a family) and social services (whose role is to ensure vulnerable families keep their accommodation).[14]

One of the first efforts at measuring cost-effectiveness was undertaken by Southwark Mediation Centre in London.[15] This analysed several cases and in one typical case showed that a neighbour dispute referred to them had already cost £395 in visits and calls from the police, the housing department, environmental services, race relations and an advice centre. If the dispute continued over a further year, it would have cost a further £655. The total cost over a year would be over £1,000. If mediation had been involved at the outset, at the approximate cost of £300 per case, this case would have saved over £700.

More recently Mediation UK has set up a cost-effectiveness research project, currently being undertaken by Sheffield University, jointly funded by the Lankelly Foundation and the Department of the Environment.[16] This research hopes to compare the cost of mediation and the cost of other processes used to resolve disputes, and also the cost of disputes which are allowed to continue without resolution. It will also cost the time involved, so that it can be estimated how far 'cost-effectiveness' depends on the use of volunteers and how far on the economies of the mediation process itself. The final report should be available in early 1996.

The importance of this research will go far beyond just 'proving' (or not, as the case may be) whether community mediation saves money. It will develop methods of measuring the costs of conflict and its resolution, in terms of both financial and human resources. These methods will have a wider application to many other kinds of mediation and conflict resolution, which may in turn develop from community mediation.

Legal Aid: Targeting Need

Almost simultaneously with the Woolf inquiry interim report, the Lord Chancellor published a green paper on legal aid.[17] This proposes among other things that there should be block funding from legal aid for a variety of non-legal services. There is no reason why mediation should not be one of the services supported in this way.[18] This would provide a possibility of funding local mediation services to take cases which would otherwise go to court. Mediation UK pointed out several features of mediation which make it amenable to block funding. First, its speed and simplicity make the costs easier to calculate. Second, block funding could make local services viable and then able to take on further work of different kinds of mediation. This viability would also help ensure high standards could be maintained.

The inclusion of mediation in the legal aid budget would be an additional cost to the current system; however, the cost of assisting mediation is relatively small and would save funds and time for the legal system as a whole as well as for other tax-supported bodies such as local authorities, the police and citizens' advice bureaux. Currently neighbour disputes consume vast amounts of agency time and funding. Legal aid would have a substantial role to play in ensuring the existence and stability of local mediation services. Legal aid funding should be available to provide part (up to 50 per cent) of the block contract funding for each local service, both where they exist and as they develop. This would ensure that mediation services can continue to offer a quick and simple method of resolving disputes; to provide a more effective solution in many cases than the legal system; and to keep inappropriate cases out of the court system. Other sources of local funding such as local authorities, housing and environmental health departments should also contribute as is currently the case. Mediation UK has suggested a pilot programme for local services, along similar lines to the one submitted to the Lord Chancellor in 1991.[19] Mediation UK also mentioned its own need for funds – to ensure smooth co-ordination of local services, and to continue its work in promoting mediation and developing accreditation programmes. A precedent was set for this with the Lord Chancellor's Department providing financial support to National Family Mediation for their accreditation programme.

These two strands show that there is a definite movement towards mediation, together with a realisation that if such a movement is to be encouraged, then there needs to be a way of paying for it. It is important that mediation services for neighbour disputes are free at the point of delivery, because otherwise neighbours will continue to use the free statutory adversarial complaints systems, with no encouragement to try another way.

Conclusion

Community mediation has moved swiftly from being an 'optional extra' alongside the legal system to being asked to take an ever-increasing proportion of neighbour and community disputes. It has gained ground rapidly because there is a felt need for it. The time has come to make more viable arrangements as a society, to ensure that mediation is freely available to all individuals and to all agencies working in the community.

There is already a growing network of independent community mediation services. Mediation UK believes that it should be extended. This network urgently needs recognition and long-term, stable, adequate funding; both national and local government have a role to play to ensure that this happens. With a relatively small input of resources, community mediation services will save time, money and heartache to many members of the community.

Acknowledgments

I would like to acknowledge the help and information received from several members of Mediation UK in preparing this paper.

Mediation UK can be contacted at 82a Gloucester Road, Bishopston, Bristol BS7 8BN, phone 0117 924 1234 and fax 0117 944 1387.

References

1 Mediation UK, *Mediation UK Practice Standards* (1993), *A Guide to Starting a Community Mediation Service* (1993), *Accreditation Pilot Scheme* (1993).
2 Institution of Environmental Health Officers, *Environmental Health Statistics 1992–93* (1994).
3 See D Hughes, *Environmental Law* (Butterworths, 1992).
4 S Farrant et al, *Managing Neighbour Complaints in Social Housing: A handbook for practitioners* (Aldbourne Associates, 1993), V Kahn et al, *Neighbour Disputes: Responses by social landlords* (Institute of Housing, 1993).

5 *Re D (minors) (conciliation: disclosure of information)* [1993] 2 All ER 693, CA.
6 *Guardian* 31 May 1994.
7 *Western Daily Press* 17 March 1995.
8 *Today* 27 April 1994.
9 National Consumer Council, *Civil Law and the Public* (1995).
10 Mediation UK, *Submission to Lord Woolf's Review of Access to Justice* (1995).
11 Para 18.21.
12 A F Acland, *Resolving Disputes Without Going to Court* (Century, 1995).
13 Para 18.30.
14 R Simpson, *Promise and Pragmatism: Community mediation in the nineties,* Mediation UK conference paper, 1992.
15 *Cost Savings through Mediation* (Southwark Mediation Centre, 1994).
16 See J Dignan et al, *First and Second Interim Reports on the Findings of the Community Mediation Service General Survey* (University of Sheffield, 1995).
17 *Legal Aid: Targeting Need* (HMSO, Cm 2854, 1995).
18 Mediation UK, *Submission on the Green Paper, Legal Aid: Targeting Need* (1995).
19 Mediation UK, *Submission to the Lord Chancellor's Department: Proposal for an experimental project for the diversion of civil court cases to community mediation schemes* (1991).

CHAPTER 8

Mediation: forming a view

ANNE GROSSKURTH

Anne Grosskurth, who has made a special study of the use of mediation in the United Kingdom and was LAG's policy officer from 1988 to 1995, looks at the issues that arise in relation to the introduction of mediation into domestic civil non-matrimonial proceedings.

A large amount of this book has concerned the development of techniques of alternative or appropriate dispute resolution in England and Wales and in the United States. This reflects its importance as a new development about which understanding is important and on which policy decisions must soon be taken.

Enormous claims are made for ADR. Over the past few years, enthusiasm for alternative dispute resolution in general, and mediation in particular, has grown at an astonishing rate. No sooner did the government's white paper on divorce extol mediation as the ideal constructive alternative to fighting out marriage breakdown with lawyers through the courts[1] than the legal aid green paper proposed diverting legal aid funds to mediators in other types of cases.[2] Hard on its heels came Lord Woolf's interim report on civil justice reform, in which an entire chapter is devoted to ADR, despite its absence from the original terms of reference. Although he stopped short of recommending a court-annexed system, Lord Woolf strongly endorsed the use of mediation as an alternative to litigation, and called for parties to be urged at an early stage to consider ADR.[3]

Strong support for ADR is also a central theme of the Labour Party's manifesto for reforming civil justice, approved at its annual conference in autumn 1995. This called for ADR's extension into areas beyond divorce, arguing:

> The benefits of mediation can be harnessed not only to allow more people to resolve their disputes more appropriately, but also to help change for the better the current culture of conflict resolution.[4]

The popularity of ADR among the legal profession is also rising, at least if the growing caseloads of, and demand for training from, the Centre for Dispute Resolution and the ADR Group can be relied on as an index. A spate of recent reports emanating from the legal profession has given serious consideration to ADR and exhorted practitioners to use it.[5] Working parties on ADR in the profession are currently investigating the field. Many long-time sceptics are taking the first tentative steps in trying out alternatives to litigating and conventional settlement. Local law societies, like that in Bristol, have instituted special educational, promotional and referral programmes to encourage members to make greater use of mediation. Much of the plenary session at the 1995 Bar conference, including the speeches by Lord Woolf and Lord Alexander, addressed barristers' concerns about ADR. An entire session was devoted to a simulated mediation and attracted more participants than any other. Over 200 City solicitors attended a special meeting on ADR in November 1995. Increasing numbers of solicitors are training as mediators, making their service available through the national ADR Net, which currently has over 300 members.

In the courts, there has also been some recognition of the benefit of ADR. A first official boost was given in early 1995 when the Lord Chief Justice published a practice direction (the 'checklist direction') which requires that parties in the Queen's Bench and Chancery Divisions show the court that alternatives like mediation have at least been considered.[6] A similar, albeit unofficial, directive was the subject of a brief experiment, known as the 'gold form scheme', in Bristol-area county courts for several months in 1994 and 1995. Parties in disputes before the Official Referee's Court and the Commercial Court have, for several years, been urged to consider alternatives to litigation.

A growing number of large multinational corporations stipulate in contracts that mediation should be used as the first step in resolving disputes. The Department of Health is piloting mediation in medical negligence cases in two regions. Local health authorities are experimenting with mediation in disputes between family practitioners and their patients. The recently-established Housing Association Ombudsman runs a mediation option for landlord and tenant disputes. An increasing number of education authorities are running peer mediation programmes in local schools to resolve bullying problems and conflict between students and teachers. Probation services for some years have been using mediation between victims and offenders with the aims of securing just reparation and rehabilitating offenders.

Environmental disputes, which might otherwise go to long and costly public inquiries, are instead being mediated. As leading independent mediator, Andrew Acland, told the 1995 conference of Mediation UK: 'We can no longer be regarded as a bunch of lunatics on the fringe. For the first time, there are real prospects of integrating mediation into the mainstream.'

ADR, then, has a considerable head of steam behind it, both in terms of support for it as an ideal and as a material practice. As can be seen from the two US contributions to this book, ADR has even greater momentum there than in the UK. With far worse problems of delay in the courts (see pp67 and 93) and with a no-costs rule that lessens the all-embracing value of winning a case, ADR has made enormous strides in terms of being incorporated within court procedures. Barbara Stedman's programme in Middlesex County just outside Boston, described in chapter 5, represents one of the most sophisticated attempts to integrate ADR within a trial court. Carrie Menkel-Meadow argues that proper incorporation of ADR into the court process offers the possibility of transformation of the nature of the litigation process (p100).

What should we make of such claims? Although research evidence is lacking, it seems quite possible that ADR has proved itself in both a community, almost a 'sub-legal', context and between certain commercial organisations. In addition, the best court-annexed ADR schemes in the United States, Barbara Stedman's Middlesex Multi-Door Courthouse among them, undoubtedly appear to lend an added value to the process of adjudication.

Examination of ADR is fraught with problems. Publication of the results of two major research projects is awaited in the United States (see p43). Previous reports on mediation or conciliation in matrimonial cases have, however, been notably ambiguous. A large study, funded by the Lord Chancellor's Department, reported in 1989 with some ambiguity that the establishment of a national conciliation service was 'a matter of political judgement'.[7] Its findings suggested that conciliation did generate certain 'important social benefits', on the one hand, but, on the other, 'involves positive resource costs'.

This chapter looks at one aspect of the ADR debate, the potential role of mediation. For this purpose, we can adopt the definition given by Barbara Stedman (p127). Mediation is 'a voluntary process in which a neutral third party assists the participants in resolving their dispute through a series of joint sessions and private caucuses'. As US interviewees told Roger Smith, mediation is the 'sleeping giant' of the civil justice system (in the words of Professor Frank Sander). As

North California's ADR suprema Stephanie Smith wryly commented, ADR is so important because 'people define it so broadly that everything is included' (p48). Indeed, one mediation can be very different from another. The concept includes a variety of techniques on a spectrum from 'facilitative', encouraging the parties to put forward their cases and to work out their own solutions in the mediation, and 'evaluative', with the mediator ultimately being unafraid to announce his/her own view on the parties' respective merits.

Caution

ADR in general, and mediation in particular, need considerably more examination and consideration than they have so far received to merit the unqualified support that now seems – somewhat unthinkingly – near universal. This is not to take a negative approach to ADR and mediation in principle. It is absolutely clear from the three contributions of ADR practitioners to this book that ADR and mediation can, in the right circumstances, have an enormous value. We need, however, to be very clear about the nature of those right circumstances.

Debate about the subject is hindered by the dearth of empirical research about mediation both in Britain and elsewhere. While small local studies on community mediation have been done, and research has begun on a national basis, there have been no thorough appraisals of the effectiveness of the process. We know little about the relative merits of outcomes in cases resolved by ADR as compared with litigation and conventional settlement. Without that evidence, assumptions about the value of mediation are based on largely anecdotal evidence, by reference to work on quite distinct areas like family mediation, or on work done elsewhere like Australia or the United States.

The absence of serious research reinforces what has been largely uncritical enthusiasm for the process. Studies, like the recent *Law in Action*/National Consumer Council survey,[8] may well show that many people would prefer to settle disputes amicably around a table than by going to court. But it is essential for people to realise precisely what mediation involves, what its limitations are, and what its appropriateness to given disputes is, before such results can be regarded as an unqualified public endorsement of mediation.

Proponents of mediation in Britain have a disturbing tendency to generalise. Are there two sides to every story in every case? What about the illegally-evicted tenant whose landlord has violated the provisions of Housing Acts? What about an employee who has not been paid according to contract? Generalisation also extends to client groups: if mediation works well for corporate executives represented by top solicitors, say ADR enthusiasts, might it not be equally effective for poor tenants in dispute with institutional landlords? If mediation has a good track record in clearing up disagreements between quarrelling neighbours, could that experience not be replicated in resolving other types of disputes in many other areas?

Two worlds

Discussion about mediation in England is often confused by conflating the experiences of two different spheres – mediation for the well-off and mediation for the poor. On the one hand, there are the wealthy corporate commercial bodies or disputants with the means to pay privately for dispute resolution. Many are served by mediators referred by CEDR, by the ADR Group or the national network of lawyer-mediators, ADR Net, for up to £1,000 a day. Such parties may have considerable knowledge of the issues in dispute and the wherewithal to get expert advice and representation. Many such disputes have a substantial legal element. For such disputants, and the lawyers who advise them, mediation truly is an alternative to the courts or to the conventional settlement process that happens in some 94 per cent of cases. The merits of court-mandated mediation are particularly relevant to these disputants.

By contrast, there is the far greater number of ordinary people with disputes arising from everyday problems of personal and social life – neighbour nuisance, particularly noise, boundary disputes and insulting behaviour, bullying at school, poor communication with doctors or arguments with landlords. While there are some common issues – how should mediators be trained, accredited and regulated, for example – there are specific questions arising from the two areas. Should volunteers drawn from the community be relied on to mediate in disputes involving their neighbours? Should limited discovery be allowed in complex business dispute mediations?

As Marian Liebmann's chapter makes clear, much of the growth in alternative dispute resolution over the past ten years has been in services providing mediation in social and personal disputes, many of which serve only council tenants by virtue of their location and funding. It is mediation for poorer people involved in essentially non-legal disputes and without the means to take cases to court or get legal advice. Community mediation services provide not so much an alternative to the courts – most of the disputes dealt with would not go to court in any event – but alternatives to doing nothing, to letting disputes fester and escalate. Certainly, some disputes with neighbours do end up in the courts. Marian Liebmann provides some shocking examples. But in neighbour disputes, cases are more likely to end up in the magistrates' court if an injunction is sought by the local authority or if, as happens not infrequently, one of the parties becomes aggressive and assaults the neighbours.

Mediation: the key issues

At this stage of the development of mediation, the appropriate response seems neither to dismiss it out of hand, a knee-jerk reaction to something new, nor to welcome it as the answer to all the problems of the civil justice system. Lord Woolf may well have struck the right note in welcoming ADR while taking a 'wait and see' attitude. As the contributions to this book make clear, mediation is still a young movement. It has existed in this country for little more than a decade. There is a danger that changes to legal aid might mean that ADR schemes become a way of diverting poor people's cases which should be heard in the courts away from them. In these circumstances, the way forward lies in careful examination of issues raised by mediation. We need to identify those issues and to work out solutions. We should not rush into over-eager implementation of any particular scheme. Addressing these questions will require properly considered and resourced pilot programmes.

The key questions in mediation appear to be the ten following points. For those concerned primarily with the poor or legally aided litigant, the first two have particular importance.

(1) Do weaker parties suffer?
Some critics argue that imbalances of power and resources may be exacerbated in mediation, even in the community mediation field where most parties are relatively equal in circumstances. The more articulate or assertive party will have the upper hand in getting the settlement terms which it desires. This is an issue which needs careful research. It is, of course, likely that weaker parties suffer in litigation anyway. Weaker parties may benefit from the greater ease with which they are able to tell their story and make their demands in a more

informal setting than that provided in a court. Courts would certainly have to ensure that mediation services were of the 'high quality' required as one the 'points of agreement' identified by the Federal Judicial Center in the United States (p47). This might well mean that the multi-door courthouse model of in-house provision provides the best way of implementing a court-annexed service.

(2) To what extent can two-tier justice be avoided?

There must be a real danger of a two-tier system of justice developing under a system in which legally-aided parties have no choice but to use mediation while privately-paying parties can afford the option of litigating through a state-funded civil justice system. The undoubted benefits that mediation can bring in some disputes arise precisely because the parties want to participate in solving their problems. If mediation is to be introduced into the domestic legal system, then a pre-condition must be that all parties, including those who are legally aided, have a genuine choice and give their genuine consent to participation.

Consideration would have to be given to the practicalities of implementing one of the other measures on which the Federal Judicial Center found clear agreement: 'The outcomes of court-based ADR procedures, particularly mandatory procedures, must be non-binding and must preserve access to trial without penalty, unless the parties voluntarily agree to a binding outcome' (see p47). For legally aided litigants, this requires that mediation be an additional process, acceptance of which has no effect on entitlement to legal aid, ie, the litigant could continue with the case if the mediation process proved unsuccessful. This means, of course, that cost savings may still be made as the result of litigants' choice but, equally, that some cases might cost more if mediation failed and litigation recommenced.

Notice must also be taken of the view reported by Roger Smith (p49) that mediation and ADR provide alternatives to courts, not to lawyers. Many in the field argue that lawyers should be retained during mediation and, indeed, it should be noted that lack of legal representation was regarded as a contra-indicator of suitability for mediation by at least some experienced US ADR practitioners.

(3) What is the right sphere of mediation?

It is frequently argued that mediation is unsuitable for some disputes and in certain circumstances. Medical negligence, public interest and multi-party actions, racial harassment and domestic violence are sometimes cited as examples of cases which should be resolved through the courts rather than mediation. However, experience in the United States and to a lesser extent in Britain suggests that there are some cases in these areas that are amenable to mediation.

The brief experience in Britain under the Department of Health pilot schemes suggests that mediation in medical negligence cases is considerably cheaper and faster than the typically protracted and exorbitantly expensive court proceedings in such cases. However, a fuller assessment awaits the results of monitoring now being undertaken and outcomes in a greater number of cases. Mediation has never been a popular option for medical negligence plaintiffs in the United States because of the need for expert reports and large quantities of complex documentary evidence.

Groups like the Newham Conflict and Change Project in east London are mediating cases in which racial harassment is deemed to be at a relatively low level – insulting behaviour and cultural misunderstanding. Any cases in which violence is threatened or carried out are passed to the police. Ethnic and racial disputes in the United States have been dealt with through mediation since the late 1960s under the aegis of the Justice Department's Community Relations Service.[9]

The British organisation Environmental Resolve offers mediation through 'consensus building' in multi-party environmental disputes. Such an approach is an alternative not to litigation but to a public inquiry – an equally long and expensive process. In the United States, several major environmental cases have been successfully resolved through mediation, including the siting of the Storm King Dam on the Hudson River and the development of Environmental Protection Act rules on clean air. Rather than removing such cases from public view, the American Federal process appears to have ensured that a far greater range of interests are represented than would otherwise be the case.[10]

There may be dangers that some terms of mediated settlements are of wide public interest – changes in hospital practice, for example – and are not fully aired or disclosed by virtue of the confidentiality of mediation. The proposed answer of some, notably the National Consumer Council, to this problem – a public register of mediation agreements – seems impracticable. Such issues need further thorough consideration.

(4) Does mediation disguise responsibility for some disputes?

By focusing on grievances between two people, mediation may deflect attention from the more fundamental source of the dispute.

Neighbour noise disputes on council estates often have much to do with inadequate soundproofing, disrepair or misjudged allocation. Mediators have told LAG about problems of mediating in cases where black tenants have been housed in largely white estates, with little support from social services or housing departments. 'One of the limits of mediation', Andrew Acland told the last annual conference of Mediation UK, 'is the sticking-plaster effect, keeping the lid on conflict. You end up with everyone in a block of flats wearing ear-muffs rather that getting the council to soundproof the building.'

Again, the policy implication is that mediation may be unsuitable for some types of case, particularly where there is no back-up from an agency like a law centre or CAB which might help in solving the problem for *all* the affected parties.

(5) Are important legal problems overlooked?

There must be fears that legally unqualified mediators taking an impartial role may fail to identify critically important legal aspects of a dispute. Even in apparently non-legal disputes like those over neighbour noise, there may be legal aspects or remedies which will go unrecognised unless informed legal advice is also available. The employment of lawyers as mediators, as in the Middlesex Multi-Door Courthouse, might go some way to prevent this. So too would legal representation throughout the mediation. This is, after all, what happens in most commercial mediations.

(6) Is mediation antithetical to the enforcement of rights?

Mediation has been criticised for militating against the enforcement of rights. Where people are up against a hostile landlord, employer or spouse, there is arguably an urgent need for someone to champion their case. As a Liverpool solicitor wrote to *The Guardian* in October 1995, 'If you have a problem, you want somebody on your side, not somebody in the middle.' This objection could, to some extent, be met by ensuring that mediation follows an evaluative model, ie, reflects an objective legal position, rather than a facilitative one, simply allowing the parties to negotiate in the light of subjective assessments of their cases. Legal representation and lawyer mediators would also help in this regard.

(7) Are untrained, unsupervised and unregulated mediators dangerous?

The answer to this question is clearly 'yes'. There are insufficient controls over the training and supervision of mediators, despite the efforts of groups like CEDR, the ADR Group and Mediation UK. The quality of mediation services may be variable and unpredictable. Anyone can hang a shingle outside the front door advertising mediation services. There is no protection for parties and no redress for dissatisfied disputants against incompetent mediators. These issues would have to be addressed if mediation were to be incorporated within a court-annexed service. So too would related matters, such as duties of confidentiality.

(8) Are there forms of alternative dispute resolution, not recognised as such, which are more appropriate for some disputes and which ought to be developed further?

There has been a trend over recent years to establish ombudsman schemes in an increasing number of areas – particularly in the financial service sector. The long-standing Local Government Ombudsman has been joined by the Housing Association and Legal Services Ombudsmen among others. By offering the potential of thorough, independent investigation of disputes between ordinary people and professionals or large institutions, ombudsmen have established a commendable record in dispute resolution and probably offer the best alternative to litigation or other forms of ADR for many types of disputes. The Housing Association Ombudsman is unique in offering complainants a range of dispute resolution methods including arbitration, adjudication or mediation.

The model of dealing with complaints by way of an internal complaints procedure and an external ombudsman has proved its worth and should be encouraged. In this context, persistent rumours of potential attacks on the Local Government Ombudsman by a government-appointed investigation are worrying.[11] The role of ombudsmen has developed from a concern with administration to a form of arbitration linked with an investigative procedure. This is desirable, provided that the courts retain an overall supervisory jurisdiction.

(9) Mediation may provide an alternative to courts, but to what extent does it provide an alternative to lawyers?

This is, in many ways, the crucial question. Matrimonial legislation introduced in the 1995–96 parliamentary session envisages the transfer of legal aid funds to mediators in divorce cases. The government's green paper on legal aid suggests legally aided mediation in a wider range of cases. Yet it is the clear lesson, both from the United States and commercial use of ADR in this country, that mediation and other

ADR techniques work best if the parties retain legal representation and thus engage in ADR fully informed of their legal rights and well within, in a famous phrase, 'the shadow of the law'. The availability of legal representation may help to allay fears about the likely fairness of the process. The US experience reinforces the view that mediation is no substitute for legal advice and representation.

(10) What can be said definitively about mediation without proper research?

Very little. The United States is yet to receive the results of two major research projects on ADR by the RAND Institute and the Federal Judicial Center (see p47). Roger Smith's observation on the United States is that mediation, like ADR as a whole, is, as yet, within the 'pre-institutional charismatic phase' (see p49). The success of ADR may still be critically dependent on the skills, personality and enthusiasm of individual neutrals and the directors of programmes.

Conclusion

Mediation presents considerable opportunities for a quicker, more accessible and sometimes cheaper alternative to litigation and conventional settlement. Work in the ADR field, both in the UK and in the United States, has highlighted the value of resolving disputes through mediation. However, it is essential to recognise the possible limitations and dangers of the process – particularly for poor and legally aided disputants. Thoroughly assessed pilot programmes are essential. We need to know considerably more about the operation of mediation in different types of legal disputes, and for different client groups, before any new national or mandatory programmes are introduced.

The government's intention to divert divorcing couples to mediation may yet show the dangers of acting before adequately piloting. In any event, it will be an important testing-ground for the use of mediation in legal disputes affecting a great many people. Caution is essential: this will be *family* mediation and lessons from such schemes should not be applied too readily to other areas.

Above all, it must be recognised that mediation does not offer easy savings. If properly implemented, with good systems of regulation, training and accreditation, it may even be more expensive, in the early stages at least. Neither is it a cheap substitute for expert legal advice and representation. And to have the radical, transformational role claimed by supporters like Carrie Menkel-Meadow, mediation must remain voluntary. It must be a participative, consensual process which empowers litigants rather than diminishes their options. In practice, these considerations may considerably reduce its attractions for government.

References

1 Lord Chancellor's Department *Looking to the Future: mediation and the grounds for divorce – the government's proposals* (HMSO, Cm 2799, 1995) pp39–43.
2 See in particular paras 7.12(iii), 7.15 and 7.18.
3 Report, chapter 18.
4 Labour Party, *Access to Justice: Labour's proposals for reforming the civil justice system* (1995), p6.
5 H Brown, *Alternative dispute resolution* (A report prepared for the Courts and Legal Services Committee of the Law Society, 1991); General Council of the Bar, *Committee on Alternative Dispute Resolution: Report of the Rt Hon Lord Justice Beldam* (1991); General Council of the Bar and the Law Society, *Civil Justice on Trial: The case for change*, Independent working party of the General Council of the Bar and the Law Society (The Heilbron-Hodge report, 1993).
6 *Practice Note (civil litigation: case management)* [1995] 1 WLR 262, checklist paras 10–12.
7 University of Newcastle-upon-Tyne, *Report to the Lord Chancellor on the Costs and Effectiveness of Conciliation in England and Wales* (1989), para 20.48.
8 National Consumer Council, *Seeking Civil Justice: a survey of people's needs and experiences* (1995).
9 L Singer et al, 'Alternative Dispute Resolution for the Poor: What ADR processes exist and why advocates should become involved', *Clearinghouse Review* (vol 26, No2) May/June 1992, p143.
10 Ibid, pp142 and 150.
11 See, eg, January 1996 *Legal Action* 4.

CHAPTER 9

Changing priorities

ROGER SMITH

A common thread of argument runs through all the contributions to this book. The problems of civil justice cannot be narrowly defined as 'cost, complexity and delay' and solved by reform of court procedure. This is not only because such an attempt denies any question of inadequate access to justice, as argued in the first chapter. It is also inherently illogical, for reasons to which Carrie Menkel-Meadow refers in considering the work of the American scholar, George Priest (p99). Solutions to the three problems in the official litany could well prove to be contradictory. Bringing down cost is likely to increase volume rather than decrease delay, which may well find its own equilibrium not far from the present position. This phenomenon could well prove to be the undoing of Lord Woolf's proposed 'fast track'. If this is successful, it might bring into the court system a whole range of litigation where currently the parties consider it uneconomic to take this course of action. This, as Carrie Menkel-Meadow suggests, could increase access to justice (though whether it is the poor that will seek to take advantage of the opportunity rather than commercial interests might be doubtful), but as likely a result is that it would ultimately bring the procedure into disrepute as the fast track slows under the weight of work.

The approach espoused by the Civil Justice Review and Lord Woolf's Inquiry is just not fundamental enough. A much broader vision is required, both in the analysis of the underlying problems and their solutions. What is the most effective way of dealing with the kind of civil disputes that are unavoidable in a complex modern society, particularly as they are likely to be experienced by the poor who are unable to buy the kind of tailor-made, private solutions provided by sophisticated alternative dispute resolution that extend, at least in California, to being able to 'rent-a-judge'?

As a way of widening an appreciation of what is to be done, it might be helpful to adopt the presentational technique of the long-range planning documents produced in the United States (p35). Let us follow the Committee on Long Range Planning of the Judicial Conference of the United States and present two scenarios, the good and the bad, for the future, as imagined (a little less ambitiously) in the year 2006. Even by this time, the information revolution will no doubt have developed in ways currently unimaginable. For this purpose, which is to prepare the ground for a discussion of contemporary policy options for civil justice, imagination has been restricted to the level of technology and innovation already available, much of which is described in the report on developments in North America (chapter 2).

A vision of 2006

It is 2006. A young woman has problems. She has broken her leg in a road accident; cannot watch television because her newly installed satellite dish fell down in a gale and the installer will not put it back; thinks she has been wrongly dismissed from her last job; cannot get her local authority to provide what she thinks is adequate assistance to her elderly father; and is seeking to join with other fellow sufferers to challenge the drug company who distributed pills to which she has, until lately, become addicted. Faced with this composite of potential civil disputes, she may well despair; but there are options in the resources that government policy can place at her disposal.

In the optimistic version, the woman has some background of understanding. She took law as part of the national curriculum while at school. Like a student in today's British Columbia, she had attended two courts and participated in a mock trial. From her own computer or that in the local public library or her local court, she can access a vast array of material developed by the Court Service and what is now the Lord Chancellor's Department. This includes interactive video presentations of courts and court procedures, using an approach recognisably developed from North Communication's QuickCourt (p41). She can also access material on law and procedure, using hypertext on-line similar to that available in Arizona today (p39). She uses the court-based small-claims procedure successfully to obtain redress against the satellite dish installer. She found the official leaflets helpful and was able to obtain copies from her local court because the numbers in stock were continuously monitored by computer so that replacements were provided whenever needed. More generally, she was aware of some of the background issues about courts and their alternatives as a reader of newspapers and watcher of television. She had seen coverage of several recent reports by the Judicial Commission on developments such as alternative dispute resolution.

For those of her problems that she does not feel that she can handle herself, she consults the court or locally-based advice service, being referred to a lawyer for her personal injury, community care and product liability litigation. A specialist lay adviser helps her through the industrial tribunal hearing of her unfair dismissal case. The personal injury action proceeds relatively easily under the now well-established fast-track procedure, though the idea of a court-appointed expert had led to too much secondary litigation and been replaced by the less ambitious reform of open disclosure of all communications with each party's expert (p73). She had attended an ADR screening session and opted to proceed with an attempted mediation involving the other parties to the dispute, including the insurer, which was assisted by the presence of her own lawyer funded by legal aid. This was unsuccessful in resolving the whole dispute, though it had isolated the one issue in contention which went forward for determination.

Both the community care and product liability litigation had been assisted by information which would previously have been the subject of complicated discovery provisions but was obtained from publicly available sources provided under the Freedom of Information Act. The community care dispute is still awaiting the decision of an independent administrative tribunal on the reasonableness of the local authority's refusal. The product liability case is being taken within a class action against the manufacturer. It had been certified as such by the judge allocated to its management and received finance from the special fund allocated for such cases by the Legal Aid Board, resembling the equivalent provisions in Quebec (see p54). It is due for hearing soon in what had been the Queen's Bench Division of the High Court and is now a specialist division of the unified court structure, though it will be heard by a Category 1 judge, the highest tier of the first-instance judiciary.

There is, of course, an alternative future. The young woman has received no education in law during her schooling and does not know where to start with her problems. New technology has been installed in the courts, but only to assist lawyers, judges and administrators. Advice provision in her area is virtually non-existent. She did go to the court and her library for help, but both had run out of the relevant leaflets. She loses her industrial tribunal case because she is unrepresented against the Queen's Counsel who is acting for her multinational former employer. It cost her £200 to get the satellite dish put up again, but this is less expensive than the court fee for issuing small claims proceedings and having an arbitration hearing. She gets legal aid for the personal injury case, but is then required to attend mediation without her lawyer. In this session she is persuaded to accept a settlement well below the going rate in court. There is no appeal against the decision of the council about her father: the head of social services agreed that he needed help but said that he had no funds left to provide it. She consulted a lawyer, but the relevant statute made it clear that this decision was perfectly legal. The drug case fizzles out when the Legal Aid Board refuses funding on the ground that it would be too expensive. As a citizen without large means, she feels alienated from the legal system. It has little to offer her. She does not know, nor really care, that in fact judges decide very few civil cases because of the pressure of criminal work. The consequent delays in deciding litigation do not really bother her, as she was not involved in any.

Recommendations

From these contrasting tales, ten propositions may be derived.

(1) The policy objectives of the Lord Chancellor's Department must be widened

The adoption of modern management techniques by government has bequeathed a plethora of goals set out in a hierarchical structure in a strategic plan and repeated in a variety of subsequent documents, including the annual report of the 'Lord Chancellor's Department Court Service'.[1] These appear to be an uncontroversial, and indeed unpolitical, statement of goals. Their selection, however, necessarily involves the making of choices which are, at least implicitly, political in the widest sense. As such, they need to receive consideration and debate. Those currently in place are far too limited and betray too narrow an imagination in relation to what could be done.

The current pyramid of goals for the department begins with a fundamental aim ('to ensure the efficient and effective administration of justice at an affordable cost'); proceeds through a 'strategic priority' (keeping cost down); goes through six 'guiding principles' (including the somewhat mystifying 'to ensure openness, subject only to exceptions necessary to protect individuals and the public interest') and ends up with six 'key challenges'. By this time, the goals take on much of the flavour, and usefulness, of professing to be against sin and for motherhood and apple-pie. Nevertheless, a point can be made by examining the wording of these 'key challenges':

- 'to ensure access to justice while reducing its cost to the parties and the taxpayer';
- 'to sustain improvements in the quality, efficiency and effectiveness of the courts';
- 'to gain control of the overall cost of legal aid while ensuring an adequate level of publicly funded services related to solving legal problems and disputes';
- 'to support improvements in the appointment and training of the judiciary';
- 'to develop a range of policies which contribute to the protection of the rights of the individual, the family and property and, where appropriate, to support these policies with an effective law reform process';
- 'to build structures and mechanisms, within planned levels of re-sources, to enable the Department to meet its key challenges and carry out its other functions'.[2]

Linked to the first two 'key challenges' are the Court Service's five 'objectives':

- 'to enable parties to resolve their disputes more speedily';
- 'to adapt and simplify court procedures to optimise access to justice';
- 'to ensure that the distribution of courts and centres for resolving disputes allows for optimal access to justice';
- 'to meet Court Service operational standards and the targets pub-lished in the Courts Charter';
- 'to control costs in the Court Service'.[3]

On reflection, this list of goals presents some difficulty. For ex-ample, both use the phrase 'access to justice' without definition, rais-ing problems discussed earlier (p19). Some have a positively Orwellian ring. For instance, as we have seen, there is no improvement in the county courts' efficiency to sustain: what Garry Watson calls 'court-based delay' (p67) is getting worse (p11). The provision of courts by the Court Service to provide 'optimal access to justice' appears to justify a programme of closure of the smaller courts (see p11).

The kind of general goals that would be set by an administration that accepted the argument of this book would be as follows:

- to seek the attainment of an equal access to justice by all members and interests within society;
- to attack the barriers to such access that arise from exclusion and excessive cost, complexity and delay;
- to adopt an approach which integrates court policy with that in other relevant areas, such as legal aid, advice and education;
- to provide a democratic framework for the appointment of a high-quality, independent and properly resourced judiciary whose members are as representative as possible of the population as a whole;
- to provide a system for the adjudication of civil disputes which is based on the needs of the parties concerned and not those of lawyers, other representatives or the judiciary and which provides appropriate types of adjudication and remedy at an appropriate level of cost for different types of disputes;
- to take account in considering any court reform, including the imposition of charges, both of the interests of parties and the public at large in their determination;
- to ensure through the provision of legal aid, advice and education that no dispute is decided by the comparative wealth, power and privilege of one party as against another; and
- to ensure that the operation of civil justice is properly monitored and researched and, in particular, that any proposed reform has been adequately considered and, if necessary, piloted, before implementation.

In such a listing, the control of costs would not be listed as a policy objective in itself but seen as a restriction on the means to be deployed.

(2) There must be better provision of adequate advice, information and legal services, using the full range of possible ways in which provision of assistance may be made

The Lord Chancellor and the Courts Service need to consider the full consequences of the changes that have been, and are being, made in the intended role of publicly funded legal services over the last decade as eligibility has slumped for both legal advice and legal aid. The consequences of a fundamental restructuring need to be understood.

It is no longer, even in theory, possible to argue that the function of legal aid is, as announced by the Lord Chancellor's Department in 1948:

to provide legal advice for those of slender means and resources so that no one will be financially unable to prosecute a just and reasonable claim or defend a legal right . . .[4]

Support for this formula was repeated by the Royal Commission on Legal Services in 1979:

> Financial assistance out of public funds should be available for every individual who, without it, would suffer an undue financial burden in properly pursuing or defending his legal rights.[5]

The government's 1995 green paper calls explicitly for 'a different approach . . . to restructure the scheme throughout'.[6] The first principle of the consequent brave new world of legal aid is that 'funds must be targeted on needs and priorities'.[7] This is a euphemism for rationing. The government proposes the cash-limiting of available resources and their distribution to legal aid providers who will ration services accordingly.

In fact, the change proposed in the green paper makes clearer the *de facto* situation that has developed because of eligibility cuts (see p4). Potential litigants are manifestly now being excluded from access to justice because they cannot afford to pay privately, and yet legal aid will pay neither for their legal advice nor their court actions. As one might predict, it is the advice sector that is best placed to monitor the consequences of these policies. A recent report from the National Association of Citizens' Advice Bureaux (NACAB) quotes a list of the kind of cases now being picked up by the citizens' advice bureaux around the country, eg: 'a CAB in Essex reported a client who was involved in a serious accident at work, and as a result spent eight weeks in intensive care. The Health and Safety Executive were expected to prosecute the employer. The client did not qualify financially for legal aid, and could not afford to pay a solicitor to start proceedings, so had decided not to pursue his claim.'[8]

This case graphically illustrates the imbalance between criminal proceedings, which were expected to be taken, and civil proceedings, from which the client was excluded because of poverty. It also hints perhaps at the kind of lateral solution that might be possible for some types of case in an age when funds are limited. The problem would be solved if it was routine for the Health and Safety Executive to combine the civil claim with the criminal prosecution. A successful prosecution could then lead to an award of compensation to the victim of the accident equal to the damages that might be received in civil litigation and an award of costs sufficient to cover the Executive's total expenditure. If this was the case, then the divisions between criminal and civil proceedings would break down. We need to look more closely at the benefits of establishing representative enforcement agencies that can not only take on the public burden of pursuing criminal proceedings but also seek compensation for individuals aggrieved. Indeed, in France, the victim of many crimes becomes a 'civil party' in the prosecution and the court expects to deal with compensation at the same time as sentence.

We have to face up to the consequences if governments are to run down eligibility for civil legal aid so that it can no longer guarantee sufficient advice, assistance and representation to the poor. In a variety of ways, courts will have to play a greater role than previously in helping litigants. It was precisely this lack of affordable legal assistance that encouraged the courts of Arizona to take the initiatives detailed in chapter 2 (p38). Courts must reconsider their services from the point of view of the litigants in person who will become an increasingly important proportion of their customers. This means examining their practices on the assumption that lawyers or other intermediaries will not be involved. The consequences, as in Arizona, may be dramatic. They should also be widespread, beginning with court procedure and going far beyond, as in the suggestion of broadening the role of enforcement agencies above.

First, courts are going to have to re-orientate themselves to the caller in person. Courts must have, as NACAB recommended in its recent report on 'barriers to justice', 'an information desk where both personal callers and people making telephone inquiries can obtain accurate advice and information on court procedures.'[9]

Second, courts are going to have to produce accessible information in written and other forms. Some current leaflets are of a reasonably high standard, such as that on pursuing a small claim. However, courts tend to be unevenly effective in distributing and displaying such documents. The computer-tracking of stock introduced in British Columbia provides a model to be followed (p41). Furthermore, the value of interactive video material has been proved in the United States (p41). It is time for a domestic pilot of the same sort of service aimed at the individual litigant.

Third, there needs to be more integration of advice provision into the courts. In-court provision of independent advice in the form of a duty scheme for certain types of case was recommended by the Civil Justice Review. Lord Woolf repeated the proposal in his interim report: 'There should be a duty advice scheme funded by legal aid at each of the courts identified as handling substantial levels of debt and housing work.'[10] So there should. Indeed, some busy courts should extend duty schemes, available only at specific times when certain types of cases are heard, into court-based provision, like that in the Royal Courts of Justice and a handful of county courts, which is more widely accessible.

Fourth, more needs to be done to provide physical access to the courts if there are to be more litigants in person. The Court Service should accept NACAB's recommendation that it introduce 'a comprehensive improvements programme and where necessary, alternative arrangements to make services accessible to disabled people on equal terms, to ensure that all court services are made fully accessible to disabled people by 2000.'[11] The CAB service also correctly asked for the 'power and resources' to be given to county courts 'to appoint interpreters, including sign-language interpreters, to service in cases'.[12]

Fifth, the issue of fee remission and reduction has to be taken seriously. This is particularly important as the Court Service moves to increase fees sharply in order to cover the full cost of the courts, a policy which should be reversed (see p23). If, however, fees are raised substantially, as planned, then detailed means-testing rules become unavoidable unless additional financial barriers to justice are to be condoned. The present County Court Rules illogically allow fee exemption only for recipients of some means-tested benefits.[13] This should be extended to all benefits, in particular including family credit. A more structured approach should be taken to fee remission and reduction than the current discretion in the event of 'undue hardship'. This is unsatisfactorily vague. In addition, NACAB's recommendation on publicity should be implemented: 'an application for fee remission should be included on the request for summons, and notices about fee remission should be prominently displayed at all courts'.[14]

Sixth, court documents have to be examined from the point of view of the needs of litigants in person. This is not just to ensure that they are written in plain English. Courts and judges could learn a lot from the experience of tribunals in, for instance, the notification of decisions. Model rules from the Council of Tribunals suggest that tribunals should produce written decisions with written reasons. The practice of the Independent Tribunal Service has become to use a form which records evidence submitted and findings of fact as well. This both helps the parties to understand what the tribunal has decided and why. This is good practice for the decision-makers just as much as it is helpful to the decision-receivers.

Finally, and in a wider context, the need for integration of funding and procedure must be better recognised. One example where this is clear is in is the experience of various Canadian provinces in class or multi-party actions (see pp51–59). For almost a decade, our domestic legal system has struggled with an approach in which consideration of these has been divided (see p28). Some adaptation of the Quebec approach seems desirable. This has produced a procedure in which the equivalent of a Legal Aid Board deals with decisions on funding and a judge handles issues about the nature of the litigation. LAG hopes to return in detail to this issue, but the general lines of any solution to the problems of litigation is clear. There must be an approach which provides such a link and which administers legal aid with the greater flexibility required to meet the specific requirements of this kind of action. Another example is provided by the link between small claims cases and legal aid. The merits test for the latter should be regarded as automatically met where a case is transferred out of the small claims procedure because it is too complicated or otherwise unsuitable.

(3) There should be a review of the operation of the costs rules
Litigants may find that one of a number of different rules apply in relation to their potential liability for the costs of their opponents. The impact of the 'indemnity cost rule' is another issue that requires examination unless legal aid eligibility is to be restored to previous levels. Prospective liability for a double set of costs, one's own and one's opponent's, is a major barrier to justice. The approach of the United States, where civil legal aid has always been available on a very restricted basis, has been to rely on generating adequate access to justice by a combination of contingency fees to meet the litigant's own costs and to avoid having a general liability for opponent's costs. The British government has moved significantly towards the introduction of the first part of this package by allowing conditional fees. The latter now needs consideration.

The principle of proportionality in costs accepted by Lord Woolf, ie, that size of costs should rise and fall with the seriousness of the case, must be right. There are problems in how to implement this fairly. For instance, both the introduction of a fast-track procedure and the extended small claims procedure may increase the power of wealthy litigants against poor ones because they may well be willing to spend more on a case than they can recover in costs from the losing party simply to get their way. There is no easy way of stopping this, but it may be that the limit on costs should apply to the successful litigators as well as the losing parties, ie, the legal representatives would face the same limit on what they could charge the successful party who is their client. This would not inhibit a large organisation with an in-house litigation facility, like a government department or a major commercial company, but it might prevent some of the power imbalance otherwise likely.

The government considered the position of costs in small claims when it extended this jurisdiction from £1,000 to £3,000 on 8 January 1996. The full rigour of the rule was to continue to be mitigated. Small claims litigants are liable for a maximum of £200 for expert's fees and, in cases relating to injunctions, specific relief or similar cases, a maximum in legal costs of £260.[15] The extension of the small claims limit in this way was opposed by many housing practitioners and the Law Society. The chair of the Law Society's civil litigation committee argued: 'The changes to the small claims procedure will worsen the imbalance of power between tenants and their landlords – and could give an unfair advantage to landlords in the courts.'[16] Such a result would, presumably, be regretted by Lord Mackay who professed his intention in making the change to be his belief that 'This increase in the small claims limit will be of great benefit to litigants who wish to bring straightforward claims in this less formal and less costly forum'.[17] He has made no public estimate of the savings to be made to legal aid nor, indeed, publicly acknowledged that there will be any. It may, therefore, be that this formed no part of his motivation in implementing this one recommendation of Lord Woolf's report before any of the others. Costs in small claims cases can now amount to significant amounts. The daily fee for attendance by a witness can be £50. Thus, a one-day case may well cost over £500, if lost. Many small claims litigants do not realise their potential costs liability. It is time to consider whether legal aid should be available in certain circumstances to cover such costs, much the same as presumably it will be for fast-track cases.

This rule change should be examined after, say, two years to examine its effect. It may have widened access, as Lord Mackay hopes. In this case, it should be regarded a success. On the other hand, it may have the consequences feared by the Law Society and LAG. If so, there should be a reconsideration of returning to a lower small claims limit for injunction and specific performance cases, particularly those which relate to housing disrepair.

Such a review of the incidence of costs could encompass other issues. It may be that some forms of litigation, say environmental actions taken in the public interest, should be exempt from the indemnity costs rule and perhaps also able to benefit from a provision that granted legal aid without contribution in such cases. Lord Woolf has himself raised the issue of whether legal aid should pay the costs of successful unassisted litigants.[18] So too does the green paper on legal aid.[19] These issues also could be swept up into a general inquiry into costs.

(4) The advantages and disadvantages of alternative dispute resolution, and in particular court-annexed mediation, should be properly researched

It must be recognised that the introduction of ADR, if properly done, will offer no savings of government resources and may, in fact, be more expensive than current practice. See chapter 8.

(5) The courts should be brought within a unified structure, possibly incorporating tribunals as well

Lord Woolf has, perhaps understandably, stepped somewhat gingerly around one of the most obvious ways to simplify civil proceedings: the elimination of unnecessary distinctions between different courts. History is strewn with similar failures to make fundamental reform of the fundamental structure of the courts. The Civil Justice Review recorded the failure of the Judicature Commissioners to see through their proposal for annexing the county courts to the High Court made in 1872.[20] In the course of its own consultation exercise, it was forced to renege on its own proposals for amalgamation (issued in a paper on general issues) by judicial opposition to loss of status. Its final report puts the case for a unified civil court: 'it would enable judge power to be allocated to cases on an ideally flexible basis'.[21] A unified court would divide cases between judges at three levels – the equivalent of High Court, circuit and district judges – rather than between two levels of separately administered courts.

The logic of this proposal is such that Lord Woolf cannot avoid reconsidering it and, indeed, records his acceptance that it 'would be an additional step in reducing the complexity of the system'.[22] The distinctions between the two levels of court are identified as rights of audience, the grant of Mareva and Anton Piller injunctions and defamation actions. He recommends overlapping jurisdiction in Mareva and Anton Piller orders, disposing of that difference. Defamation actions hardly seem a big problem: they could stay with top level judges. The nub is rights of audience: 'There are difficulties in amalgamating the High Court and the county courts which go beyond my remit. In particular, there is the problem of rights of audience, which is subject to a separate statutory regime.'[23]

Such reasoning is wrong on grounds both of principle and practice.

It is absurd that the Bar's interest in restricting rights of audience in the higher courts should prevent discussion of reform of the court structure. Furthermore, Lord Woolf's argument can be stood on its head. Precisely because the Courts and Legal Services Act 1990 now provides a statutory regime for rights of audience, it is not necessary for courts to be structured to perform the same purpose. Even if the argument for maintaining current rights of audience was accepted, then restrictions would be better retained by reference to the type of case rather than by the level of court.

The potential problems created by side-stepping this issue are enormous. Anomalies will remain in the apportionment of cases. Large commercial lenders will continue to use the High Court procedures for relatively small debts, while personal injury cases involving much larger amounts continue to be diverted to the county court. A quite unnecessary degree of inflexibility is maintained in the management of judicial time. Many otherwise suitably qualified solicitors still do not have rights of audience in the High Court.

An issue of structure exists at the base of the adjudication structure: tribunals. At the moment, the Lord Chancellor is responsible for seven permanent tribunals in England and Wales. Their work and efficiency appears to be falling. In 1993–94, total caseload dropped by 13.4 per cent over the previous year and disposals by 14.2 per cent. The Council on Tribunals, responsible to the Lord Chancellor for England and Wales, oversees the operation of a total of around 50 tribunals. Many tribunals are beginning to coordinate their work much better, and the Council on Tribunals and Property Holdings, responsible for government premises, jointly produced a central register of tribunal accommodation for the first time in 1994.

There must be a strong case for consolidation of the tribunal network. While the specific subject matter of each tribunal is clearly different, there is surely benefit to be obtained, not least financially, from centralising training on such matters as enabling unrepresented parties to present their case and on ensuring fair procedures. A stronger tribunal organisation would make it easier to use tribunals to select and encourage people into the judiciary who might not otherwise consider it.

Consolidation should be considered not only at the primary level of decision-making. At the moment, separate appellate provision is made for a number of specialist jurisdictions, for example, employment, immigration and social security. It must be worth at least reviewing whether there are advantages from the sort of reform undertaken in Australia where such appeals are heard by a common administrative review tribunal which can then develop a coherent approach to good practice. What is more, suitably resourced, such a tribunal might, in time, take over a wider range of appeals which currently proceed to judicial review, such as questions that arise under a variety of local authority duties. Such a reform would fit well with the proposals for administrative law set out below.

(6) Judges should have greater administrative responsibilities; the consequences of this need to be carefully considered

Both Lord Woolf and the Civil Justice Review have seen judicial case management on the North American model as the saviour of the deficiencies of the court system. This has major consequences that need to be considered. Training will certainly be necessary. More fundamentally, a shift to a more managerial role may require a different sort of person to be appointed as a judge. Trial advocates will have much less experience of complex case management than their instructing solicitors.

What is more, serious consideration should be given to the mechanism for tightening judicial control over cases. This probably requires the allocation of cases to individual judges. This would follow practice in the United States. It would individualise responsibility; give a sense of personal ownership to the judiciary of their caseload; and surely provide an incentive for good management.

Some mechanism is certainly required to encourage change in a judiciary that historically has devalued administration in favour of adjudication. The practice of sending High Court judges on circuit might make individual allocation meaningless: at that level, it may be that judges should operate in small teams which are responsible for a defined part of the overall caseload. Failure to introduce such reforms may well foster the situation considered by Carrie Menkel-Meadow (chapter 4), where procedural judging and judges come to assume a lower status than more traditional activity and judges.

Furthermore, if judges are to move towards a managerial role then account needs to be taken of how they are organised. In *Shaping the Future: new directions in legal services*, Professor Martin Partington set out the lessons that might be transferred to the courts from the organisation of tribunals.[24] This would be to give much more administrative autonomy to the judges, grouped under presidents who are accountable for overall standards. Ultimately, such a model might lead to a pattern of organisation much more like that of the United States where the executive is responsible for overall policy and resource allocation but, within the consequent democratic perimeters, the judiciary has a greater degree of autonomy. At the extreme, the Court Service would be transferred from the Lord Chancellor's Department to some form of judicial commission. Such an idea certainly raises constitutional issues which merit consideration.

(7) There should be greater commitment to research and evaluation of reform and an institution should be created to undertake and further this role

The clear burden of the contributions from North America in this book is the need for painstaking research, careful formulation and diligent monitoring of reform. This was also the burden of Cyril Glasser's chapter in *Shaping the Future*.[25] Lord Woolf calls for some form of consultative council on civil justice in his interim report. A period of change appears inevitable for the courts, if for no other reason than continuing pressure on resources. There is a desperate need for a permanent body with responsibility for overseeing reform and research. This might begin as the free-standing committee envisaged by Lord Woolf rather than a fully fledged body like the Federal Judicial Center in the United States (see p34). Ultimately, its function could be assumed within a judicial commission if one is created to oversee the appointment and functioning of the judiciary.

(8) The benefits of a strong administrative law jurisdiction of the courts should be accepted and built upon

The kind of wholesale attack on the administrative jurisdiction of the High Court made by the Labour Party's Lord Irvine (see p14) is completely misplaced. There clearly is an issue about the extent to which judges may assert supra-parliamentary principles. However, there should be no dispute about their role as lions under the parliamentary throne. The executive invites judicial review, and should get it, if it acts outside the content or spirit of legislation. Nothing but good would appear to come from a strong judicial line in protecting the quality and competence of tribunals and other sub-judicial decision-making. The executive should, indeed, have the same. It could promote this by such initiatives as developing the kind of internal guidance which has been circulated to civil servants, such as the booklet entitled *The Judge over your Shoulder*,[26] into an administrative code recommended as governing decision-making in all public bodies. Reforms of this kind would have the effect of developing an administrative law jurisdiction recognisably akin to European models, such as that in France. A strong constitution surely requires a commitment to an effective separation of powers and there can be no widespread objection to developing a strong judiciary, capable of preventing abuse and stimulating good practice, yet limited by the sovereign nature of parliament. For example, judicial examination of secondary legislation may be inconvenient for politicians but it is required as a protection against the over-weaning power of the executive over the legislature.

(9) There should be a number of improvements to procedure, undertaken on a properly researched and monitored basis

Lord Woolf's approach to civil justice reform in his interim report is essentially threefold: there should be a shift to court-controlled rather than adversary-controlled litigation with individual management of larger cases; costs should be kept proportionate to the value of what is at stake in the litigation, largely through increase in the small claims jurisdiction where costs are not awarded at all or are minimal, the introduction of the 'fast-track' procedure for cases worth less than £10,000 where costs will be limited and the reduction of certain rights, eg, of discovery; and lawyers should undergo a 'change of culture' so that they see litigation as solution-finding rather than problem-setting in which the encouragement of private ADR techniques will be helpful.

The difficulties with this package of proposals have been well raised in chapters 3 and 4. To take but one example, lawyers are bound by both self-interest and professional duty to act in the interests of their clients. As a result, those acting for, say, insurance companies will always face commercial pressures to delay and minimise payments to be made by their clients. It is what those clients need to do in order to ensure maximum profitability. It is not abuse of process to use procedures to further one's clients' aims to the greatest possible extent; it is completely naïve to suggest that clients of any sophistication want any other goal. The use of procedure in this way can be minimised by tightly drafted rules. A co-operative approach to problem-solving can be encouraged among lawyers by exposure to ADR and the sort of education and training suggested by Carrie Menkel-Meadow (see p106) but, ultimately, the interests of lawyers' clients will out. The danger in major changes to existing rules must be recognised. If rules are shortened and generalised and judges given greater powers of discretion, then attempts to maximise the possible advantages of imprecision and obscurity are absolutely predictable by more 'professional' litigants such as insurance companies.

A general point can, therefore, be made. Reform of procedure may be better undertaken in small, incremental steps which are piloted and monitored before universal implementation. The example of the rule changes in 1992 over witness statements (p23) should stand as a dreadful warning of what can happen to an attempt to find a broad and easy solution to complex problems. The idea of the 'fast track' is not to be rejected, but, just as is argued above for the small claims changes, it should be piloted on a time or court-limited basis. We can then study its effect in practice without running the risk, manifest in the witness statement débâcle, that a reform designed to reduce delay and cost in fact has the reverse effect. What is more, the monitoring of a fast-track pilot would have to be sufficiently sophisticated to identify such issues as whether the limitation on costs benefited large commercial litigants (for whom they were financially irrelevant) at the expense of poorer individuals for whom they imposed, in reality, a limit on the costs that could be incurred in pursuit of the litigation. Furthermore, we need to know how well proposed monetary limits represent the real value of litigation. Fast-track and small claims procedures may reflect a proportionate response to different sizes of contested credit-card bills, but are they appropriate for deciding litigation over repair of a roof which has a low monetary value but which makes a crucial difference to the home life of the tenant underneath?

Similarly, reform is likely to be the better for being incremental. Before implementing court-appointed experts, let us follow Garry Watson's advice and deal better with party-appointed ones. The first step should be a requirement of full disclosure of all party correspondence with all experts. Reform has also to be based on a detailed analysis in order to avoid the kind of unintended consequences that have bedevilled some previous efforts. Court-appointed experts may be satisfactory in some cases. In others, court appointment may give the appearance of a spurious objectivity to an expert who has merely, if subconsciously, given a subjective opinion on a matter where no objectivity is possible. Furthermore, the likely consequence of appointment of experts by court is that only well-resourced litigants would be able to afford a second opinion; legal aid would not pay for this. We have to look no further than the various miscarriages of justice in the criminal field to see how fragile can be the substance of claims to expertise.

Judicial case management would also be best explored by its introduction in a small cross-section of cases before being applied wholesale to all cases in very broad categories. This is surely a very clear lesson to be learned from North American experience with the same idea as, for example, that described by Carrie Menkel-Meadow on p94. Gradual implementation will also answer for us the crucial question as to whether we in England have sufficient judicial resources to make this change of approach work or not. It might also be helpful to consider the extent of existing problems of discovery in cases other than commercial litigation before making any detailed changes from current rules. Government departments and small businesses, for example, will predictably use any restriction on discovery simply to assert that no relevant evidence exists. Time and time again, the result of cases involving individual litigants against big battalions turns on the information that they have been able to prise out of their opponents by way of discovery. Reduction of the chances of obtaining information in this way will simply lessen access to justice.

(10) There should be more education, both in and out of schools, about the operation of the courts and the legal system

LAG has consistently argued for more attention to be given to education about the law both in schools and less formally. In *A Strategy for Justice*,[27] LAG argued this in relation to legal services, demanding:

> a much wider commitment to education and information than simply more advertising for legal aid. Such a commitment can be seen in the examples of education work undertaken by the *Commission des Services Juridiques* [the equivalent of the Legal Aid Board] in Quebec and the Australian legal aid commissions. Furthermore, the Office of Fair Trading, with a range of clear and attractive material on the subject of consumer rights, provides a domestic example of what can be done. There needs to be an institution which takes a similar role in relation to the rights of citizens more generally, a function widely known abroad as 'public legal education'.

This was followed by three chapters in *Shaping the Future: new directions in legal services* which illustrated the work done by British Columbia's People's Law School as well as British-based law centres and the Citizenship Foundation. LAG continued to argue that 'legal education and information should be seen as integral to the provision of publicly funded legal services'.[28]

What is true of legal services is also true of the courts. There must be a greater commitment to education in the law and legal process. British Columbia provides a wonderful example of what can be done; an enormous amount of goodwill and energy among the judiciary and the courts is tapped by the provision of an in-court education facility linked to a province-wide commitment to legal education (see pp36–38).

Conclusion

Three principles should guide the search for a civil justice system which provides dispute resolution appropriate for the 1990s and beyond. First, there is a need for an approach which is a particular mixture of vision and empiricism. We need new ideas grounded in a real understanding of how they would work in practice. Second, we must pay attention to the experience of other jurisdictions which provide the opportunity for much more experiment and innovation than could be possible domestically. Third, we need to inject into debate a commitment to equality of access to justice which is too often lacking. Reform of the civil justice system is not just a matter of shifting and limiting resources: it requires acceptance of the fundamental purpose at stake, the creation of a fair society for all its members. One of Lord Woolf's express goals for his inquiry is to raise the 'low priority and low status of civil work'.[29] His report, like the Civil Justice Review (see p10), is to be commended to the extent that it achieves that goal. This book represents, however, an attempt to broaden a debate on the reform of civil justice which looks to be at risk of becoming too narrow.

References

1 Lord Chancellor's Department, *A Programme for the Future: Strategic plan 1995/96–1997/98* (HMSO, 1995) and *Annual Report 1994–95* (HMSO, 568, 1995).

2 *Strategic Plan* as above.

3 *Annual Report* as above.

4 Lord Chancellor, *Summary of the Proposed New Service* (HMSO, Cmd 7563, 1948).

5 Royal Commission on Legal Services, *Final Report*, Volume 1 (HMSO, Cmnd 7648, 1979) para 5.3.

6 Lord Chancellor's Department, *Legal Aid – Targeting Need* (HMSO, Cm 2854, 1995) para 4.1.

7 Ibid, para 4.2.

8 NACAB, *Barriers to Justice: CAB clients' experience of legal services*, 1995, para 2.57.

9 Ibid, para 4.26.

10 Lord Woolf, *Access to Justice* (Woolf Inquiry Team, 1995) recommendation 56.

11 NACAB (note 8 above), para 4.47.

12 Ibid, para 4.57.

13 County Court Fees Order 1982 SI No 1706, as amended.

14 Note 8 above, para 4.65.

15 Lord Chancellor's Department Press Notice, 4 January 1996.

16 Phillip Sycamore, quoted in Law Society Press Release, 4 January 1996.

17 Note 15 above.

18 Woolf Report (note 10 above), Recommendation 123.

19 Note 6 above, para 12.27.

20 Civil Justice Review, *Report of the Review Body on Civil Justice* (HMSO, Cm 394, 1988) para 3.16.

21 Ibid, para 3.104.

22 Woolf Report, para 12.6.

23 Ibid, para 12.12.

24 (LAG, 1995) chapter 18.

25 Ibid, chapter 15.

26 *The Judge Over Your Shoulder: judicial review of administrative decisions* (Cabinet Office, 1987). This was the first edition; another has now been published.

27 (LAG, 1992) p114.

28 (LAG, 1995) p88.

29 Woolf Report, para 1.50.

Index